YOUR HIDDEN POWERS

Intercepted Signs and Retrograde Planets

by Joanne Wickenburg

American Federation of Astrologers, Inc.
PO Box 22040 6535 South Rural Road
Tempe, Arizona 85285-2040

First Printing 1992
ISBN Number: 0-86690-405-0
Library of Congress Catalog Number: 91-77412

Cover Design: Lynda Kay Fullerton

American Federation of Astrologers, Inc.
PO Box 22040
Tempe, AZ 85285-2040

Printed in the United States of America

This book is dedicated to

Sharon Gillum

There is nothing so special as friendship

Other Books by Joanne Wickenburg

Journey through the Birth Chart
In Search of a Fulfilling Career

co-author of

The Spiral of Life
The Digested Astrologer
When Your Sun Returns

Joanne has also designed a complete Corresondence Course in Astrology. See back page for further details.

TABLE OF CONTENTS

RETROGRADE PLANETS--Your Hidden Powers

TO THE READER

Because of the limited published information on intercepted signs and retrograde planets, their significance is often either misunderstood or overlooked by students of astrology. In many texts, both interceptions and retrogrades are clumped together with scanty, incomplete, or superficial definitions. Often both "conditions" are defined as weaknesses in the chart, suggesting repressions or "hang-ups." It is not unusual to find only one brief paragraph in astrological literature addressing life issues brought to play because of retrograde planets and intercepted signs. The advise frequently given regarding both factors is: Develop the functions of your retrograde planets and intercepted signs within. But what does that mean?

I have included both retrogrades and interceptions in this book not because they function the same way, but because many people believe this to be the case. My intent is to define how they differ, and to introduce some new ideas about retrograde planets and intercepted signs with hope it will be useful in your astrological work.

While there is "nothing new under the sun," I hope the material introduced in this volume will give you some food for thought. You might find that some of the information I have presented, especially on retrograde planets, seems incongruent with what you have read elsewhere. In reality it neither negates nor contradicts their generally accepted interpretation. It does, however, encourage you to view their functioning from a perspective seldom suggested in other literature.

Much of the material I offer here is not new. Many of the ideas I am presenting on retrograde planets, for example, originated from the works of Dane Rudhyar, offered in his books as brief statements packed with substance that provided a whole new way of perceiving the significance and power of retrograde planets. I have expanded on his observations.

Regarding intercepted signs, even less concrete information has been handed down by the "masters." To a large degree, the conclusions I have reached regarding their significance in a horoscope are based on theory and observation.

This book is not designed to simply look up the meaning of a particular intercepted sign or a retrograde planet in a particular house. It is important that you read all materials prefacing each such section in order to understand the full significance of the astrological premise being discussed. Many wrong conclusions can be formed if you reach only for the "trees" in a chart and miss the "forest" entirely. Isolating specific features, and making judgments on them without taking the entire chart into consideration, can be dangerous. This is a trap many students fall into when relying on "cookbook" definitions of any kind.

For example, some definitions of how retrograde or intercepted planets might operate when located in a specific house or sign are offered throughout the book. This, in itself, is "cookbook" astrology. I have made considerable effort to make these examples as universally significant as possible. You should realize, however, when reading these sections, that each individual experiences a specific planetary placement in his/her own unique way, as shown by other features in the horoscope. This is where experience in reading the *whole* chart becomes essential. While specific examples are necessary as part of the educational process, they must be considered only as guidelines.

A point you will find emphasized throughout both sections of this book is: Don't take for granted the power of retrograde planets or intercepted signs. They make the chart unique. They make life complex. They describe powers and potentials waiting to be unleashed. While it is true that in some way you will stand apart from the "norm" if you have interceptions or retrogrades, who wants to be lost in the masses?

PART ONE

INTERCEPTED SIGNS: Environment vs Destiny

INTRODUCTION TO INTERCEPTED SIGNS

Intercepted signs...they presented such a dilemma to me when I first began my trek into the world of astrology. Wherever and whenever I looked for information regarding their interpretive significance, I'd only find a sentence here, a paragraph there, in the many books I reviewed. Nothing of substance was available regarding their importance in chart interpretation. In my early years, the only books covering interceptions presented them in such a way that readers were left feeling inadequate, seriously handicapped or in some other way cursed if intercepted signs were in their charts. The general consensus on interceptions was enveloped in one or two sentences. 1) Interceptions were said to create limitations and delays. 2) They had "karmic" implications. The reasons given for these beliefs varied from author to author.

Some authors suggested that intercepted signs describe qualities that have been developed in past lives. For that reason, they are held in abeyance during this incarnation until you equally develop other personality characteristics. Other authors suggested the opposite, implying that intercepted signs describe qualities that were *not* sufficiently honed in previous lives and therefore are difficult to access in the current incarnation. Information presented in still other literature suggested that intercepted signs describe "sins from the past" catching up with the individual in this life time. So many contradictions! And all are abstract.

In all cases one factor remained constant. Intercepted signs were considered taboo. They were said to cause frustration and inhibition in the areas of life described by the house in which they were "trapped" and in the expression and development of the sign qualities. Planets in intercepted signs were considered to debilitate the chart further.

Fortunately astrology has evolved over the last few decades. We no longer look at isolated facts in a chart and consider them benefic or malefic. For example, we now recognize the square aspect as representing challenges rather than evil influences. We are now looking into the psychology of astrology rather than viewing horoscopes in only black and white terms. What was once considered a detriment beyond control is now defined as a challenge to grow. Astrology now gives us *choices*. At one time, because of society's limited understanding of the workings of the human mind and emotions, astrology, influenced by the mentality and belief structures of the era, took people's choices away.

Even in today's more sophisticated world, many remnants from the "old school" remain in our psyches. We still fear a transit of Uranus moving to square our natal Moon. We still look forward with avid enthusiasm to the day when transiting Jupiter conjoins natal Venus. In reality neither aspect *must* function more positively than the other. The outcome of the Uranus square, for example, may be of greater benefit than the promises shown by Jupiter. It's all a matter of perspective. It's all a matter of attitude. Its all a matter of understanding the energies operative in our lives and learning to work with them.

Likewise, intercepted signs in a chart do not have to result in permanent repression as implied in many of our early teachings. I think you will find, after having considered the information provided herein, that intercepted signs and planets present some rather unique and exciting possibilities. They show special qualities about an individual that stand out in some important way. Interceptions can result in originality. They can point to unique, creative skills.

It is true that intercepted signs suggest stress. Just as many other features in a chart present challenges to the developmental process, interceptions contribute to considerable frustration. It is often only through struggle that we bring their powers to the surface. The intercepted condition throws the basic synchronicity of the horoscope off balance. Once the challenges of intercepted signs and planets are met, however, the results are seen in people's unique abilities to become more than what was expected of them, or taught to them, in their early formative years.

CHAPTER I

What is an Intercepted Sign?

A sign is intercepted when its full 30 degrees fall in a house having another sign on its house cusp. It is literally "trapped" in a house between two other signs on consecutive house cusps (see figure 1 on the following page).

That intercepted signs own no house cusps in the chart is significant from an interpretive sense. Before going further with this concept, some basic astrological facts should be noted.

It is important to realize exactly what the houses represent and how they differ in interpretation from signs and planets. The houses of a horoscope describe specific areas of life activity. These fields of experience are universally available to everyone on the planet.

Houses set the structure for life. Signs on houses begin the process of personalizing the activities ruled by each house. For example, we all have a persona we project to others. We all have a specific mask we wear when meeting the world. The *door* to the outside world is represented by the first house cusp of the chart. Each of us approach life differently and present a different persona when meeting new experiences. This "dressing" is described by the sign on the first house cusp. It describes how others see us based on our individual self images and the way we have been taught to present ourselves to the world. The first house rules the "generic" persona. The sign on the cusp of the first house, the Ascendant, describes the persona. The planet ruling, and planets in, the first house further characterize the personality.

Likewise, we all have a past, a family that provided the foundations upon which all future activities in life will be based. This past is designated to the fourth house of the horoscope. To describe the family's impact and the home environment of your past, the sign on the fourth house cusp, its planetary ruler, occupant planets and their aspects must be considered.

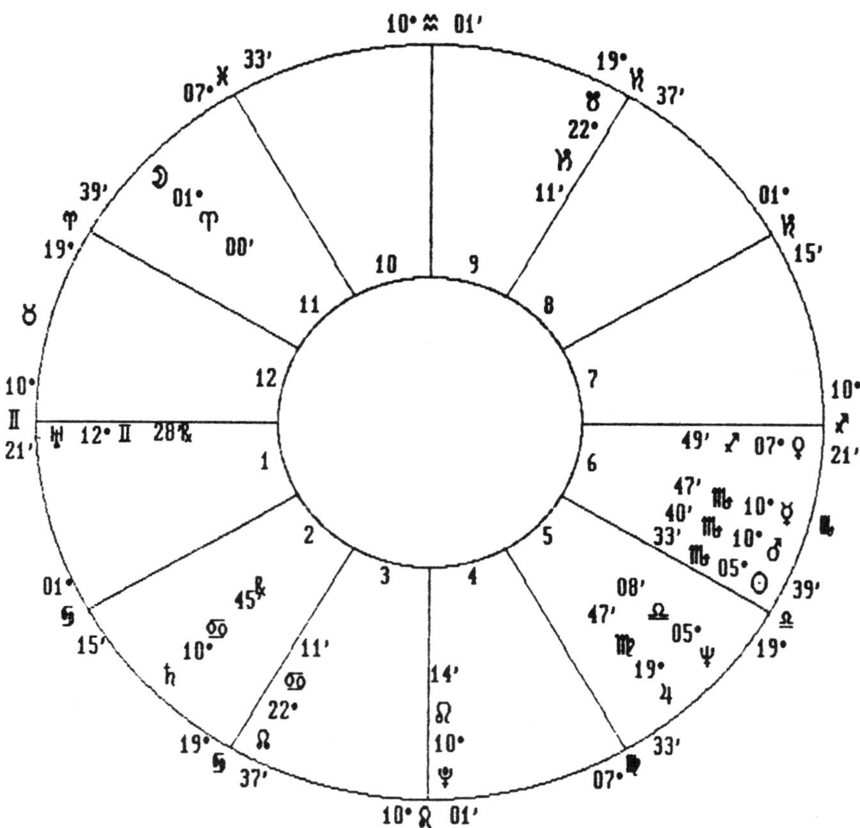

Figure 1: All 30 degrees of Scorpio are intercepted in the 6th house. Taurus is also intercepted.

Planets put the chart in motion. They describe actions taken throughout life that either lead to the development of the personality and its potentials, or detract from success and potential growth.

Seen from another point of view, houses represent territory ... external fields of experience. The signs on their cusps describe the territory based on your individual needs, tastes, and environmental conditioning. Each sign is ruled by a specific planet that will probably be located elsewhere in the chart. This ruling planet describes the energy that must be used, and the field of activity where it must be spent (its house), to acquire what is needed in the house it rules. A "partnership" is evident between signs on house cusps and the planets that rule them. If you are not familiar with rulerships, the Table on the following page will be useful.

House *cusps* represent *doors* leading into the life experiences ruled by houses. Planets ruling signs on house cusps represent the *keys* that must be used to open the doors to the realms of life described by the houses they rule. Planets provide the energy to get the process moving, to experience life.

SIGN	RULER
Aries	Mars
Taurus	Venus
Gemini	Mercury
Cancer	Moon
Leo	Sun
Virgo	Mercury
Libra	Venus
Scorpio	Pluto/Mars
Sagittarius	Jupiter
Capricorn	Saturn
Aquarius	Uranus/Saturn
Pisces	Neptune/Jupiter

Intercepted Signs are not found on these house cusps. While intercepted signs describe needs of the personality, the individual has a difficult time accessing and developing these needs. There are no obvious doors (cusps) leading to the experiences required. Lack of a doorway leading into any "room" of life creates a dilemma when attempting to discover what lies within.

The first quandary regarding intercepted signs lies in defining what astronomical factors create the doors (cusps) that invite you to enter and participate in what the world has to offer. You must also examine the astronomical factors that cause no doors to be present for a sign to find release.

The circle that contains the horoscope represents the ecliptic, or the Sun's apparent pathway around the Earth. The ecliptic is divided into 12 equal sections that represent the signs of the Zodiac. Zero degrees of Aries is located at the point where the ecliptic and celestial equator (the earth's equator as it would be if extended into space) intersect. This is the point of the spring equinox. The fall equinox, represented by zero degrees Libra, begins when the Sun, moving into the southern hemisphere, crosses this intersection at the opposite point. Our current calendar is based on these astrological principles.

All signs contain 30 degrees of space. This is a constant in astrology. The houses, however, are divided by more complex mathematical formulas and therefore might contain any number of degrees (unless, of course, you are dividing the wheel using the Equal House system). The *latitude* of the birth place plays a strong part in determining house size.

To determine the signs and degrees occupying the various house cusps of the chart, you must first find the points on the ecliptic representing the Ascendant and the Midheaven. The Ascendant is located where the local horizon, if extended into space, intersects the ecliptic. The Midheaven is found by determining where the meridian of the birth place intersects the ecliptic.

The Midheaven should not be confused with the Zenith. The Zenith is the point directly overhead at the time of birth. The Sun is only directly overhead between latitudes 23 1/2 degrees north or south of the equator. The Sun will never be directly overhead if you live in Seattle. You would have to locate it in the sky by looking south from where you stand.

Once the separation between the Ascendant and Midheaven has been determined, the intermediate house cusps are ascertained based on the house system of your choice. *All house systems share the same Ascendant and Midheaven.* Only the intermediate house cusps change based on the house system used. More specific information will be provided on house systems later in this chapter.

Keep in mind that there are always three houses in each quadrant of the horoscope, and there are always 30 degrees in each sign. When the separation between the Ascendant and Midheaven does not equate to 90 degrees (three signs), interceptions often occur. For example, if the Midheaven/Ascendant separation has been determined to be 60 degrees, it is impossible to put three signs of 30 degrees each in that limited space. Likewise, if the distance between the Ascendant and Midheaven is greater than 90 degrees, the houses in that quadrant must be greater than 30 degrees each. More than three signs will tenant these houses. This distortion is largely based on the latitude of the birth place.

Intercepted signs are common in charts of people born in extreme northern or southern latitudes. The farther north or south an individual is born from Earth's equator, the more likely s/he is to have intercepted signs in the chart. Charts of people born in New York, for example, have a greater probability of having interceptions than charts of those born in Florida or southern California. It is not uncommon for individuals born in Alaska or northern Europe to have multiple interceptions. If you were born at one of the Earth's poles, the Midheaven and Ascendant would be the same! The horizon and the meridian of the birth place would intersect the ecliptic at the same place. If you were born near the equator, however, the houses would be more evenly divided.

To get a different perspective of how intercepted signs occur, take a moment and refer to your Tables of Houses. Notice that under any given sidereal time listed, the Midheaven sign and degree remains constant regardless of the latitude being considered. All other house cusps, including the Ascendant sign and degree, change with a change in latitude. The farther north or south you look from the 0 degree latitude point, the greater the house distortion becomes. (See figure 2.)

The Midheaven, simply by its position in the chart, represents, from an interpretive point of view, the highest rung attainable on the ladder to social success. It describes, by sign, your destiny with regard to social accomplishment. This is not "destiny" relating to personal soul growth, as that shown by the Sun. Nor is it the destiny statement made by Pluto, i.e. one's individual role in the larger evolution of the planet. The MC represents your ability to find your place in society. It represents your importance within society's structure. It is the point of social attainment.

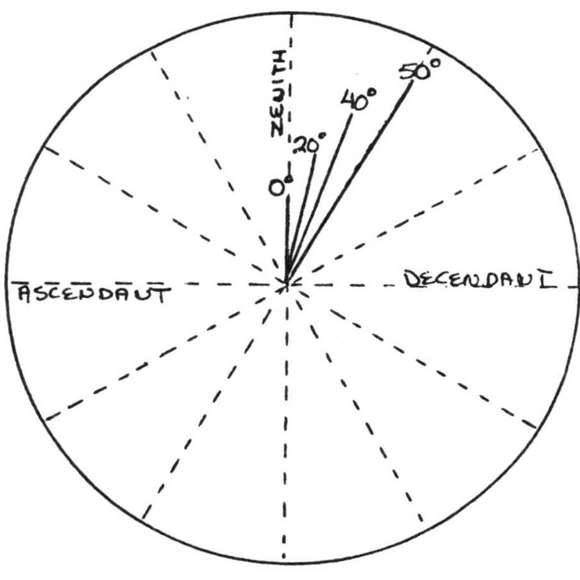

Figure 2: Note the difference between the Zenith and the MC at Sidereal Time 0:33:44. * _____ = MC

The chart promises, regardless of the house system you use, that no matter where you were born, you will experience opportunity to fill this important role in your life. No matter where you were born, or what house system you use to calculate the chart, the Midheaven remains constant. Fulfillment of your "destiny" is not denied because of your birth location. However, because of the external conditions in your particular environment, the *path* you use to reach this destiny will differ from those of another person sharing the same Midheaven sign and degree, but born in another region. It is my belief that intercepted signs in a birth chart suggest conflicts exist between personal destiny and birth location.

The fact that the Midheaven remains constant regardless of the house system used, while the Ascendant and other house cusps change according to the latitude of the birth place, presents another interesting question regarding the interpretation of interceptions.

How can location play a part in defining an individual's destiny? Consider those born in the extreme northern section of our globe where weather conditions limit the quality of life and the external activities available for experience. Survival would not be possible in some areas on our planet unless food and other life-supporting products were brought in from the outside. The environments' of these locations simply do not accommodate human life. The idea that environment plays a strong role in life is of core significance when evaluating the meaning and importance of intercepted signs. One could go so far as to say that:

ENVIRONMENT VS DESTINY.

HOUSE SYSTEMS

Methods of house division are a matter of frequent debate among astrologers. There are dozens of house systems, some currently in use, others considered obsolete and rarely used.

The Placidus house system is the most widely accepted. Until recently, most of our published Tables of Houses were designed around this method of division. It is the system on which most astrologers cut their teeth. Recently, the Koch system has gained in popularity. Porphory is another still in use. Rudhyar promoted the Campanus house division in some of his writings, while other noted astrologers support the Equal House method.

What house system is an accurate one? They all are. They are all mathematically sound, but determined by different means of intersection, projection or other mathematical formulas. They all share the same Ascendant and Midheaven. No matter what house division you use, the Ascendant and Midheaven will always be the same. The intermediate house cusps differ, however, based on the method of division. This causes frequent instances where actual signs on intermediate house cusps change from one house system to the next. Also, intercepted signs may occur in one method of division and not in another. Or, you may find one set of intercepted signs in one system of house division and another set in the other. In my own chart, Virgo and Pisces are intercepted in the Placidus house system. In the Koch, Aries and Libra are intercepted. In the Campanus house system, Leo and Aquarius are intercepted. Also, stelliums of planets move from one house to another when different house divisions are used. What a dilemma!

To date, there is no consensus on which house system is more accurate in an interpretive sense. Only you can decide what house system works best for you. You may find, after having experimented with several house divisions, that more than one describe your life. In my own experience, I have found that the Placidus house system serves me well.

The questions presented by house division are baffling and may never be completely resolved. I feel that several of these house divisions work. In some way, each method needs to be linked to a particular approach to interpretation. For example, one method may be better to evaluate mundane issues with astrology while another may address psychological factors more precisely. One may be more appropriate to use when considering a chart for spiritual advice, while another may be more suitable when working with the world of finance.

The interpretive sections of this book are based on charts calculated using the Placidus house system. If you use another house division in your chart construction, I recommend that you adapt these interpretations to your particular approach to astrological interpretation. It is my premise that the basic concepts brought out with intercepted signs work with various methods of house division and that you will undoubtedly choose the house system that accommodates your style of analysis.

CHAPTER II

GETTING STARTED

House cusps represent the doors that lead into the various areas of life awaiting to be explored. For example:

First House Cusp: Your door to the world. The window through which you view life. Your persona or mask. Your outlook on life. Your self image.
Second House Cusp: The door to survival. Financial acquisitions. Issues of worth (material, psychological, spiritual, emotional). Your resources, assets and talents.
Third House Cusp: The door to your community. Learning facilities available for use in the community. Basic education. Mobility. Relationships with siblings and neighbors.
Fourth House Cusp: The door to your home. Security issues. The emotional foundations upon which all life is supported. Family involvement. Nurturing parent.
Fifth House Cusp: The door to creativity. Creative and recreative activities. Children. Your legacy. Personal and creative procreation. Entertainment. Speculation. Romance. Play.
Sixth House Cusp: The door to employment. Your job. Routine responsibilities to health and daily life maintenance. Service and productive performance.
Seventh House Cusp: The door to relationships. The others with whom you interact. Partnerships, marriage, and all relationships requiring equality in interacting. Competition.
Eighth House Cusp: The door to rebirth. Circumstances requiring sacrifice in order to achieve intimacy or unity with others. Regeneration, sex, taxes, recycling, the psychological processes of death and rebirth.

Ninth House Cusp: The door to the larger world. Foreign involvement. Higher education. Philosophy. Religion. Knowledge available from outside the community. Travel.
Tenth House Cusp: The door to success. Social standing and achievements. Your place in the social structure. Authoritive parent.
Eleventh House Cusp: The door to friendship and social awareness. Humanitarian involvements. Goals for the future. Friends and group activities. Social causes to which you are drawn.
Twelfth House Cusp: The door to the past. The door to spiritual truths. Services given out of love. Karma confronted. Institutions providing services and rehabilitation. Volunteer services. Meditation. Privacy.

The signs describe personal needs. These needs stimulate urges to move into the world to find satisfaction. When signs are located on house cusps, experiences that can fill these needs are easy to locate. When a sign is intercepted, the doorway to external opportunity is hidden.

An intercepted sign can be equated to a closet in a room. You must enter the room before the closet is evident. This same concept applies to intercepted signs. You must move into the experiences ruled by the house, via the sign on the cusp, before you recognize that a "closet" exists that contains something you never knew was available to you before entering the room. This closet could contain many treasures that must be discovered and put to use before your life can be complete, well balanced and fulfilled. The Astrologer's job is to lead the client into the room and then bring to his, or her, attention what lies hidden within.

To do so, the key to the original door must be located via the planet ruling the sign on the cusp. Once used to open the door, attention must be drawn to the hidden contents of the "closet" or intercepted sign. Several astrological factors must be considered to get this far.

For an in-depth examination of how rulerships operate in natal chart interpretation, I refer you to my book "A Journey Through The Birth Chart." Following, however, is a brief review for those who are not familiar with this interpretive principle.

ARIES: The need to be independent. You need to approach the experiences of this house with courage and initiative. Each new experience encountered here contributes to your self image. By cultivating courage to "do your own thing," you become aware of your identity as separate from others.

The Key: Mars. The power of desire. The motivating force. The physical urge to move aggressively to get what you want. The drive to act on personal desires. By courageously following your instincts here (house), you fulfill your Aries search for identity.

TAURUS: The need to be productive. In the house of Taurus, you need to acquire physical substances that not only prove your worth, but enable you to sustain life independently. By developing perseverance here (house), you recognize your life as worthwhile and valuable. You validate your importance in the world and learn to be self sustaining.

The key: Venus. The power of love. The attraction force. Your urge to acquire what you want from the outside world to accommodate comfort and build self worth. As you learn to appreciate the sensual, physical enjoyments available here (house), you fill your Taurus-need for self gratification and personal acquisition.

GEMINI: The need for variety that contributes to intellectual curiosity. Your need to remain mentally open to information provided by the experiences encountered in this house. Here (house) you need to acquire fresh ideas and communication skills. By remaining adaptable to the variety of experiences and knowledge life has to offer, you grow in self understanding.

The Key: Mercury. The power of the intellect. The mental force. The urge to accumulate information that builds intellect. As you seek new information, and learn to appreciate the value of knowledge, you fill the Gemini-need for intellectual stimulation.

CANCER: The need for security and emotional protection. As you learn to nurture and be nurtured through the experiences available in this house, you grow in your sense of belonging. Here (house) you learn to protect yourself from the elements, and build emotional strength.

The Key: Moon. The power of emotion. The nurturing force. The urge to find security and establish protective barriers in life. Here (house) you must learn to adapt to the changing currents of life in order to maintain your emotional equilibrium.

LEO: The need to be important. You need to shine in this area of your life (house), to stand out as important, as significant. You need to approach these experiences with confidence and flair. You need to project yourself strongly into all that you do in order to validate your importance.

The Key: Sun. The power of will. The life force. The urge to find personal purpose in life. The need to shine. By developing consciousness and a sense of purpose in this area of your life (house), you fill your Leo-need to stand out and be important.

VIRGO: The need to perfect. The need to develop analytical skills that enable you to adjust to your surroundings. In this area of life (house), you need to use information in practical ways. Here you need to understand the importance of detail, techniques and complex systems.

The Key: Mercury. The power of intellect. The mental force. The urge to accumulate information to be classified, perfected, and put to practical use in your Virgo-ruled experiences. Here (house), as you accumulate data, you find information that needs to be analyzed, perfected, and applied for daily life maintenance in your Virgo-ruled activities.

LIBRA: The need to interact. The need to work as an equal with others and to find harmony with what is non-personal. You need to share information and experience regarding this area of life (house) in order to cultivate objectivity and an understanding of others' needs and rights.

The Key: Venus. The power of love. The attraction force. The capacity to attract others with whom to interact. As you learn to appreciate the importance of interaction and attract relationships into your life, you fill your Libra-need to share and establish harmony with the outside world.

SCORPIO: The need to experience intimacy and the rebirth or regeneration resulting from it. The need to look under the surface of life to find answers to life's mysteries. The need to experience depth of emotion that cultivates depth in understanding.

The Key: Pluto. The power of change. The regenerative force. The urge to regenerate emotions of the past, and to unite with others to experience intimacy at some level. As you look into the depths of your emotional make-up, you unleash or release intense emotions requiring regeneration.

Mars is considered a secondary ruler of Scorpio. The physical desires of Mars must be regenerated before intimacy can be experienced. Also, Mars provides incentive and physical drive to create changes that have a profound impact on life.

SAGITTARIUS: The need to look beyond the immediate to understand ideas and issues that are "foreign" to your community. The need to understand theory as well as fact. By expanding your horizons and experiences in this area of life (house), you learn to appreciate the vastness life has to offer.

The Key: Jupiter. The power of expansion. The urge for more! As you develop optimism regarding the future and acquire insight regarding what is possible, you fill the Sagittarius-need to develop a broad, philosophical outline for living.

CAPRICORN: The need to appreciate structure, and the importance of the laws pertaining to your society. By establishing a place for yourself in society, and learning the rules that apply to that space, you build a sense of worldly importance and become secure with your social identity.

The Key: Saturn. The power of discipline. The structured force. The urge to belong in a social sense and to earn the respect you seek in your Capricorn-ruled activities. Here, structures for social living are necessary in order to fill your Capricorn-need to establish your social territory.

AQUARIUS: The need to develop originality and cultivate humanitarian principles. Here (house) you are challenged to break free from social limitations and explore the unknown. Here you are encouraged to develop originality and become a unique individual.

The Key: Uranus. The power of individuality. The rebellious force. The urge to become more than what you were taught to be by your early conditioning, and to experiment with new ideas. The urge to tear down obsolete structures that inhibit progress and to discover, as a result, your uniqueness rather than your similarities with the mainstream of society. As you break new ground for progress to be experienced, you fill your Aquarius-need to explore the unknown. **Saturn** is considered a co-ruler of Aquarius. Saturn gives direction and discipline to the reforming zeal of Aquarius. It also points to the structures you need to reform.

PISCES: The need to cultivate faith in an unknown future. Here (house) you are challenged to let go of the past and move into the undefined future. You need to consider your oneness with humanity rather than your separateness from it. In this area of life (house), you need to make a commitment to serve humanity at some level.

The Key: Neptune. The power of faith. The dissolution force. The urge to dissolve structures that separate you from the masses. Here (house) you are challenged to let go of any over-attachment to the material world to experience spiritual development. **Jupiter** is considered co-ruler of Pisces. It provides perspective and perception regarding future possibilities, along with the optimism needed to move into the unknown.

As you enter these doorways (house cusps) you meet external experiences that result in objectivity. For every action you initiate in life, an equal reaction is experienced. This reaction is provided in the form of feedback from others regarding the value of your independent undertakings. Whether from overt feedback, or as subtle reactions shown by others' silent responses to you, there will always be a result for each independent action you take.

Action versus reaction is the basis of all oppositions in the horoscope ... the opposition aspect, the opposition of the signs, the opposition of one house to another. Oppositions breed objectivity. They provide awareness of the importance of balancing personal desires with those of others, sharing personal assets and talents with others, integrating your knowledge with the knowledge of others, and so forth. One of the most powerful polarities providing personal objectivity through feedback is seen in the relationship established between the first and seventh houses of the chart. Through the doorway of the first house, you move into the world. You project yourself into new experiences. As a result, you meet others (7th house) who respond to your projection. You learn to see yourself through others' eyes. You grow as a result. In some way it is this objectivity (so important to a well-balanced life) that is stifled when intercepted signs are present in a chart. Frustration and lack of direction often result.

There is usually no apparent problem acknowledging the needs and developing the attitudes of signs occupying house cusps, or in eliciting feedback from others that encourages objectivity regarding the needs and potentials described by signs on house cusps. However, when signs are intercepted, instead of providing constructive feedback and encouraging you to investigate the needs of your intercepted signs ... to delve more deeply into the experiences available through your intercepted signs ... to uncover the hidden potentials they define ... the environment challenges you to move on to the next *obvious* step in life (the experiences of the next house). The environment simply does not see, or understand, the degree of complexity involved with finding fulfillment in the areas of life shown by houses containing intercepted signs. Due to the lack of encouragement, feedback, or role models offered by the outside world, the needs of these signs are often hidden until later in life when some crisis (brought on by transits) brings them to the surface. The needs and potentials of intercepted signs, and the powers of intercepted planets, are sometimes delayed in expression because of lack of external stimuli.

Even after having recognized the underlying needs evident in this area of your life, they are difficult to access because of environmental limitations. When you attempt to bring them to the surface they, at first, operate without objectivity because the environment does not provide the feedback, encouragement, or role models you need to project these qualities in a well balanced manner. The environment cannot encourage or support something it does not recognize.

The environment does not offer the experiences, or teachers, necessary to adequately help you develop the qualities of your intercepted signs. Social structures are not available to facilitate full use of the signs and/or planets. Therefore, you are left with a need (sign) in a particular area of life (house) with few, if any, external facilities or resources available to use the potentials represented by your intercepted signs. This dilemma can be likened to the prospective astrology student unable to locate a teacher due to the environment's lack of acceptance, or knowledge, of the value of such information. Interceptions advise you to look in obscure areas to find the tools you need to unlock the potentials and fill the needs they represent. As you look out to your world, you discover that the environment does not have the facilities *you* need to answer *your* questions, or to help you fill *your* needs regarding the matters ruled by houses containing intercepted signs. Delays in personal fulfillment are often experienced because the schools (3rd house), the family (4th house), the church (9th house) or the relationships in your life (7th house) do not offer what you need for personal growth.

It is important to understand the dilemma between the environment and the self, as experienced with intercepted signs. When considering the environment's significance and influence on personal fulfillment, realize that references in this book to "environmental limitations" are based on *your* specific experiences and the way *you* view life around you. In childhood, the environment is your neighborhood, your family, your circle of friends, your church. This environment expands as you mature. When making references throughout the book to your relationship to the environment, I am referring to an environment that is qualified by *your* perspective of it. All references are directed to an environment, or circle of activity, that is uniquely your own because it is colored by your association with it. The opinions of others who share your environment will differ from yours due to their particular orientation toward it. Therefore, when making references to the "limitations of the environment," I am referring specifically to the limitations you associate with it due to your perspective of it and your personal experience within it. Realize that any conflicts evident between personal need and environmental facilities are founded on your perspective of what the environment holds for you. You may feel that it does not support your unique needs. Your siblings, on the other hand, may not experience it in the same way even though they shared your same physical space. In reality, the environment may contain what you need for growth. The question is: can you locate what you need within it? Keep this in mind as you consider the material offered in the following chapters.

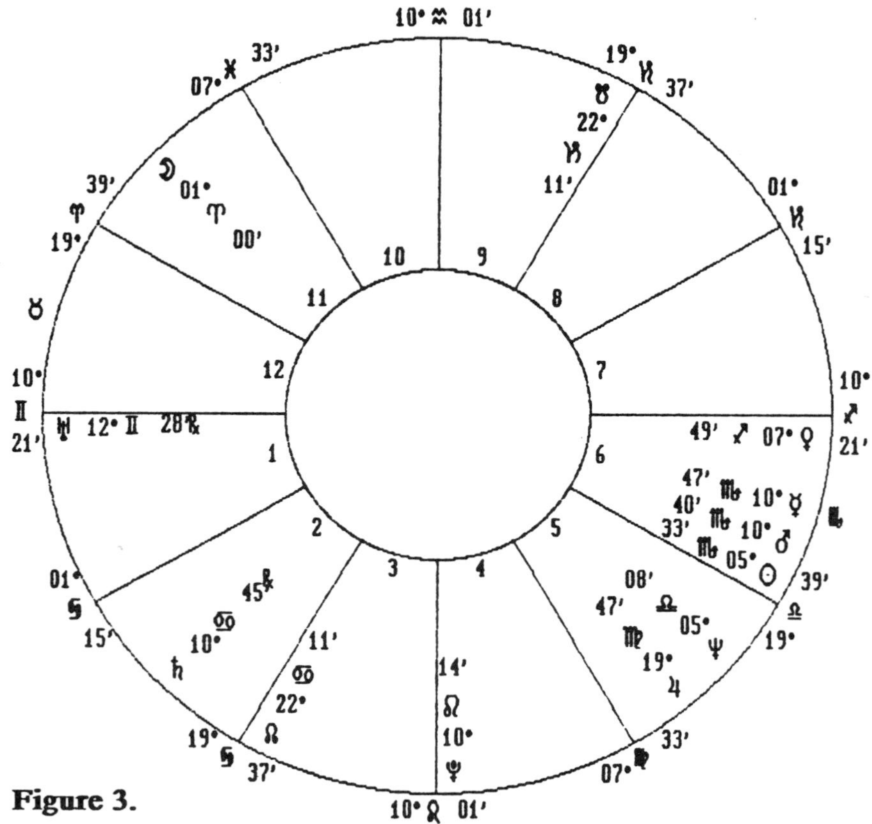

Figure 3.

As an example, consider the chart of a woman having Scorpio intercepted in the sixth house, with Sun, Mercury and Mars therein. (See figure 3). These planets are particularly important in the chart. Not only does the Sun describe her urge to shine and find purpose and importance to her life, but Mars co-rules her Scorpio Sun, and Mercury rules her Gemini Ascendant. The latter strongly qualifies her self image and the way she wants to present herself to the world.

The emphasis of Scorpio planets describes this woman's potential to have a powerful influence in her work environment (6th house). These planets, however, are intercepted in a house having Libra is on its cusp. She was encouraged by the environment to approach daily routines in a manner descriptive of Libra: be congenial, share responsibilities, learn to compromise and promote harmony. She was encouraged to interact with others and to respect the rights and privileges of her co-workers and the people she routinely encountered (Libra on 6th house cusp). She was taught to be diplomatic.

Her environment did not encourage her to seek employment. In fact, her husband, whom she married soon after she graduated from high school, did not want her to work. Her daily responsibility, in his eyes, was to be a wife, a partner (Libra). The environment did not recognize her more powerful needs ... the hidden intensity lying under her surface (Scorpio). She had an inner urge to merge with others in work experiences and to pursue an intense, emotionally-motivated drive to play a part in creating change in people's consciousness. It was not until after she experienced a Libra-routine that she, herself, recognized the power she possessed to create, or contribute to, regeneration. Once the door to employment was opened to her, she discovered an intensity she never knew she possessed. She discovered a need for a work place that encouraged depth of perception and an emotional commitment on her part (Scorpio intercept). As her world did not recognize or understand this powerful desire, it did nothing to encourage its development or expression. Frustration was the result.

Had Scorpio been on the cusp of this house, she would have been led to a job that encouraged the use of her Scorpio energy. She would not have had to struggle to bring her Scorpio intensity to the surface. The feedback she would have naturally attracted would have brought her Scorpio-urges to her attention.

Because Scorpio is intercepted, however, she had to discover them on her own. Rather than having the environment enlighten her to her powers of regeneration, she had to enlighten her environment. But first she had to discover these traits on her own. The only way that this was possible was to first experience the Libra-energy in relation to the work experience. For this reason, interceptions imply some delay experienced in the objectification and unfoldment of intercepted signs' potentials and needs.

This woman, once having experienced the essence of a Libra vocation (a wife and partner), found she was not satisfied. After struggling between inner desire and environmental lack of encouragement, she finally chose to pursue a career in psychiatric nursing. She wanted to delve under the surface of peoples' minds and explore the mysteries therein. She wanted to participate in the potential regenerative processes.

Scorpio encourages an individual to deal with issues of re-birth. It brings to the surface, to be confronted and regenerated, powerful energies from the unconscious that influence people at core levels. This woman's environment did not recognize the intense drive lying hidden under her surface. The intercepted planets suggest the intensity is very potent. Her very purpose, or sense of self importance (Sun), is dependent on her ability to work with Scorpio energies through sixth house activities ... the job. It wasn't until Uranus transited Scorpio that she rebelled against the constraints of her environment and demanded an opportunity to explore her Scorpio power and potential in reference to work. As she did so, multiple areas of her life were affected.

Her home life was disrupted (intercepted Sun rules 4th house). Her self image was radically changed (intercepted Mercury rules the Ascendant). She began to explore her creative potentials (intercepted Mercury also rules 5th house). Her identity, formed around services she provided to others (intercepted Mars rules Aries on the 12th house), was released. She surprised her environment (and herself) by exhibiting a power no one had previously recognized.

When her intercepted signs first began to emerge (out of the closet), they were expressed erratically and with little objectivity. She had never received "tutoring" or feedback regarding the outer expression of Scorpio energy. She was unable to unleash the power in a knowledgeable, well-balanced manner. This is typical of the emergence phase of intercepted signs and planets. Balance comes from objectivity and objectivity comes from opposition or feedback.

When considering the development of signs on house cusps, balance and integration is found in the polarity established by a sign's opposite (Aries-/Libra, Taurus/Scorpio, Gemini/Sagittarius, Cancer/Capricorn, Leo/Aquarius, Virgo/Pisces). In the case of intercepted signs, the opposites are also intercepted.

Just what are the issues involved with the Taurus/Scorpio polarity? In the next chapter, all sign polarities will be covered in depth. To fully of understand the dilemma set up in this particular example, however, a brief description is in order.

Lessons brought out by the Taurus/Scorpio polarity involve accumulation versus regeneration. When these signs are intercepted, people often have difficulty knowing when to accumulate and add on to the resources they already own (Taurus), and when it is appropriate to let go, or eliminate (Scorpio). This woman, once she became aware of her need to make changes in her daily routines (6th house), was not only compelled to change vocations, but, due to lack of objectivity, felt compelled to eliminate (Scorpio) conditions in her life that still had value (Taurus). The tendency of this polarity, when intercepted, is to either eliminate indiscriminately, and therefore destroy what still has potential value in life, or to focus too strongly on Taurus at the expense of Scorpio, and attempt to hold onto, or to control, what no longer has meaning or value. The challenge of this polarity is "regeneration versus accumulation."

When intercepted signs begin to emerge, their outer expression is often out of balance. As people do not receive the type of feedback, encouragement, or tutoring needed from the environment in this area of life, the intercepted sign is unable to function in harmony with the needs described by its opposite sign. The polarity seems, at first, to be non-existent. Because of the lack of objectivity, due to lack of environmental teaching, we try to express the qualities of one intercepted sign at the expense of the opposite. It finally becomes necessary to force ourselves on the environment in order to get a response from it. Often we do so without knowing how out-of-balance this projection manifests, because we are not attune to the polarity of the intercepted pair. In the following chapter, you will find some of my observations regarding the resulting conflicts.

CHAPTER III

POLARITY OF THE SIGNS

ARIES/LIBRA POLARITY

Aries, the first sign of the zodiac, symbolizes the power of the pioneer. It is a sign of leadership and shows where (house) you need to be assertive and spontaneous in your behavior and independent in your actions. You need to approach the experiences described by this house with the future in mind. A pioneering, adventuresome attitude must be developed if fulfillment is to be attained. Here, by being assertive, you discover who you are. You begin the important process of developing a self image. You prove to yourself, and those around you, that you are able to function independently. With each new venture you undertake in this area of your life, you discover a new adjective for your self description. By courageously plunging into new experiences you learn, as a result of others' reactions, that you are capable of functioning as an independent being. You discover that you have a particular role to play in life's drama.

Aries, in itself, is concerned with action for actions' sake. The need here is to prove to yourself that you need not be dependent on what others provide. Here you develop the courage to pioneer territory you have never before explored.

When Aries occupies a house cusp, these needs and potentials are an obvious part of your external projection. The environment recognizes your need to do your own thing in the area of life described by its house.

Others' reactions to your assertive behavior is found in the polarity provided by Libra, the sign opposite Aries in the zodiac. Libra's role is one of cooperation. It shows where the outside world provides feedback for the Aries-aggression. Libra encourages you to maintain independence while functioning in a socially acceptable framework. When viewed in polarity with Aries, Libra encourages you to share your Aries-identity with others. It tempers the Aries tendency to be over-aggressive or to demonstrate overly selfish or rash behavior.

When Aries is intercepted, you do not receive, in early life, the feedback or encouragement from the environment needed to integrate your Aries-urge for independence with the lives of others around you. Nor do you receive the encouragement you need to develop confidence in your ability to plunge into new experiences independently. The desire for independence in the Aries-ruled area of your life is present, but hidden. External stimulation needed from the environment is not available to encourage you to prove your independence in the outside world.

Under the surface, you are a leader, a pioneer of thought when involved in the matters ruled by this house. At the surface level, however, you cannot at first find a structure through which to express this pioneering energy. When struck with an urge to move ahead to conquer new territory, the environment does not facilitate or encourage your desires. Frustration results.

Toward experiences ruled by the house containing intercepted Aries, you need to be confrontational. Your world, however, has never taught you these skills. This dilemma can lead to one of two things. You could be spontaneous and confrontational and "do your own thing" in the area of life described by the house of Aries, but manifest these traits in a manner considered unacceptable by others in your environment. This is a result of lack of environmental guidance regarding appropriate techniques of self assertion. Or, you may fear taking independent action due to lack of encouragement from others, thus inhibiting your Aries-identity and innate leadership potential.

Aries deals with the development of the identity. When intercepted, you find it difficult to define who you are as separate from others around you. Your identity is submerged. It is important to realize that Pisces is on the cusp of this house. It describes your initial approach to these experiences (and therefore how others see you functioning here) as imaginative, universal, and somewhat selfless. Others see your role in this department of life as that of an idealist, acceptive and passive. Inside, however, you possess a powerful drive to function in an aggressive, self-proving manner. Initially you approach these experiences with faith and an idealistic outlook. You have a vision (Pisces) that you want to explore. Once having formed the vision, however, the hidden Aries-needs begin to emerge, creating a desire to play an *active* role in pursuing your Piscean ideals. The environment recognizes your idealistic tendencies (Pisces on cusp) but assumes you are content living in your dreams. As a result, you may find it necessary to force yourself on the world to prove your independence within it. You could easily become overly aggressive in your attempt to make an impact on your environment and to function independently within it.

When Aries is intercepted, it is important to realize that Libra is captured on the other side of the wheel. In Libra's house you experience a need to share, but may feel the opportunity to do so is not available within the confines of your environment. When intercepted, Libra does not benefit from the experience gained by its partner, Aries. No obvious doors exist to link these experiences. For this reason, you may find difficulty acting on decisions regarding the matters of Libra's house. Instead, you look to others to make your choices.

Aries, in polarity with Libra, provides the initiative to act after balancing the pros and cons of any given situation. When intercepted, this polarity does not function objectively. As a result, you vacillate, unable to make decisions independently. You look to others for leadership rather than sharing responsibilities in the Libra-ruled area of your life. You may feel, at times, as if you are standing on a see-saw, afraid to move one way or the other for fear of losing your balance. You could become so entrenched in compromises in an attempt to maintain relationships that you forget who you are as a separate individual.

An interesting phenomenon results. In the house containing the Aries interception, you tend to do your own thing without considering how your actions affect others. At the same time, when involved in the experiences described by Libra's house, you may do nothing at all, afraid to move ahead without permission from others. You could easily lose your identity (Aries) to relationships (Libra). Or, when operating in reverse, you may lose your capacity to form significant relationships (Libra) because of your desire to maintain independence (Aries).

When Libra is intercepted, Virgo occupies the cusp of its house. An analytical, discriminating approach to the area of life described by this house has been encouraged by your environment. It is natural for you to organize, analyze, and criticize when dealing with this department of life. But it is difficult to share the results of your analysis. You have not learned these skills. Is it possible that the environment is not equipped with the types of people you need to complement your identity? Could it be that others expect you to have all the answers and therefore consider it unnecessary to share their knowledge? Others may simply not volunteer their opinions or encouragement. In some way, the environment does not offer the sharing experiences you need for fulfillment in this area of your life.

Even though you need a complement, a person to be your mirror, this person does not appear when functioning in this department of your life. The house containing intercepted Libra shows where sharing is needed most. Frustration is experienced when the people you meet do not offer what you need because they are unaware of who you are or what you want.

Because of the lack of objectivity evident with intercepted signs, you may not consciously recognize these needs until frustrating experiences bring them to the surface. In later chapters, I will offer some suggestions for resolving the problems posed by intercepted signs.

TAURUS/SCORPIO POLARITY

Unlike Aries, a sign showing the need to be initiating and spontaneous, Taurus points to an area of life requiring a practical, persistent, and stable approach. In Taurus you need to see something of value and substance result from the goals that came to life through the Aries experiences. You are concerned no longer with action only, but in getting material, tangible, or concrete results for all actions you initiate, for all projects you undertake. In Taurus you develop personal strength and endurance. You acquire material, physical, psychological assets. Here you experience the urge to accumulate. Questions needing answers from Taurus activities include: What gives *me* a sense of personal worth? What can *I* do to establish roots that provide stability in my life? What do *I* need, in a physical sense, to enjoy the pleasures available on this planet? What must *I* do to guarantee survival?

When Taurus is intercepted, the answers to these questions are not easily found. Your environment does not offer the structures, or facilities, you need to build self worth. You are challenged to acquire substances that prove your value by looking into more obscured channels.

Taurus shows where (house) you are concerned for your own physical safety and comfort. Here you learn to survive in the physical world. Taurus reminds us that "God helps those who help themselves." Without concern for self ... without drive to create personal stability ... you do not have the personal endurance, or a sufficiently powerful sense of your own value, to find fulfillment in intimate relationships. Without self worth you would have nothing of value to offer others once functioning in the world of relationships.

Scorpio provides the polarity needed by Taurus. It's house defines an area of life where you want to merge with others. By uniting your resources (material, emotional, physical or spiritual) with those of others, you are able, through the merging, to accomplish goals greater than what is possible independently. When involved in experiences described by Scorpio's house, you are challenged to join forces with another, or others, in an attempt to produce more than what you alone could accomplish. But to contribute something significant to any joint enterprise (Scorpio) you must have something of personal value to offer (Taurus). Also, any merging requires certain personal sacrifices.

Scorpio represents the reactions of others to your Taurus assets and accomplishments and the practical use you have made of them. Others, through their feedback (polarity), enable you to objectively see the value of your life. They show you, through their responses, how you have used or abused your material, mental, physical, emotional or spiritual assets. Scorpio is the sign of regeneration. Its house describes an area of life offering regenerative experiences. It shows where rebirth can occur. Intense involvement in the activities described by Scorpio's house "move" you to make significant changes in your life. Scorpio challenges you to look under the surface of the experiences it provides. Its house describes where you have the power to penetrate and regenerate.

In Scorpio you have the power to control. You can use this power to control others, or you can use it as a positive force by contributing to the world around you, supporting required change. The power, or intensity, of Scorpio is absorbed from the energies of those surrounding you. The ultimate challenge of this sign lies in the need to channel this power back to those from whom it came in a way that you both, or all, benefit through the experience.

Scorpio follows Libra in the zodiac. It describes the *value* of shared (Libra) experiences. You need to delve deeply into the experiences ruled by Scorpio's house to find what lies at the very core. This investigation ultimately leads to your own rebirth. It has been said that the house of Scorpio points to an area of life where you experience both the heights and depths of emotion and reality. These extremes in emotion result from interaction with others. Some are intensely satisfying; others are difficult. The relationships formed in the arena described by Scorpio's house strongly influence your life. They are so powerful, in fact, that you could repress feelings regarding their importance. These feelings, if not acknowledged, can fester until they erupt in explosive behavior either initiated by you or provoked by others. The eruption of repressed emotion creates a cleansing or rebirth.

Through the polarity established between Taurus and Scorpio, you learn to balance your personal survival needs with the need to merge resources and energies with others. Without both signs working in partnership, significant imbalances occur. Survival is the keynote for both of these powerfully important signs. In Taurus you need to accumulate the substances and skills required for your own physical, psychological survival. In Scorpio you must develop concern for others. You must be willing to share your personal strengths (Taurus) to assure survival of the significant relationships in your life.

When these signs are intercepted, there is a conflict between the Taurus urge to accumulate and Scorpio's need to regenerate or eliminate. There may be difficulty defining what rightfully belongs to you versus what assets must be shared. This is rarely, however, a conscious imbalance. There is a tendency to accumulate personal substances through the Taurus experiences without accessing Scorpio's awareness of the need to eliminate once the personal assets have served their purposes and hold no further value in your life. Instead of knowing how to let go or change when appropriate to do so, you tend to stand firm and hang on to outdated assets or fixed opinions long past the time of their usefulness.

The possessive tendencies so often associated with both Taurus and Scorpio are emphasized when these signs are intercepted. Here we find possessiveness in a material sense in Taurus, and a tendency to be overly possessive in relationships with Scorpio. Balance does not come easily when defining what assets or energies rightfully belong to you with what belongs to others. Conflict results because of the environment's lack of receptivity to your internal state. When Scorpio and Taurus are on house cusps, the environment recognizes your intensity and potential possessiveness in dealing with the issues of their houses. Lessons are provided regarding give and take. You are taught to recognize what has value and what has become obsolete in life.

Scorpio reveals to Taurus when it is time to clean house, when it is time to give up or let go, when it is time to unite resources, talents, energies with others in order to reach some powerful outcome. When intercepted, this polarity does not function objectively. In Taurus you may try to ingest more than what you are capable of digesting. In Scorpio you may try to digest "food" providing no real substance or value to personal growth.

As Aries is on the cusp of the house containing intercepted Taurus, your initial approach to this arena of experience is progressive and instinctive. The environment views your role here as that of a pioneer, courageous and daring. Even you, at first, may not recognize your inner need to not only initiate new experiences in this area of your life but to get *results* for your efforts. The environment supports your urge to be a leader here, to be assertive and independent. It may not provide the stability, the tools, or the role models you need to develop endurance to see projects through to completion. Once having moved into your Aries-experiences, you discover that you need to accomplish something having value here. However, because of the intercepted condition of Taurus, it is difficult to locate the substances or tools you need to acquire tangible results that make you feel resourceful. This dilemma can be likened to having a pocket full of money in an environment having no stores with merchandise that meet your fancy. What you feel is valuable, an important personal asset, may not be equally appreciated for its value by others.

The Scorpio interception creates another dilemma in another area of life. Here (house) you have power, but have difficulty finding an outlet for its expression. You want to experience intensity and intimacy, but the environment is unable to facilitate that need. Due to the environment's lack of support for your intensity and depth, the power evident in this sign can be repressed or turned inward. Until you have found a vehicle for its expression, it can surface as a subtle control over others or excessive self control leading to repressed emotions.

When Scorpio is intercepted, there is a tendency to attempt to change, or eliminate, what still has value because of the lack of value-consciousness available from the Taurus polarity. You recognize a need for change in the way things are normally managed in this area of your life, but rather than retaining the value of what has already been established, you may choose to destroy the whole thing ... to throw the baby out with the bath water.

The sign on the cusp of this house is Libra, suggesting your initial approach to this area of life is based on a desire for harmony, cooperation, and balance. It is important that your Scorpio power does not become suppressed entirely in your attempt to maintain harmony and balance in this area of your life.

Your environment recognizes your need for cooperation and shared experience. It may not, however, recognize your inner need to be "re-born" as a result of the relationships formed here. You attract others with whom to share ideas and experiences (Libra). These sharing involvements dredge up power from your unconscious that also need an outlet for expression. A problem results because the environment does not accept, or acknowledge, your power. Therefore, it has not taught you how to direct it. Some suggestions for resolving the conflicts posed by the Taurus/Scorpio polarity will be provided in later chapters.

GEMINI/SAGITTARIUS POLARITY

When involved with the activities ruled by the house of Gemini, you need variety. Here you are curious, communicative, and sometimes naive. You need mental stimulation and freedom to pursue your varied ideas and accumulate information that cultivates self understanding. In your Gemini activities you learn to recognize the contrasts and similarities evident in all of life's experiences. You discover the similarities and differences between yourself and others and begin to understand and appreciate the many contradictions in your own personality.

Gemini is concerned with accumulating and communicating information that is based on concrete fact. Sagittarius, its opposite sign, opens your awareness to the value of theory, principles, and abstractions. Without this polarity operative in life, the information received through the Gemini experience has no real value (Sagittarius). The words provided by Gemini are meaningless without the understanding made possible by Sagittarius. As in all polarities, there can be a conflict between action and reaction. Sagittarius represents others' reactions to your communications. When intercepted, this response is not obviously given or received.

Through the experiences ruled by the house of Sagittarius, you learn to view life from a broader frame of reference than what results from your Gemini activities. Sagittarius provides wisdom. Gemini provides the language used to share that wisdom with others.

As symbolized by the archer, Sagittarius is associated with future aspirations. Through experiences in its house, you become aware of tomorrow's possibilities rather than remaining trapped in the realities of today. Gemini, in its relationship to Sagittarius, shows where you apply future ideals and goals in daily living. Sagittarius enables you to make value-judgments around the information accumulated through your Gemini associations.

When this sign polarity is intercepted in the chart, there are no doors (cusps) through which to project their needs and capabilities into outer fields of activity. This does not mean that no projection is going on here, but there is little objectivity regarding the give-and-take required between these two areas of your life (houses). Due to the lack of feedback or encouragement gleaned from the outside world, you have problems communicating your ideals or expanding your understanding of the significance of these areas of life. A common dilemma associated with this intercepted polarity involves: When you have questions, no one has answers. On the other hand, when you have important answers to life's questions, no one asks.

When working with an intercepted Gemini, you need to ask yourself the following questions: Do you have a tendency to speak without first considering the value of what you are saying? Do you feel others are not interested in what intrigues you? Or, that others aren't hearing what you have to say? Are you often misunderstood? Are you obsessed with words, using them superficially or indiscriminately? Or, at the other extreme, do you fear communication because of the confusing responses you receive from others?

When Gemini and Sagittarius are intercepted, frustration in communication and feedback are often experienced. In Gemini's activities you may experience difficulty finding answers to your questions. The environment may respond to your quarries, but because it doesn't fully understand what you are asking, it provides unacceptable answers. Typical problems associated with this intercepted polarity involve communication frustration. You could have trouble presenting information in a manner that has meaning to others. Or, you may have difficulty finding meaning in the answers your environment gives you. You may understand, but be unable to find the words to express it.

When Sagittarius does not function in cooperation with Gemini, the power contained in the spoken word eludes you. When the environment furnishes you with information, the data presented does not "speak" to you in a way that has meaning. Or the environment, in attempting to respond to your questions, fails to understand exactly what you want to know. The resulting frustration can lead to one of two things. You may fear communicating your ideas due to an apparent lack of understanding, or encouragement, from your environment. Or you could develop a tendency to communicate indiscriminately without concern for others' desire to hear.

It is important to realize that this interception does not imply that you lack the abilities described by these signs. It suggests that the environment around you is not sufficiently set up to accommodate your educational needs. Because of lack of environmental input, you must learn to access information from obscure areas rather than expecting the environment to sate your intellectual hunger.

Intercepted Gemini suggests that answers to your questions are not available through "normal" channels in your community (school, neighbors, siblings). You must find your answers through more unconventional, unique or obscured areas. On one hand, you could rebel against your surroundings, demanding the kinds of feedback it is not normally equipped to provide. Or you may choose to keep silent, locking your ideas safely within the closet of the intercepted sign to avoid intellectual confrontation.

Taurus occupies the cusp of this house. It describes your initial approach to its experiences and therefore how others see you operating here. Based on what they see, they make assumptions that are not always correct. When first approaching this area of life, you are looking for stability, something offering practical or physical results for the efforts you put forth. After entering these experiences, you discover something new about yourself that others have never recognized. Curiosity invites variety here, encouraging you to seek new information, to discover the multiple avenues available for exploration in this area of your life. As the environment does not recognize your intellectual yearnings, it does not provide the variety of information you need for mental stimulation and growth. As a result, you may rebel against the confines of your environment and demand the variety it cannot offer. Or you might choose to remain silent about your interests to the degree you could suppress your curiosity altogether.

Gemini intercepted by no means implies impairment of the mental or communicative functions. It does, however, challenge you to find answers to life's questions with little objective feedback or educational direction provided by your environment.

On the other side of the chart, Sagittarius is intercepted in Scorpio's house. Here, you need to reach out to a larger world to expand your level of awareness regarding all things "foreign" to your conditioned environment. The role of Sagittarius is one of expansion. When intercepted, your urge to expand is not recognized by those around you. Therefore, it is difficult for you to define your philosophical beliefs and ideals regarding the future. Lacking objectivity normally provided by the Gemini polarity, it is difficult to mold your ideals, goals, and philosophical ideas into well-formed structures. You have not been taught methods to communicate your abstract thoughts.

When occupying a house cusp, Sagittarius shows an area of life around which you form philosophical attitudes. When intercepted, it is not, at first, easy to project these philosophies to the world around you. You have strong principles and goals regarding this department of life, but find difficulty communicating, or defining, these goals in concrete terms. At first you lack the Gemini-objectivity to communicate, or live out, your ideas in the here and now. It is easy to become caught up in a fanatical approach to these experiences to the degree you cannot objectively communicate your beliefs.

Having Scorpio on this cusp, your initial approach to this department of life is intense, deep and powerful. The environment recognizes your intensity and potential power. It may not encourage you to reach out to acquire a more expansive understanding of what future possibilities are available to you in this area of life. You are left with two obvious choices. You could rebel against the community and the limitations it imposes, and demand the freedom you desire to spread your wings, to broaden your horizons and expand your life. Or, you might choose to suppress your expansive urges altogether, allowing the environment to control your affairs, squelch your enthusiasm, and inhibit your goals for the future.

In later chapters, I will offer some suggestions for resolving the conflicts posed by intercepted signs.

CANCER/CAPRICORN POLARITY

More than in any other area of your life, when meeting the experiences ruled by the house of Cancer, you need security. Here you need to be nurtured; you need to belong. Once some degree of personal security has been established, you experience an urge to nurture others, first at a personal level, then at a social level, potentially evolving further to reach the level of universal "motherhood."

At first you tend to be vulnerable here ... sometimes even defensive ... out of fear of losing those things to which, or people to whom, you have become emotionally attached. You could cling to the substances or people represented by this house, looking to them to protect you instead of finding personal security through the experiences they provide.

The natural caretaking instincts of Cancer have been, in the past, related only to the nurturing of home and family. We now realize that Cancer's urge to protect functions at other levels. A great artist, for example, might feel toward his, or her, creations as a mother would toward her child. A businessperson having Cancer on the 10th house is protective and nurturing toward the business and his/her social accomplishments. The house of Cancer describes where your natural nurturing instincts are expressed, even though you may not consciously associate your involvement here as being "maternal."

Both Cancer and its opposite sign, Capricorn, are concerned with security, but at two different levels. In Cancer, you need personal security. In Capricorn you are concerned with social security and acceptance for the place you fill within the social structure. Capricorn describes the need to define your social territory to find security within your particular social realm. Its house describes where you are territory-conscious, where you need to feel secure at a social level. Here you need respect, recognition, and approval from the outside world to validate your importance within it.

The polarity offered by the Cancer/Capricorn partnership deals with personal security and emotion versus social security and ambition. When functioning objectively, Cancer helps you build the emotional strengths needed to support your Capricorn social image and accomplishments, and to define and defend your social place. When these signs are intercepted, this polarity does not, at first, function naturally. You could concern yourself with acquiring personal security in Cancer's house at the expense of reaching your social potentials (Capricorn). At the same time, in the Capricorn activities of your life, you might block the emotional, sensitive side of your nature entirely out of fear of social ridicule.

With Cancer intercepted you are, at first, unable to structure your emotions creatively. You either over-react to emotional experiences or inhibit emotional expression altogether. As the environment does not offer the security you need in this area of life, you are challenged to build emotional strengths and stability on your own. You may find it necessary to break from old attachments in this house in order to find yourself.

As occurs in the case of all intercepted signs, there is no door (cusp) through which to apply these qualities into external affairs. Others may not recognize your emotional needs, your sensitivity, your emotional vulnerability in the Cancer ruled area of your life. Gemini occupies the cusp of the house containing Cancer, suggesting that the environment recognizes your apparent flexibility and skill in adaptation. It is not attuned to your need to set emotionally safe limits. Due to the environment's lack of perception regarding your Cancer-ruled needs, it does not offer the help you need to fill them.

Gemini is a detached, mental sign. It describes a cerebral approach to the experiences it rules. It is not until you are actively involved in the activities ruled by this house that you confront your own emotions. Because this happens at such an internal level, the outer expression of these emotions lacks objectivity and may seem erratic.

You probably felt that your early environment did not offer the kinds of experiences you needed to feel grounded in this area of your life. As a result, you could develop a tendency to cling to possessions and/or people associated with the house even more strongly than if Cancer were on the cusp. The kind of nurturing you needed in youth may not have been available to you from the environment or your family. What you needed to develop security was not recognized by those around you.

Your initial approach to this area of life is one of accumulating ideas and experiences (Gemini on cusp). Your mind is active. Your ideas are dualistic and versatile. However, with Cancer intercepted here, you may attempt to hold on to each experience you encounter until a psychological "overload" is reached. Thus, it becomes necessary for you to define boundaries, to set limits, to learn to let go. Having Capricorn also intercepted, this is no easy task.

While Cancer needs the structuring provided by its opposite sign Capricorn, Capricorn needs the warmth offered by Cancer. When Capricorn is intercepted, it is often difficult to project warmth and understanding when working within the parameters of the house in which it is entrapped. Because you don't feel the emotional warmth of Cancer when operating here, one of two things could result. Either you could build your Capricorn walls so rigidly that you find yourself imprisoned within them, or you could fail to build any emotional structures in this area of life and therefore find yourself left out in the cold.

If you have Capricorn intercepted, and the first example rings true in your life, ask yourself the following questions: Are you overly concerned with what people might say in response to any emotional display on your part? So much so that you suppress your true feelings about the experiences described by this house? Are you afraid to bend here, to reveal your own vulnerability and sensitivity? Are you living in a jail built by your own rigidity? Have you become so dependent on society's approval and opinions that you are neglecting those who love you the most? Has social protocol become more important to you than the projection of human warmth?

On the other hand, you might ask yourself: Have you failed to define the social significance of what you are expressing and experiencing in this area of your life? Have you failed to build structures that merit social respect? Do you feel you are not receiving the recognition you need here? Are you unable to define your social place?

Having Sagittarius on the cusp of this house, it is important to set future goals regarding these experiences. However, with Capricorn intercepted, you must go one step farther. You must build the kind of structures necessary for those goals to be met and realized at a practical level. You need freedom in this area of life to expand outside the limits of your environment (Sagittarius). You also need to know when to stop expanding and begin building something solid from your ideas (Capricorn). If a pilgrim never reached the end of his/her journey, s/he would never establish a homestead, nor would s/he ever know, or own, what rightfully could belong to him/her. The ideals of Sagittarius need to become realities in Capricorn. When Capricorn is intercepted, the process of definition may not be an objective or easy one. It is difficult to define your social place because your environment never made that place known to you.

You may find that your social ambitions have no place in your particular environment. If this is the case, you need to break from tradition, or conditioning, and build your reputation around something more unique or individualized.

Because Cancer and Capricorn deal with parental archetypes, your relationship to parents, or the relationship between the parents themselves, may have been illusive or incongruent in some way. Their influence on your life is more important than what you might, at first, recognize, especially when considered with regard to how their relationship influenced your goals and needs in the areas of life described by the houses of your Cancer/Capricorn interceptions.

In later chapters, I will offer some suggestions for resolving the problems or conflicts posed by intercepted signs.

LEO/AQUARIUS POLARITY

Through the experiences encountered in the house ruled by Leo you see a part of yourself reflected in everything you do. Here you need to stamp your identity, or leave your mark, on all that you touch and all that touches you. By doing so, you prove to yourself, and to those in your surroundings, that your life has value. It is purposeful. You have a definite or special role to play. For this reason, when functioning in your Leo-ruled activities, you need to occupy center stage.

The experiences available in this house help you to develop self confidence and to design creative modes of self expression. As you see your importance reflected in your creations, and in others' responses to your expression, you become illuminated to personal potentials and/or problems you had not previously recognized.

Ruled by the Sun, the center of our solar system, Leo describes an area of life (house) where you outwardly express your inner sense of purpose and importance (Sun). Here you need to take pride in what you accomplish. You need to be recognized and appreciated for all that you do.

Without the polarity offered by Aquarius, it is easy to become trapped in the wonder of your own importance and go overboard in expressing your will, or to demand unmerited attention to feed your ego. Aquarius is concerned with social needs and causes. It represents group reactions to your Leo ego-expression. Aquarius provides an opportunity to play a significant part in filling social or group needs. But you must draw on experiences cultivated in Leo's house for the *product* of that contribution. As with all oppositions, Leo and Aquarius must operate together to produce something purposeful, or special, to contribute at a social level.

Aquarius has been called the sign of the "rebel." Its house shows where you need to break free from conditioned attitudes about yourself and society and express your true individuality, unconditioned by outside circumstances.

In Aquarius you rebel against personal or social injustices. However, to do so constructively, you must call on the polarity of Leo to provide a purpose for the rebellion. Without Leo, you become a "rebel without a cause."

When these signs are intercepted, their natural polarity does not function with full consciousness, and personal frustration is experienced when attempting to integrate them in your outer life. In the house containing intercepted Leo, it is difficult to find experiences that make you feel important and successful. Others may not recognize your need for attention and recognition here. You may feel unappreciated, as others tend not to verbalize their gratitude for your generosity. You need "strokes" here. You need to feel proud of the quality of your life, but have difficulty attracting appreciation from others for your accomplishments.

Cancer occupies the cusp of this house, showing your initial approach to these experiences is sensitive and nurturing. Inside, however, where others cannot see, you are proud and powerful, strong willed and creative. Because others fail to recognize your Leo-strengths, they don't respond to your need for power. And, because they don't recognize your need for attention in this area of your life, they do not offer you the stage. You react to this in one of two ways. You could demand attention by exhibiting excessive behavior, or you might inhibit your Leo creativity altogether.

When Leo is intercepted, it is necessary to break from your environment's conditioning in order to find and express your sense of purpose and importance in life. While in the process of doing so, you, at first, have a tendency to project your ego without concern for others, without the polarity of Aquarius. As the environment does not offer the facilities you need for purpose-fulfillment, you are challenged to either break away from it, or find areas of expression through more obscured channels.

While you have a significant role to play in this area of your life, you find difficulty locating external facilities that accept your creative assets or encourage their development. As a result, you either rebel against society's lack of receptivity to your offerings, or you begin questioning the value of your talents to the degree you could suppress them entirely.

As mentioned earlier, Leo shows where you see yourself reflected through others' responses, and through your own creations. When intercepted, the "mirror" is defective in some way, showing only a foggy blur that distorts the true essence of your creativity.

On the other side of the chart, Aquarius is intercepted in the house ruled by Capricorn. Two very contradicting needs influence your experiences and attitudes toward the experiences ruled by this house. Abstractly, Aquarius could be considered the ruler of intercepted signs. As interceptions refer to qualities that only surface out of rebellion, they have a special affinity to what Aquarius represents.

Aquarius shows where (house) you need to break free from rigid social patterning and express your unique, individualistic self. Here, you discover that you can be more that what you were taught to be. You don't have to be a product of your environment. When intercepted, the process of breaking free creates a crisis. You experience difficulty locating external channels that enable you to develop your individuality or encourage you to become unique.

As Capricorn is on the cusp of this house, respect and recognition are important to you when meeting the experiences it rules. Under the surface you are a rebel, an investigator, and an inventor of new ideas. To express these qualities you must defy the expectations of others. Others may think of you as conventional, while inside your ideas are quite the opposite. The question here is: Do you dare risk your social reputation by outwardly expressing unconventional attitudes and proving the need for reform? Must you break from your environment and its influences in order to be yourself?

Your needs in this area of life are indeed complex. You want to become a part of the social structure. You want to achieve and to know where your particular social territory lies (Capricorn). But you also need to be "different." You need to be a part of the structure and still feel free from it. You need to be a rebel without risking your reputation.

In early life, the surroundings did not encourage you to develop your inventive faculties. In time it becomes necessary to break away from these surroundings, at least at a psychological level, to find who you really are. A dilemma is confronted as you attempt to break from rigid conditioning of the past. You might try to rebel, but as you look around you, be unable to find anything to rebel against. Or, society doesn't recognize the form your rebellion takes and therefore can offer no feedback.

In later chapters, I will offer some suggestions for resolving the conflicts posed by the Leo/Aquarius interception.

VIRGO/PISCES POLARITY

Just as Virgo rules the physiological digestive processes, it also deals with mental digestion. Its role in the chart is to provide the capacity for discrimination between valuable information and superficial nonsense. It enables you to separate and digest, eliminating waste material while organizing and retaining information that has potential meaning in your life.

Through the experiences met in the area of life described by Virgo's house you learn to analyze, discriminate, and eliminate non-essentials. You learn to use knowledge. You learn to criticize, to ask questions and, by doing so, you continually adjust and perfect your skills. In Virgo you are looking for the best way to use your potentials, an acceptable way of expressing your Leo-ego, a well-defined awareness of your life purpose.

Virgo has an innate ability to identify incongruities and to recognize imperfections. Its purpose lies not simply in identifying problems, but in developing techniques for perfecting. Pisces, its polar opposite, is not concerned with details but looks for the total significance of an experience or an idea. Pisces is concerned with universal ideals rather than concrete data. While the lessons of Virgo lie in areas of analysis, discrimination, and perfection, Pisces' lessons are acceptance and faith. This polarity enables you to work at perfecting your life and to accept your imperfections.

When intercepted, Virgo and Pisces function separately, against one another rather than cooperatively as a team. This leads to mental frustration, tension and confusion. In the house containing the Virgo interception, you over-criticize, over-analyze, over-classify to such a degree that you lose the overall significance of the experiences at hand. There is a tendency to take things apart, only to find yourself unable to put the pieces back together. In the process of your dissection, you forget the Piscean image of the goal you are striving to reach. You lose the Pisces vision of wholeness. Therefore, rather than perfecting with your Virgo energy, you are ultimately destroying, or shredding, the true essence of the experiences the house holds for you.

Pisces provides the ability to see a "vision" of a finished product or an ideal. Virgo sees the details, or the parts, needed for construction. When Virgo is intercepted, you see only fragments, while in the Pisces interception you have an abstract vision of the whole, but lack the practicality or technicality needed to build something tangible out of your dreams. You could be totally unrealistic in the area of life described by the house of Pisces, while at the same time be overly realistic in your Virgo experiences. The natural objectivity provided by this polarity is not functioning in your outer world. When this occurs, you fail to see things as they actually are.

Leo occupies the cusp of the house containing the Virgo interception. Others see you, as you function in this area of life, as confident, reliable, proud, generous, and probably rather fixed. Inside, however, you question, you criticize your performance, you try to perfect your expression, but you lack a clear vision of what you could become. You lack the Piscean faith required to make the adjustments you inwardly know are necessary. Without a door (cusp) through which to express and develop your Virgo skills, others do not recognize your need for detail and organization. Without role models to show you how to organize your life, confusion reigns.

Virgo shows, by house, where you have questions. When intercepted, you may feel that no one truly comprehends the questions you ask and therefore no one can provide answers. You must look for your answers within. As occurs with all intercepted signs, one of two things could result when Virgo is intercepted in the chart. You could become excessively critical due to your inner frustrations, or you could stop attempting to perfect your skills because of the environment's lack of encouragement. You could be excessively critical about the matters of this house, sometimes even demanding, or you could fear outwardly criticizing those things you know are in need of repair. You might mentally dis-assemble things ruled by this house only to find yourself left with a multitude of nondescript pieces. Or, you might fall into a pattern of accepting the unacceptable. The way the system taught you to organize your life doesn't work for you.

When Virgo is intercepted, Pisces is also captured on the other side of the chart, posing a completely different challenge. As you lack the balance of Virgo here, you tend to be overly nebulous toward these experiences ... too unrealistic, living too much in a world of dreams with no real substance. While Pisces calls for faith in the unknown, when intercepted this faith is easily misplaced. You may lack discrimination here, giving indiscriminately of your time, services, money, or whatever things are ruled by the house in question.

The ability to analyze, organize, and use discrimination is obscured by the lack of Virgo objectivity. Therefore, you may accept your inadequacies in this area of your life without ever trying to perfect them.

Pisces and its ruler Neptune rule both fear and faith. When intercepted it is easy to become obsessed with unrealistic fears. This results in either neglecting responsibilities entirely and escaping into an unreal world, or in hanging on to things that have no real value due to an over-attachment to the past and fear of the future.

Aquarius is on the cusp of this house. Others are aware of your unique ideas for handling these affairs. They view you as progressive, a humanitarian, possibility an eccentric, as they see you go about functioning in this area of your life. They fail to recognize your ideals and emotional vulnerability. There comes a point in everyone's life when they must stop giving and let others take responsibility for their own lives. This seems an especially important lesson to be learned when Pisces and Virgo are intercepted. The same could be said in reverse.

It is the role of Pisces to provide the faith required to move forward into the unknown. When intercepted this faith must be developed with little help from the outside world. This does not mean that everyone will oppose you. It could simply indicate that the responses of others are not adequate. Others find it difficult to identify with, or to understand, those things that inspire you. As it is difficult for you to define your goals, others are unable to encourage you to pursue them.

In later chapters, I will offer some suggestions for resolving the problems associated with intercepted signs.

CHAPTER IV

RULERSHIPS AND INTERCEPTIONS

Planets operate to energize life. Each planet has a specific role to play, a specific job to perform, to keep your life moving. Part of each planet's responsibility is to acquire the kinds of experiences, through the house it occupies, that will bring fulfillment to the area of life described by the house it rules.

The energies of two planets are required to fill your complex needs when a sign is intercepted. The planet *ruling* the house cusp acquires experiences that encourage you to enter the house activities. Once the door is opened, a new need is met that was not known to you prior to the time it was exposed by the cusp ruler. This is shown by the intercepted sign. The planet ruling the intercepted sign must then work to find other experiences (its house) that help you elicit and utilize the resources described by the intercepted sign. Certain frustrations are experienced in the process.

Planets ruling intercepted signs point to experiences (house) that may have played a strong part in contributing to the repression or suppression of the signs' needs. For example, if the ruler of an intercepted sign in the second house, confusion regarding money, self worth, or the importance of acquiring resources independently might have caused you to suppress needs and urges regarding the house containing the intercepted sign. The only way you can bring the positive qualities of this sign to the surface is by developing a new, more individualized, less conditioned outlook toward all second house matters. The following outline briefly describes other possible manifestations of dilemmas experienced regarding the house placements of planets ruling intercepted signs.

RULER OF INTERCEPTED SIGN IN 1ST HOUSE: Self image not adequately supported by the environment. You need to define yourself in new terms. Problem: Early excessive, or lack of, attention placed on appearance or personality.

RULER OF INTERCEPTED SIGN IN 2ND HOUSE: Self worth and capacity to maintain life independently not adequately supported by the environment. You need to discover personal strengths and resources beyond what you were taught you possessed. Problem: Early excessive, or lack of, attention placed on economical stability or personal worth and talents.

RULER OF INTERCEPTED SIGN IN 3RD HOUSE: Educational requirements not adequately supported by the environment. You need to acquire information from sources beyond what was provided by your communities' educational facilities. Problem: Early excessive, or lack of, attention placed on academic skill, intelligence, or community participation. Problems with siblings.

RULER OF INTERCEPTED SIGN IN 4TH HOUSE: Personal foundations and a solid sense of where you "belong" not adequately supported by the environment. You need to build security around experiences other than those provided by family. Problem: Early excessive, or lack of, attention placed on security or family background.

RULER OF INTERCEPTED SIGN IN 5TH HOUSE: The urge for creative expression and the desire to reproduce yourself through external activities not adequately supported by the environment. You need to find creative and recreative interests beyond those defined by your environment. Problem: Early excessive, or lack of, attention placed on creativity, procreation, recreation, sports or entertainment.

RULER OF INTERCEPTED SIGN IN 6TH HOUSE: The desire for a meaningful routine and the need to feel useful when approaching daily activities not adequately supported by the environment. You need to define your usefulness in your own terms. Problem: Early excessive, or lack of, attention placed on work, health and/or routine daily management.

RULER OF INTERCEPTED SIGN IN 7TH HOUSE: The urge to interact with others in sharing experiences not adequately supported by the environment. You need to redefine the importance of interpersonal relationships in a way that holds meaning to you rather than relying on the environment's interpretation of who you need to complement your life. Problem: Early excessive, or lack of, attention placed on marriage (this can be marital problems between parents) or teamwork.

RULER OF INTERCEPTED SIGN IN 8TH HOUSE: The urge to merge with others or another to experience intimacy and create needed change not adequately supported by the environment. You need to investigate the deeper meaning of life in ways not encouraged, or recognized, by your environment. Problem: Early excessive, or lack of, attention placed on sacrifice, sex, separation or intimacy.

RULER OF INTERCEPTED SIGN IN 9TH HOUSE: The urge to broaden your understanding of life and explore what lies beyond not adequately supported by the environment. You need to establish principles and philosophical ideals that extend beyond those introduced by your environment. Problem: Early excessive, or lack of, attention placed on religion, higher education or the existence of prejudice.

RULER OF INTERCEPTED SIGN IN 10TH HOUSE: The urge to find your "place" in the world to secure success not adequately supported by your environment. You need to define success in terms not understood or encouraged by your environment. Problem: Early excessive, or lack of, attention placed on success, recognition or authority.

RULER OF INTERCEPTED SIGN IN 11TH HOUSE: The urge to interact with the larger community and to define goals for a personal and social future not adequately supported by your environment. You need to find a social cause not yet recognized by your environment. Problem: Early excessive, or lack of, attention placed on social interaction or goal setting.

RULER OF INTERCEPTED SIGN IN 12TH HOUSE: The urge to investigate the mysteries of life and to understand the impact your personal and social past has had on your life not supported or recognized by your environment. You need to define spirituality, karma or service in terms not familiar to others in your environment. Problem: Early excessive, or lack of, emphasis placed on privacy, secrets or social services.

Rulers of intercepted signs not only suggest conditions that contribute to the frustration defined by interceptions, but indicate what must be done to rectify the potential problems. Like falling off of a bicycle, your only recourse for overcoming the resulting fear of repetition, frustration, or lack of environmental support and understanding, when dealing with the experiences defined by the house holding your intercepted ruler, is to try again under different circumstances. Try again, but on your own terms.

It is possible to find the ruler of an intercepted sign also intercepted. When this happens, the entire concept built on intercepted signs is intensified. It is particularly important, when this occurs, to find alternative means of filling the needs of the intercepted sign and directing the energy represented by its ruler. Inner probing can result in a unique definition of what you need for personal fulfillment apart from what you have been overtly or covertly taught. Once you recognize, and accept, that your familiar world may not provide the experiences you need for personal fulfillment, your process of self discovery begins. Your self concepts (1st house), sense of productivity (2nd house), search for knowledge (3rd house), sense of emotional belonging (4th house), creative capability (5th house), sense of usefulness (6th house), capacity to find fulfilling relationships (7th house), ability to regenerate (8th house), philosophical concepts (9th house), capacity for success (10th house), desire to connect with others at a social level (11th house) or urge to contribute through service (12th house) must be defined in terms other than what has been introduced to you through early, formative experiences. Your answers lie within. If you seek fulfillment in these areas of your life through traditional channels, you will always find missing links exist that keep you from fully integrating your life.

CHAPTER V

DUPLICATED SIGNS OR INTERCEPTED HOUSES

Whenever you find intercepted signs in a chart, you will also find a set of "duplicated signs," or two houses, side by side, having the same sign on their cusps (see figure 4 on the following page). Whenever a sign is duplicated on two consecutive house cusps, its opposite sign will also occupy two houses.

Each sign contains 30 degrees. When the same sign is found on two house cusps, the house containing the lesser degree is obviously smaller than 30 degrees. What you are seeing when you find duplicated signs in a chart are intercepted *houses*. The sign is intercepting the house. The house containing the lesser degree is intercepted by the sign.

The potential represented by the sign on these two sequential house cusps is so strong and highly developed that it carries the power to dominate the environment defined by the intercepted house. Rather than being intimidated or inhibited by the environment, such as in the case of an intercepted sign, intercepted *houses* define areas of life where you can influence the environment. Could this be the way the universe has chosen to compensate for the frustrations presented by intercepted signs?

Planets ruling duplicated signs, or the intercepted houses, must work overtime. They have twice the responsibilities of other planets in the chart. Because the functions of personality represented by these planets are highly developed, the added responsibility, while at times exhausting, is something you are capable of handling.

When *signs* are intercepted, it is difficult to locate outside structures through which to express the qualities and fill the needs they represent. When *houses* are intercepted, the opposite is true. You have developed the traits of these signs to such a degree that you can use the resulting power to control the world around you, or at least to the degree you are not intimated by it. Your needs and potentials (sign) dominate, or intercept, the environ-

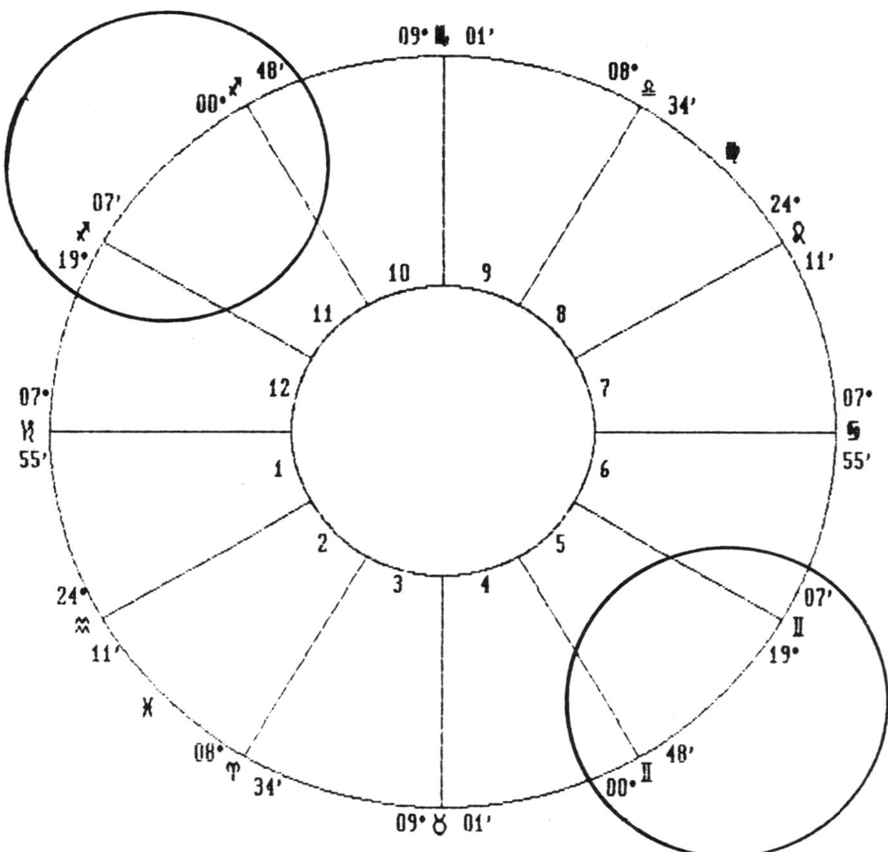

Figure 4: Gemini & Sagittarius are duplicated, intercepting the 5th house.

ment (house). Realize that this power, or potential to influence, can be projected in a positive or negative manner. Aspects to the rulers of these signs show the talents and challenges involved with the direction of the power.

The activities described by an intercepted house (the house containing the lesser degree) must be channeled into the activities of the house containing the larger degree of the same sign for fulfillment and personal growth to be experienced. You are challenged to incorporate what is comfortable and well formed (intercepted house) into a new framework for expression (following house).

According to Elan Bacher, an intercepted *house* represents the unfulfilled past seeking fulfillment or expression through the experiences defined by the house containing the larger degree. The fact that the intercepted house is in a 12th house relationship to the following seems to be of some importance in the interpretation of this configuration as well. Bacher's theory suggests that it is important to apply the experiences acquired through the intercepted house into the operations of the following. The 12th house significance suggests some spiritual, or "karmic," responsibility lies in meeting this challenge. In some way, fulfillment in the house having the larger degree on its cusp is dependent on what has been developed in the intercepted house.

An intercepted house describes an area of life where you find ease in expressing the power of the sign. Therefore, you need a new outlet for its expression to continue your growth within the environmental structure. This external outlet is found in the house containing the same sign, but larger degree. Just as the needs of intercepted signs are hidden or obscured due to the power of the environment, the external experiences represented by intercepted houses are less important to the growth process than the need of the sign. The sign encourages you to "stretch" your capabilities. It is attempting to draw you into the following house activities. In the process, it encourages you to integrate the external activities of the intercepted house (the house containing the lesser degree of the duplicated sign) into the activities described by the following house (the house containing the larger degree).

As an example, consider the chart shown in figure 4. It has 1 degree Gemini on the 5th house cusp with 19 degrees of Gemini on the 6th. The experiences described by the 5th house are intercepted by Gemini. This individual has creative skills descriptive of Gemini, i.e. communication talents of some kind. These skills are natural and require less effort to develop than what is normally the case of Gemini on the 5th house cusp. This individual has an ability to influence his/her environment by using creative talent. The challenge of this combination involves finding a way to incorporate the creative Gemini talents (5th) into 6th house work routines. In essence, this person is challenged to turn his/her hobbies (5th house) into a vocation (6th house). The efforts expended to develop and use the activities described by the intercepted house involve not developing skills within the framework ruled by the house, but finding an outlet for expression through the following house.

The activities defined by intercepted houses do not sufficiently challenge you. You are already well-versed here. You need to apply the innate abilities you possess toward meeting experiences in the house sharing the same sign, but having a greater degree on the cusp. As less attention must be focussed on developing skills in the intercepted house, you are encouraged to filter those skills into the activities ruled by the following house. Once you integrate the activities of these two houses, your intercepted signs automatically begin to emerge.

Realize that an intercepted house is smaller than most, and considerably smaller than a house containing an intercepted sign. This suggests that less energy and time must be spent focusing on external experiences ruled by intercepted houses. Transiting planets, for example, take less time moving through intercepted houses than through houses containing intercepted signs. This is congruent with the idea that intercepted houses describe fields of experience requiring less focus because you are already well-established in these areas of life. There is little need to concentrate long periods of time and energy developing something you already possess.

INTERCEPTED FIRST HOUSE: Here, we find the same sign on both the 1st and 2nd house cusps of the chart, suggesting *power of personality*. This combination encourages you to integrate 1st and 2nd house experiences ... make your personality (1st house) an asset (2nd house). Your persona is powerful. People notice you. Your challenge is to focus not on personal appearance, projection, or other facets that compose your persona. These qualities are already well developed. When being introduced to the world, you need to demonstrate productivity and exhibit your talents. You need to show the world that you can produce results in concrete terms by *using* your personal power and charisma to produce something of value.

The sign on these house cusps describes a powerful quality, positive or negative, that you possess. Because it is strongly developed, you must prove its productive potential. You must concern yourself with not how others see you (first house), but the value and substance (second house) of your projection. Incorporate the power of your personality into resourceful enterprise. The planet ruling this sign describes the energy you must use to merge these two departments of life. Experiences are encountered in the house it occupies that enable you to do so.

INTERCEPTED SECOND HOUSE: Here we find the same sign on both the 2nd and 3rd house cusps of the chart, suggesting *power of productivity*. Rather than directing your energy on acquiring material substances, you are challenged to use your resources to acquire new skills, new information, and form new community associations. Your self worth (2nd house) is strongly connected to intellectual pursuits (3rd house). Appreciate the value of information and use your innate talents to encourage others to become informed. To you, knowledge is worth the financial investment it requires. Self worth, built on possession and acquisition only, is not enough. You need to appreciate the value of information, communication and community interaction. And, you need to communicate and share with those in your environment what you have found valuable through personal experiences.

The sign on these consecutive house cusps describes a quality that is well-developed. It can easily produce the resources you need for productive living and personal survival (2nd house). It describes strengths you own that enable you to acquire the personal resources you need. These skills must also be used to acquire information that can be useful not only to yourself, but to those who share your space.

The planet ruling this sign describes the energy used to merge these two departments of life. Its house shows where experiences are available that enable you to do so.

INTERCEPTED THIRD HOUSE: Here we find the same sign on both the 3rd and 4th houses of the chart, suggesting you have *power of knowledge.* Information you possess must be used to strengthen your emotional base. Use your intellectual expertise when evaluating all security issues. You have information that needs to be used to secure your life or the lives of others, to establish foundations, to gain a sense of belonging in your environment. Strive to make emotionally satisfying contacts in your community. Security must be built on knowledge. You have good ideas. You have intellectual power to influence your community with the information you possess. Your challenge is to direct your knowledge into emotionally satisfying channels, and use it to build a solid nest.

The sign on these consecutive house cusps describes the way you process data and how you interact within your community. The planet ruling their cusps describes the energy used to merge these two departments of life. Its house shows where you meet experiences that enable you to do so.

INTERCEPTED FOURTH HOUSE: Here we find the same sign on both the 4th and 5th houses, suggesting *emotional power*. You are challenged to use the experiences you have accumulated from your past as a source of creative inspiration. Your needs regarding security and emotional safety strongly color your creative expression and recreative interests. You have a strong emotional base. You need to find creative ways of expressing your emotions.

You own inherited features that contribute to creative enterprise. Your legacy (5th house) can be built on your inheritance (4th house), or what you have acquired through genetic transfer.

The sign on these cusps describes attitudes, needs, and potentials that are strongly developed. You can use them to get what you need from your environment to acquire security and build a strong emotional base. Your challenge is to incorporate your emotional strengths into all 5th house creative, procreative, recreative ventures.

The planet ruling these consecutive house cusps describes the energy used to merge these two areas of life. Its house location describes the experiences enabling you to do so.

INTERCEPTED FIFTH HOUSE: Here we find the same sign on both the 5th and 6th house cusps of the chart, suggesting *power of creativity*. You were born with well-formed talents descriptive of the sign on these two house cusps. As these skills are natural, minimal attention must be focused on their development. Your challenge is to use your creative gifts (5th house) in productive enterprise (6th house). Incorporate your talents (5th house) into your employment (6th house). You may choose to work (6th) with children (5th). Or you might opt to seek a position that encourages other forms of creative expression. Your talents are well formed, but they will be wasted if no productive, routine outlet is designed for their expression.

You are blessed with the potential to find a vocation you love, and to work in an environment that encourages creative expression, risk, speculation, or other heart-felt activities. Negatively, you might not take your work seriously, only to meet criticism of others based on your playful approach. You perfect your creative skills by locating productive outlets that require technical application.

The sign on these consecutive house cusps describes the creative abilities you need to incorporate into daily routines. The planet ruling the sign describes the energy required to merge these two areas of life. It shows, by its house placement, experiences that enable you to do so.

INTERCEPTED SIXTH HOUSE: Here we find the same sign on both the 6th and 7th house cusps of the chart, suggesting *power of daily management*. You need to work (6th house) with people (7th house). You came into life with an innate ability to produce, handle routine responsibility, and to develop systems that fill the needs of your daily life. You grow as you use your vocational skills in harmony with others, learn to delegate work responsibilities, and share the benefits that result from good management. It is important, however, that you don't project your work ethic on all personal relationships you form.

The sign on these consecutive house cusps describes a quality you possess that enables you to handle daily requirements for life maintenance. As these traits are natural to you, they require minimal training. Once you integrate your skills with those of others, you begin the process of social integration. The planet ruling this sign describes the energy required to merge these two areas of life. It shows, by house placement, experiences that enable you to do so.

INTERCEPTED SEVENTH HOUSE: Here we find the same sign on both the 7th and 8th house cusps, suggesting *people power*. You know how to attract people. Growth comes not from the process of forming relationships (7th house), but as a result of maintaining them (8th house).

You know how to interact. This natural skill provides power to influence others. Your challenge lies in using these skills to promote, and experience, the regeneration that relationships require. You need to merge with others to share mutual skills, talents, and assets. This requires ego-detachment. Your attention needs to be focussed not on relationships only, but on what comes out of relationships ... the changes relationships invoke ... the sacrifices and investments they require.

The sign sharing these consecutive house cusps describes how you interact and a quality you seek in others. The planet ruling this sign describes the energy you use to merge these two areas of life. Its house shows where experiences are available that enable you to do so.

INTERCEPTED EIGHTH HOUSE: Here we find the same sign occupying both the 8th and 9th house cusps, suggesting *power of regeneration*. The 8th house deals with issues of regeneration, the "death" process, the need to recycle life's experiences. These issues are familiar to you. Your challenge is to focus not strictly on the process of regeneration and change, but to develop a philosophical orientation regarding its significance.

This combination induces an occult philosophical perspective toward life, and often leads to a belief in life after death. A psychological, penetrating outlook on religion, and all concepts that are foreign to the normal views of others in your environment, is evident. You must learn to be attentive to how the major changes life presents influence your beliefs and color your prejudices.

The sign sharing these consecutive house cusps describes how you meet significant life changes, the way they influence your philosophies, and how they create an urge to expand your intellect. The planet ruling this sign describes the energy you must use to merge these two areas of life. Its house shows where experiences are available that enable you to do so.

INTERCEPTED NINTH HOUSE: Here we find the same sign on both the 9th and 10th houses of the chart, indicating *power of convictions*. You have strong principles that stand behind your social reputation. You demonstrate these beliefs through the role you play in your professional arena. The quality of your morals, ethics, and social principles strongly color your professional reputation. Your focus must be placed not on proving the validity of your beliefs, but in demonstrating your principles, and level of wisdom, when functioning as a social participant or in profession.

Your understanding of "foreign" concepts, and your attitude toward ideas and people who are different from what is familiar to your environment, are solidly formed, whether positively or negatively. Your test is to live out these principles through career or other social functions. As a result, your reputation, or social standing, is strongly colored by the principles you stand upon.

The sign sharing these consecutive house cusps describes your basic orientation toward higher learning, philosophy, and career ambitions. The planet ruling this sign describes the energy you use to merge these two areas of life. Its house shows where experiences are available that enable you to do so.

INTERCEPTED TENTH HOUSE: Here we find the same sign on both the 10th and 11th house cusps, indicating *power of influence*. You have the ability to be noticed, to acquire recognition, and to gain professional status. You are challenged to use your position to contribute to social, or group, causes. You must share your success with others in order to meet some social need that requires group energy. Rather than focussing on personal attainment only, look further to find a social cause that needs your professional skills. True fulfillment comes by incorporating your inborn talent to achieve goals that extend beyond personal.

The 11th house is the house of Aquarius, representing concepts and issues involving true Aquarian-age goals of brotherly love and humanitarian progress. You need to know that your career (10th house) provides a vehicle for contributing to humanitarian goals and encourages social growth (11th house).

The sign sharing these consecutive house cusps describes how you approach professional activities and the type of group contributions you need to make. The planet ruling this sign describes the energy you must use to merge these two areas of life. Its house shows where experiences are available that enable you to do so.

INTERCEPTED ELEVENTH HOUSE: Here we find the same sign on both the 11th and 12th house cusps, suggesting *group power*. You have an innate ability to influence groups. You are aware of the importance of social causes and the power available when groups of people merge to work for social change. You are goal-oriented and concerned with the future.

You were born with an ability to work with people and to work toward social reform. Your challenge is to not simply participate in groups, but to make a commitment to serve the larger community. Don't just befriend others and interact at a social level, but be sensitive to people who have suffered or are in need of healing at some level.

The sign sharing these consecutive house cusps describes the power you have to influence others. It also describes how you approach service-oriented involvements. The planet ruling this sign describes the energy you must use to merge these two areas of your life. Its house shows where experiences are available that enable you to do so.

INTERCEPTED TWELFTH HOUSE: While little has been written on intercepted houses, (duplicated signs) in the past, there has been various materials offered regarding the significance of having the same sign on the 12th and 1st house cusps. The most common belief regarding this combination is that it describes an individual who was unable to complete an important mission, or fill an important need, in a past life and is here to "wrap things up."

There seems to be some karmic significance to an intercepted 12th house. Whether it indicates unfinished business from past lives or not, we may never know for sure. What is evident, in this life, is a need to live out your inner beliefs and commitments. You are projecting, through the ascendant, a great deal of unconscious energy. If you have a strong spiritual base, it will be evident to others who first meet you. On the other hand, others will also see your fears. The point to be stressed is that you have a powerful past to call on that needs to find an outlet for expression.

The 12th house deals with the inner life. When intercepted, the inner self is powerfully developed. The challenge is to show it to others by overtly living out what you believe.

The sign sharing these consecutive house cusps describes your inner life and how others see you projecting it. The planet ruling this sign describes the energy you must use to merge your inner and outer life. Its house shows where experiences are available that enable you to do so.

CHAPTER VI

ARE YOU "OUT OF YOUR ELEMENT?"

Another significant phenomenon occurring when signs are intercepted in a chart is that the natural sequence of Elements with the House Trinities is altered.

Houses of Life (1, 5, 9) describe areas of life that naturally encourage personal progress. This house trinity, a division corresponding numerically to the Fire Element, describes external opportunities available for the development of the life force. For example, in the first house you move into the world to experience life in its most basic form. In the fifth house you discover opportunity, through external experiences, to express yourself in some important way, and to reproduce yourself either through creating offspring or by developing talents. This house represents your legacy. In the ninth house you meet opportunity to expand beyond a limited environment and explore the vastness life has to offer, either through travel, philosophical pursuits, or extended learning. The *approach* taken to these experiences is characterized by the signs on their house cusps.

In a chart having no interceptions, signs of the same Element always occupy these three related house cusps, providing a natural unfoldment, a flowing from one experience to the next. For example, Fire signs on Houses of Life denote a need to develop a progressive, future-oriented approach to life (1st house), to reproduction (5th house) and expansion (9th house). Earth signs here define a need to develop a practical approach to life, to reproduction, and expansion. Goals pertaining to these experiences must be rooted in the physical, material, earthly plane. Air signs on Houses of Life describe an intellectual approach to the trinity of experiences described by this house division. Air shows a need to share the results of your mental explorations with others. Water signs describe the need to view the future in reference to the past. Water on Houses of Life suggests strong emotional needs surfacing around progressive issues.

Houses of Substance (2, 6, 10) rule external areas of life where you meet opportunity to accomplish in worldly terms and to succeed at a practical level. For example, in the 2nd house you develop the material substances you need for independent survival. You build and accumulate assets and survival skills. In the 6th house you develop efficient routines to successfully meet life's daily responsibilities. In the 10th house you develop your territory in the world. You seek opportunity to cultivate personal power and a position of importance in the world outside. You attain in worldly terms. A chart having no interceptions interfering with this particular house trinity indicates relative ease in acquiring techniques for integrating these experiences and finding environmental avenues that promote productivity. When no interceptions are found in the chart, signs sharing the same Element will occupy the three Houses of Substance.

Houses of Relationships (3, 7, 11) deal with areas of life encouraging you to interact with others. In the 3rd house you learn to interact with your immediate community (siblings, neighbors, etc.) and acquire information from your neighborhood's educational facilities. This leads you to close personal relationships that require sharing. In the 7th house you learn to respect the importance and needs of others who share your space. You form partnerships, you marry, and you form other types of relationships that require give and take. Next, you are led into a larger community where you learn to view your personal role from a larger, collective perspective (11th house). You learn to interact with groups and become interested in social causes that extend beyond what brings personal pleasure only.

If your chart has signs of the same Element on all Houses of Relationships, the environment presents no objections to the way you interact with others. The people you need to attract to become "relationship conscious" are available within the environment. It is easy to move from one level of interacting into the next with little confusion. One basic temperament is used when approaching all sharing experiences.

The Houses of Endings (or Houses of the Unconscious) include the 4th, 8th and 12th houses. These houses rule experiences that require emotional investment. In the 4th house you build personal foundations that provide emotional stability (a home, a family, a place where you "belong"). In the 8th house you learn to share emotions with others and experience intimacy. In the 12th house you meet opportunities to explore the hidden, emotional content of the subconscious. You discover what lies under your surface. When signs of the same Element rule these houses, you take a similar approach to all emotional experience. This makes them easier to integrate.

When intercepted signs are in a chart, the natural rhythm of the horoscope is offset or disturbed. The mode you must use to integrate personal needs (signs) to outer affairs (houses) is not easily synthesized. You will experience greater complexity than most when attempting to integrate the various levels of experiences described by Houses of Function (or House Trinities). It is necessary, due to the nature of your environment, and your relationship to it, to go "out of your element" to acquire tools, information, and skills you need to succeed in meeting life's call (Houses of Life), meeting practical or career requirements (Houses of Substance), forming meaningful relationships (Houses of Relationships) and establishing an integrated emotional life (Houses of Unconscious).

The house containing the sign that is "out of Element" in any house trinity describes where (house) your needs (sign) are more complex than normal. This house defines where you search for synchronicity. It describes where, from your perspective, your environment has not sufficiently prepared you to fill your complex needs. This can be an area of life where you confront frequent "stop signs." Life moves along flowingly from one House of Function to the next until the fluidity ceases and the tides begin to change (out of Element). You need, at this point, to "switch gears" and take on a new course of action and use a new approach in order to find personal fulfillment.

For example, you may have two Air signs on your Houses of Substance and be stopped by a Water sign on the third (see figure 5). Your basic approach to work and practical life maintenance (Houses of Substance) is intellectual and people-oriented (Air). If Aquarius is on the 2nd house, you approach matters of survival from an intellectual, humanitarian perspective. Your mind and your originality are assets that can help you acquire what you need for survival and financial stability. If Gemini (another Air sign) is on the 6th house cusp, you approach routine responsibilities met daily in the work place with an intellectual outlook that blends nicely with Aquarius on the 2nd house. When dealing with routine obligations, you seek mental stimulation and demonstrate curiosity. You thrive on variety of routine and seek job positions that promote communication and interaction. In a chart having no interceptions, Libra would occupy the Midheaven. However, with interceptions in the horoscope, it is possible to have Scorpio ruling the 10th house cusp. The energy of Scorpio is not harmonious with those of Gemini and Aquarius. Scorpio on the Midheaven indicates a need to be emotionally engrossed in professional involvement. Scorpio is intense, while Air signs denote a curious, communicative, detached approach. How can you have a varied, flexible routine while simultaneously explore the depth of, and

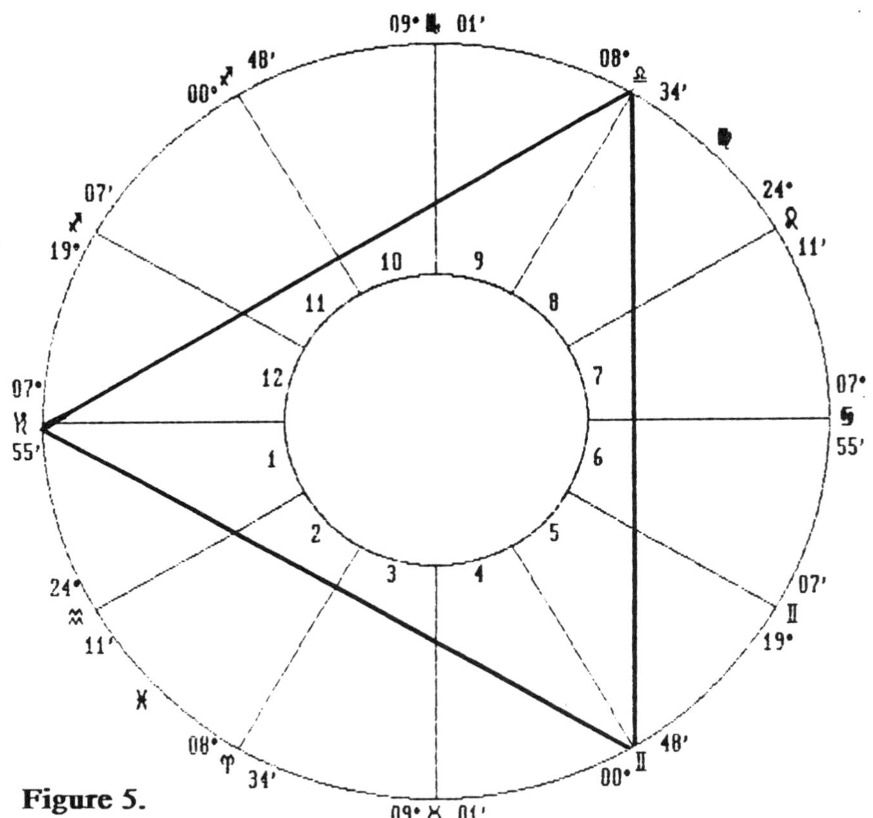

Figure 5.

develop intensity toward, career?

Society, or the environment, has provided us all with an "outline" of careers that are compatible with different personality "types." The structure it provides, while generally useful, often overlooks the exceptions life frequently presents. This particular combination suggests that society, or the environment, may be attuned to the Gemini-Aquarius urges and needs regarding profession, success and practical survival, but is unable to grasp the deeper, more penetrating needs you have regarding career, as shown by the Scorpio Midheaven. You must go "out of your Element," away from the normal strain, to integrate two comparatively compatible needs with one dynamic urge that seems to come to you from out of the blue and doesn't conform to the norm. The traits of the "out of Element" Water sign are not characteristics normally attributed to an Air sign path.

Using another example, consider what happens when intercepted signs disturb the natural elemental flow of the Houses of Relationship (3, 7, 11). This does not deny relationship fulfillment. It does, however, create complexities regarding relationships. If this imbalance occurs in your chart, you must seek avenues other than direct or taught routes, to find fulfillment and integration through relationships. What you need from others, and what you have to offer, are unique to what is considered normal by those around you. You need *more* from relationships than what others perceive. The *more* is described by the sign that is out-of-Element from the other two signs ruling the Houses of Relationships.

The following outline offers some food for thought regarding the challenges presented when intercepted signs interfere with the natural Elemental balance of the house trinities of the chart.

Two Fire Signs: Inspired by the possibilities of what the future holds, your natural approach to this trinity of experience is characterized by action based on vision and idealism. You have been taught to move forward to meet new goals, but ...

One Earth Sign: can you maintain your momentum once you meet the need to produce concrete evidence that proves your goals can be attained?

One Water Sign: can you meet the future head-on and still guarantee security and emotional safety?

Two Earth Signs: You have learned the importance of getting results for efforts expended. Your natural approach to this trinity of experience is based on productive management of time and energy. You have been taught the importance of stability and practicality, but ...

One Fire Sign: can you guarantee that tangible results will materialize from your efforts and still maintain enthusiasm and vision regarding new possibilities in the future?

One Air Sign: can you guarantee that practical results will be achieved and the seeds you have planted will bear fruit when meeting the need to delegate responsibility. Will you welcome new ideas offered by others?

Two Air Signs: Desirous of relationships and the intellectual stimulation they provide, your natural approach to this trinity of experience is backed by others' ideas that influence decisions. You have been taught the importance of interacting with others, but ...

One Earth Sign: can you maintain relationships, remain receptive to the new ideas they offer, and still root yourself in patterns that promise stability but leave little room for outside influences?

One Water Sign: can you guarantee movement and intellectual freedom to interact and still fill your need for security and emotional safety?

Two Water Signs: Concerned with security and emotional involvement, you approach this trinity of experience with caution and sensitivity. You have learned the importance of emotional commitment and the need to protect your space, but ...

One Fire Sign: can you guarantee emotional safety, form emotional commitments, and still possess a pioneering spirit regarding what the future holds. How can you guarantee security while moving toward an unknown future?

One Air Sign: can you protect what is dear to you and still interact with others who provide new ideas that challenge your security boundaries?

CHAPTER VII

THE PLANETS

Without the energy provided by planets, the horoscope would reflect only the needs of the personality and describe areas of life where these needs are met. Just as the Sun gives life to all things on our planet, the Sun, Moon, and planets energize the chart. Planets represent your capacity to act on your needs and develop your potentials. Planets represent *life*. Houses and signs set the stage for life to be experienced.

As discussed earlier, each sign is ruled by a specific planet. The nature of a particular planet is such that it complements, or feeds, the needs represented by the sign it rules. A planet ruling a house cusp represents the *key* you need to open the door to the area of life described by the house it rules.

As an example, consider the relationship between Aries and its ruling planet, Mars. Aries shows where you need to develop independence and courage. It points to an area of life (house) where you function independently in order to discover who you are as a separate entity. Aries, in itself, cannot *act* on those needs. It requires the energy provided by Mars to initiate the action that Aries needs. In the activities of your Aries house, you need to prove your existence by making an impact on the world around you. You need to take an active part in life's drama. Based on this need, you take on the role of an aggressor. Mars represents desire. It provides courage and strength required to meet Aries' challenges. Action promoted by Mars develops self awareness.

Before discussing how planets in intercepted signs operate, it is important that you understand the interpretive differences between planets ruling house cusps and planets in houses. The house ruler describes energy that must be stimulated in order to open the door to the house it rules. An occupant planet shows energy seeking an outlet for expression in the area of life described by the house it occupies. This planet needs the experiences available in the house it occupies to fill the needs and develop the potentials of the house(s) it rules. The houses ruled by occupant planets are dependent, for fulfillment, on the experiences available in the houses they occupy. A planet in a house can only function according to the parameters defined by the planet ruling the house cusp.

Seen from this point of view, the planet ruling a house is the *landlord* of the house. The occupant planets are the *tenants* that must function within the rules and regulations outlined by the landlord. The house cusp ruler represents the *key* that can help you open the door to the experiences of the house. Functions of planets in the house cannot be totally tapped or consciously expressed until the ruler has opened the door to fully expose their potentials.

When planets are intercepted, this natural unfoldment is in some way blocked. Once the house ruler has opened the door, it finds another door requiring still another key. In other words, we have the equivalent of a silent partner holding the deed on this property. Any planets contained within the intercepted sign are not only qualified in their expression by the cusp ruler, but also by the planet ruling the intercepted sign. These intercepted planets rule even other areas of life. Therefore, fulfillment in the experiences defined by the houses they rule depends on you unlocking the intercepted sign and unleashing the power of the intercepted planets. As the environment offers little assistance for developing these functions in a way that brings personal fulfillment and supports integration, you are left with a big job on your hands with few tools provided by your environment to help you get the job done.

Twice the usual effort is involved to get life functioning smoothly when dealing with houses containing intercepted signs and planets. You must work through two signs via two rulers before meeting opportunity to utilize the functions of intercepted planets in an objective manner. Intercepted planets describe functions of personality that are difficult to overtly or objectively express due to the structure of your existing surroundings. The environment does not encourage you to develop the functions of intercepted planets in a manner that is compatible with your individual, unique needs.

The following material will give you a clearer picture of how intercepted planets function. Keep in mind, while reviewing this section, the complexities involved with joint rulership.

SUN

The Sun represents the center of consciousness, the basic life force. Its house shows where you need to shine ... where, due to the solar radiance, you become illuminated to the importance and purpose of your life. It describes where purpose is cultivated and experiences are available that help you build consciousness. The Sun provides direction. Its brilliance makes you aware of your own importance, the significance of all that is around you, and your relationship to it. It represents your potential for continuous growth and enables you to control and direct all other functions of your personality (planets). It contains the power to integrate and synthesize life.

The Sun is the center of our solar system. In the natal chart, it represents the center of your personalized universe. It encourages you to keep your life moving, to grow. Just as the Sun empowers and illumines the planets in our solar system, it illuminates you to your own power and life force.

The sign containing the Sun describes a quality you must develop to integrate all other planetary energies. Its house describes experiences where you need to function with full consciousness. It describes where your sense of purpose and importance are developed. Without the Sun, your life cannot be maintained. Without the Sun watching over all products of our planet, life on the planet would not exist.

When the Sun is intercepted, this purpose ... your need to shine, to stand out, to be important ... is obscured in some way. You experience difficulty defining the true essence and importance of your life. Experiences needed to develop self consciousness are not provided by facilities in your environment. As you attempt to discover the meaning of your life, you find that the environment does not contain, or provide, experiences that make you feel important. It may be necessary to break from your surroundings to find and utilize your full potential, express the power of your will, and understand the essence of your own personality. The old cliche that states, "the answers lie within," holds great merit for you.

An intercepted Sun does not negate your importance, nor does it indicate that you will never find a direction or develop consciousness. It does, however, imply that facilities to fill your needs are not available within the pre-existing structures of your community. You are challenged to investigate concepts and create experiences independently. You are challenged to listen to an inner voice speaking to you, coaxing you to become more than what your environment is able to teach you. Your world simply does not understand you. Due to its lack of perception, you must struggle to build your ego, your purpose, your importance, on your own.

While the Sun's house shows where you develop a sense of purpose, **Leo's** house describes where this purpose seeks expression. Both houses are affected when the Sun is intercepted. It is not until after you have psychologically broken free from the limitations imposed on you by your surroundings that you find a purpose to your life and open the door to your Leo house experiences.

The sign on the cusp of the house containing your intercepted Sun describes the first step you must take to discover your importance in the world. As you become involved in the area of life described by this house, using the strengths described by the sign on its cusp, you are led to your Sun ... your purpose and your life force. Full consciousness is often delayed due to the complexity involved in reaching the Sun in the natal chart. Full power of the Solar force cannot be tapped until after you have developed the qualities of the sign on the house cusp, and opened the door to the house experiences via the planet ruling the cusp.

MOON

While the Sun rules consciousness and life purpose, the Moon represents emotional responses that have been formed from past experiences.

The Moon can be likened to your internal mother, your protector. Her role is that of the caretaker. The Moon meets responsibilities based on knowledge gained in the past and uses it as a reference for the future.

The Moon rules the brain. It holds all memories from the past and, based on these memories, provokes emotional responses whenever it senses danger or is confronted with new experiences that you have not yet learned to handle.

Not only does the Moon represent your internal protector, it describes the relationship you shared with your physical mother. From this relationship, you learned protective techniques that, positively or negatively, strongly influence your emotional life.

The Moon controls the tides of our oceans. In the natal chart, its house describes where you frequently meet experiences that require you to adapt, to flow, to move with the predictable changing currents that life presents. The Moon shows where adaptability is required to assure the security required by its sign, Cancer. If you don't flow with the daily changes life presents, in the department of life shown by the Moon's house, security will always allude you.

The Moon's sign describes how you respond when emotions are triggered. It shows how you have learned to respond to change to protect yourself and those closest to you. These responses become obsolete and ineffective if the Sun is not functioning creatively in the chart. While the Sun provides opportunity for growth in consciousness, the Moon protects you through the growth process. If the protective urges of Luna overpower the Solar force, growth is stymied due to fear of the changes growth requires.

When the Moon is intercepted, it is difficult to access memories from the past that are useful in your growth process. This could be due to confusion in early life regarding mother and her influence on your development. While emotions are strong, they are inhibited because others around you don't understand or respond to your emotional needs in a way that is helpful to you. Because you lack environmental support, or role models, you may experience difficulty dealing with emotional confrontation. You were not taught how to direct emotions into positive external channels. This can lead to the following dilemmas. Either you suppress emotions altogether, or the emotions override logic because they lack conscious direction. As your environment does not recognize your emotional needs, it could become necessary to break from its confines to find emotional fulfillment and expression.

To access these "trapped" or intercepted emotions, you must first enter the doorway to the experiences of the Moon's house via the sign and ruler of the house cusp. Once introduced to this arena of activity you meet an urge to become emotionally involved. You have learned to approach these activities in a manner described by the sign on the house cusp. Once having unlocked the door, via the cusp ruler, you find intense emotions that need to be addressed and directed into the experiences described by the house. No one has prepared you for this confrontation.

Because the Moon rules **Cancer**, the experiences of Cancer's house are also influenced by this interception. Until you access your emotions, and find constructive means of directing emotional energy, security remains illusive in the area of life described by Cancer's house.

If your Moon is intercepted, it is important for you to investigate your past because it holds hidden meaning to you. The past, as you know it, does not seem to "fit" the patterns your environment has planned for you. It is your job to investigate, integrate, and implicate what you discover.

MERCURY

Mercury provides the ability to perceive, classify, and communicate information. The role of this planet is to accumulate information. It represents your thirst for knowledge and your urge to gather data that contributes to your growth.

Mercury operates as a messenger. It accumulates information and distributes it to the other functions of personality (planets). Mercury encourages you to learn about all phases of life ... all external and internal processes that make up who you are. Mercury rules the nervous system that receives and sends signals to all other parts of the body, enabling it to function as a unit. When viewed from a psychological perspective, Mercury's role is that of a facilitator. It lets the head know what the heart is doing. Its role is to provide congruency to life.

Mercury's sign describes how information is accumulated and perceived. It shows how your mind functions and the kinds of information that interest you. Its house describes where information is available that stimulates thought and learning.

When Mercury is intercepted in the chart, frustration is experienced when attempting to acquire information. Your environment may not contain the information you seek. It does not provide the learning experiences you need for self development. Your ideas do not fit into the mental patterns set up in your community. Your urge to communicate often goes unnoticed due to the lack of interest, or understanding, of others. As a result, little constructive feedback is available concerning your interests and ideas.

The resulting frustration leads to the following dilemma. Either you chose to quit learning and communicating your ideas altogether, or you project your ideas erratically due to lack of environmental guidance regarding the appropriateness of your communication. Because you have not received the kind of intellectual input you need from your environment, your ideas, and the way you communicate them, lack objectivity. If Mercury is intercepted, you must find answers to your questions from sources alien to your environment. You must acquire information from obscured channels.

Mercury's intercepted condition does not deny intellectual power. It does, however, suggest that the information that serves you best may not be attainable through "normal" channels. For this reason, the process of creative intellectual unfoldment is often delayed. When you finally acquire information that holds meaning for you, it is often difficult to locate an outlet for it due to the limitations of your surroundings. You need to rebel against the educational limits of your community and explore ideas it has not yet developed.

As Mercury rules both **Gemini** and **Virgo**, at least three houses are affected by its intercepted condition. Gemini is dependent on Mercury's information to fill its innate curiosity. Virgo relies on Mercury's data to classify and apply the information it gathers toward self perfection. When Mercury is intercepted, it is necessary to either gather information from hidden or obscured sources, or break from your environment altogether in order to experience freedom to communicate and learn about those things that interest you. Mercury, when intercepted, can lead to the potential for genius. On the other hand, it could lead to repression of intellectual pursuits due to the frustration experienced when trying to gather information.

VENUS

Venus represents the capacity to value what life has to offer. It encourages you to appreciate life's tangible substances and to form relationships with others who share, or complement, your values.

Venus is like a magnet. You use its power to attract what you need from the outside world to find comfort and value within it. This is the planet of love, representing relationships shared with others as well as your ability to love yourself. Based on the value you place on your life, you attract substances and people that complement you.

The house containing Venus shows where this attraction or magnetism operates in your life. It describes where you use your powers of attraction to get what you want. It describes an area of life where you discover love, where you build values, and where you share experiences with others. Its sign describes how your magnetic powers operate. It shows what qualities you appreciate in others.

When Venus is intercepted, it is difficult to locate substances or people that provide sensual satisfaction. The environment is not attune to your magnetism and may be unreceptive to what you want from it. You may feel as if you are on a different "frequency" than those around you. The signals you put out are not clearly received by those in your environment. What you want alludes you because the environment is not set up to facilitate your needs. The types of people with whom you need to share may not exist in the confines of your environment. It could be difficult for you to define what you want for personal enjoyment and in relationships with others. This dilemma is experienced due to lack of information or education provided by the environment regarding the concept of sharing. What the environment encourages, or provides, is incongruent with your internal reality of what you want.

Venus rules both **Taurus** and **Libra**. When it is intercepted, all three houses are in some way influenced. Taurus relies on Venus to attract substances that provide self gratification and build self love. Libra relies on Venus to attract others with whom to share significant experiences. When intercepted, fulfillment of these needs is often postponed due to the environment's lack of compatibility with, or understanding of, your unique needs. You may find it necessary to break from your environment's attitudes regarding what is valuable to find your true worth. It is important that you don't respond to your environment's lack of perception or facilities regarding your personal wants by conforming to its expectations of you, or give up trying to relate.

MARS

Mars represents desire. It provides incentive to move into the world to get what you want from it by being assertive, courageous, daring and enterprising. Mars rules masculine energy. As ruler of Aries, its role is that of the initiator. Mars challenges you to do your own thing. Prove, through action, that you can function independently. The experiences encountered, or provoked, by Mars fill your Aries need to define your separateness from others.

The house containing Mars describes an area of life where you meet experiences that dare you to take independent action. Its sign describes the nature of your aggression. It shows how you go about initiating new experiences. It describes what moves, or stimulates, you to take risks.

When Mars is intercepted, its desire-energy is suppressed or inhibited. Your environment does not offer experiences that excite you to take independent action. The environment has not taught you creative techniques of self assertion, or how to take care of your personal needs. While you have an inner urge to prove yourself through action, no role models are available to encourage the kinds of activities you need to express this urge. Due to lack of stimulation and objectivity provided by the environment, little consciousness is evident when you do take a stand on issues. While independence is necessary to develop self confidence when meeting new situations, encouragement from your environment has not been sufficient to help you direct these energies. Due to the resulting frustration, you could do one of two things. You might avoid taking independent action to get what you want out of fear of the environment's response to such behavior. Or, you could meet your Mars-challenge with little objective direction, and demonstrate your aggression erratically due to lack of training regarding acceptable assertive behavior.

As Mars rules **Aries** and **Scorpio**, all three houses will be affected by its intercepted condition. Aries needs Mars to assist in developing identity-awareness. Scorpio uses Mars' energy and converts it into emotional power. When intercepted this power is obscured. In time you learn to rebel against society's restraints or expectations to find out who you really are apart from what you were taught.

JUPITER

Jupiter provides opportunity to expand your personal life and your realm of influence within the social structure. The largest planet in our solar system, Jupiter deals with all issues of increase. It stimulates an urge to get more out of life; reach beyond what is immediately available to find greater opportunity, more experience and expanded wisdom. It has often been associated with travel and higher education due to the natural relationship it shares with Sagittarius and the ninth house.

Jupiter has been called the "Great Benefic." Its house describes an area of life where you have a "guardian angel," a mentor providing protection while simultaneously encouraging you to grow, to move beyond the limitations evident in your life at any given time. Jupiter's house shows where opportunity for expansion is available. It shows where you experience the urge to acquire wisdom, to look beyond the immediate to gain an understanding of concepts that extend beyond basic knowledge required for survival. Jupiter represents the part of you that wants freedom to grow, to expand, to discover what truly lies at the end of the rainbow. Its sign describes how you go about the process of expansion and the psychological motivation standing behind it. It describes an element of personality that operates overtly and with confidence. A prominent Jupiter indicates a jovial personality. When not directing its energy into positive channels, it can promote excessive self-indulgence.

When intercepted, Jupiter's urge to expand is not encouraged by the environment. The world around you is not sufficiently tuned in to your needs regarding expansion and the acquiring of wisdom. For this reason, it does not facilitate your needs in this respect. The environment you live in does not understand what you need, what you are looking for.

Intercepted Jupiter does not deny opportunity to expand and grow. It does, however, indicate difficulties experienced in the process of defining what you want or need in the future. Jupiter's role is to assist in the process of expanding consciousness. When intercepted, it is difficult to locate, within the environment, experiences that encourage this growth. You need to rebel against the constraints of your environment to find experiences that provide expansion. Jupiter, even though intercepted, wants more from life. But it is difficult to locate experiences or information that encourages the kind of expansion you desire. Don't suppress your expansive urges altogether due to the lack of environmental support and understanding.

Jupiter rules **Sagittarius**. This is the most goal-oriented of all zodiacal signs. The house of Sagittarius describes where you form goals for the future, where you form principles, where you constantly seek a greater understanding of life. It is Jupiter's function to facilitate the needs of its sign. When intercepted, a challenge is met not just in the experiences described by Jupiter's house, but in filling the needs of the house of Sagittarius. Sagittarius shows where you need to develop a philosophical orientation toward life ... principles upon which to base all expansive undertakings. When Jupiter is intercepted, it is difficult to find experiences around which to define your philosophical beliefs. You must go outside the limitations of your environment, either physically or psychologically, to find principles, philosophies, and wisdom that work for you.

SATURN

Saturn represents the part of you that wants you to define your place within the social structure. Saturn requires you to be responsible and understand the laws or rules that apply to your social space. It provides discipline, both self imposed and discipline coming from outside authority figures. Saturn's role is to define boundaries. This includes social boundaries and those that separate the unconscious from the conscious mind. Saturn's job is to allow unconscious material to penetrate the consciousness only when you are ready to assimilate it.

Saturn is concerned with structure and order. Its house describes where you must function within well-formed limits to maintain your place within the social structure. It rules all authority issues confronted in life ... people having authority over you, and your ability to be an authority in your own right. Saturn provides a perspective of where you fit in life's complex jigsaw puzzle. This territory is extended as you learn the responsibilities involved with each level of social development.

Saturn wants respect. Its house shows an area of life where you need to earn the respect you seek. It defines where you must operate within the regulations described by its house to gain approval and recognition within the experiences it rules. Its sign describes an element of personality that must be expressed in a disciplined, well-formed manner. It is important, however, that you don't build your boundaries so rigidly that you repress the natural expression of this sign.

If Saturn is intercepted, you have difficulty finding and defining where you belong. As you look around your environment, you don't find a "place" that is compatible with your inner reality of where you belong. The environment does not contain the types of experiences or facilities you need to establish a social identity that is congruent with your social yearnings.

As Saturn represents the father, there may be some significant lack evident in the model he provided in your life. The structures you relied on him to provide to help you build your social identity were not presented in a way that filled your particular needs. This can result in difficulty developing skills in management, as well as in defining and defending your "territory." It is difficult to defend a territory you cannot define. It is equally difficult to objectively set limits when you don't receive the instructions or tools you need from the environment to do so. For this reason, it may be necessary to turn away from the schematics society, or your environment, has designed for you and create a new "floor plan" for your life.

As Saturn rules **Capricorn**, both houses will be influenced by Saturn's interception. Capricorn's house shows where you need to be respected for the social role you play. It shows an area of life where you must learn to play by the rules. This need is difficult to fill when Saturn is intercepted because you have difficulty defining appropriate rules due to lack of constructive environmental input.

URANUS

Uranus represents the inner urge to become individualized, to break out of patterned thinking and behavior, to rebel against restrictions or obsolete cultural beliefs, to investigate and experiment with unknown forces. Uranus is the rebel. It represents the urge to become more than what society has taught you to be, break up crystallized patterns, and know that in order to grow you must evolve and welcome change.

At first, Uranus functions unconsciously. It shows where (house) you attract abrupt changes that alter the course of your life. It rules instability and eccentricity as well as originality and inventive mental energy. When accepted by consciousness, Uranus provides an ability to recognize when intuitive flashes attempt to enlighten you to what's about to unfold.

Uranus operates with lightening force and speed. When old patterns need changed, Uranus enters your life to break up structures that prohibit new potentials. Like all of the unconscious planets (Uranus, Neptune and Pluto), Uranus does not discriminate. Its purpose is to shake you free from an old life style and awaken you to new possibilities ... sometimes by creating unexpected crises that force you to change. Other times it creates unexpected opportunities.

The house containing Uranus describes an area of life where you should be prepared for the unexpected. It shows where life challenges you to take risks and be open to change. It points to a department of life that may always be unstable. At the same time, it describes where your potential for genius can be found.

Uranus has been called the "maverick." It challenges you to detach. Uranus asks: Can you stand apart and still recognize your unique connection to the rest of the world?

When Uranus is intercepted it is difficult to locate external circumstances that teach you independence and detachment, or that encourage you to use your originality. You have not been taught to experiment in fields that enhance growth and challenge your boundaries. Therefore, it is difficult to find experiences that excite you. You either demonstrate overly rebellious behavior due to the lack of education received from your environment regarding positive rebellion, or you repress your individuality altogether and accept the boundaries and limitations society has defined as yours.

To access your Uranian energy, you must first unlock the door to the house in which it is captured via the sign on the house cusp and its ruling planet. Once this door has been opened, the unconventional, original, sometimes eccentric energy of Uranus is met. Give yourself time to become familiar with the highly charged energy of Uranus, but don't repress it altogether.

NEPTUNE

Faith, commitment, dedication, illusion, idealism, fear, altered states of consciousness, fantasy, confusion ... all illusive, intangible states ... all ruled by the powerful, yet evasive Neptune.

When fear is met and conquered, it no longer exists. When faith becomes reality, it is no longer required. When fantasy becomes fact, fantasy ceases to exist. Neptune rules all that is, yet cannot be proven real. Neptune requires faith and sometimes yields fear. Neptune rules inspiration and confusion. It encourages you to believe. To acquire faith you must experience doubt. Neptune deals with transition. It rules all that is vague.

The house containing Neptune describes an area of life where transition will be experienced. It shows where confusion will be met. It shows where inspiration can be experienced. Neptune does not require physical evidence to find satisfaction. In fact, it often dissolves attachments to physical, material, tangible realities in its process of enlightening you to the value of all that lacks substance.

When meeting experiences in the area of life described by Neptune's house, you are challenged to face and dissolve dependencies on the physical, "real" world, to define what you believe in, and to develop faith in those beliefs or ideals even though there is no evidence to prove their truth or value. On one hand, Neptune can open you up to deception and confusion. On the other, you can be in-spired (pierced by truth coming from sources beyond the ego).

Neptune offers spiritual food. Its house describes where spiritual substance is available. When intercepted, however, the illusive energies of Neptune are even more difficult to tap. As you look around your environment, you don't find the truths you seek. You may find that your physical world does not have what you need to be inspired. You have not been taught to deal with pure, positive, Neptunian concepts. Therefore, you may find it difficult to differentiate between idealism and illusion, truth and deception. You need to make a commitment to a belief, but have difficulty finding a belief that inspires you. You must look within rather than looking to the outside world to find your true spiritual source. Meditation and prayer may be particularly useful in accessing the truths you seek. Even after you have found something to dedicate your life to, it is difficult to find an environmental outlet for its expression. Your environment is not transmitting on the same channel you are trying to receive and visa-versa. The environment offers little assistance in helping you focus your images or objectify your ideals.

Neptune rules **Pisces**. In the area of life described by the house of Pisces, you seek the truths that Neptune channels. Neptune shows where old attitudes and structures are being dissolved so you can move forward toward your commitments. When Neptune is intercepted, it is difficult to determine what needs to be dissolved. Unreasonable fears or doubts may invade your consciousness, obstructing your faith in the future. When Neptune is intercepted, the house ruled by Pisces will also be influenced because the needs of Pisces are dependent, for fulfillment, on Neptune's expression.

PLUTO

Pluto represents the deep, at first unconscious, urge to participate in the process of evolution. This is the planet of rebirth. Pluto functions to alert each of us, individually and collectively, that all processes of life have a beginning and an end. It alerts us when its time to let go so that something new and more powerful can be born. It is Pluto's role to purge, to cleanse, to eliminate attitudes, behaviors, beliefs, or belongings that restrict growth. As is the case with all unconscious planets, Pluto does not discriminate. It functions beyond the personal or even social ego.

The house containing Pluto describes an area of life where rebirth will take place. A metamorphosis will occur. You will experience a complete and total change in your perspective of the importance and purpose of the experiences ruled by its house. In some way, what you live out here reflects the current level of consciousness of the world in which you live. As the world evolves and changes, you must change with it. The house containing Pluto shows where the greatest impact of society's changing beliefs and concerns influence your personal life. It describes where, whether consciously or not, you are playing a part in social evolution ... you are playing a part in determining the future growth, or deterioration, of the globe.

Pluto is associated with major upheavals, destruction, death and rebirth. Its house shows where you experience profound changes that not only influence your personal life, but the lives of others. In some way, you are setting an example through your involvements here. Others can learn from you. The results of Pluto's power, the repercussions of its impact, are always greater than consciousness perceives.

When Plúto is intercepted, its profound energies are hidden deeply within the unconscious. Inside, you feel an urge to make an impact on society. Outside, you have difficulty locating a vehicle for mobilization. You want to play a part in social unfoldment but have never been taught how to do so. You have never been led, by your environment, to experiences that offer opportunity to create significant changes. Your perception of needed social change may not be recognized by your environment. You stand alone in your convictions and, because of this sense of isolation, you have difficulty attempting to "make a difference" in the world. Your potential social contribution is difficult to define because it has not yet been recognized as a need by others in your environment.

Conditions experienced in the house of **Scorpio** are also influenced by Pluto's interception. Scorpio's house describes where regeneration is needed. It is Pluto's responsibility to bring about these changes. When intercepted, this is no easy task. Frustration is experienced not only when pursuing social causes in the area described by Pluto's house, but delays are met in filling the regenerative needs of Scorpio's house. Scorpio shows where (house) emotions have been repressed. Pluto brings experiences from the unconscious to be regenerated. When Pluto is intercepted, this process is often delayed due to lack of environmental direction.

CHAPTER VIII

ASPECTS AND PHASES

Aspects play an integral part in all chart interpretation. Aspects are determined by the angular relationship formed between planets at the time of birth. They describe how your various planetary energies operate together.

The planets of our solar system, Moon through Pluto, can be likened to a "family" consisting of multiple people, each one operating on a different energy level. To maintain the family unit (the chart) these energies must operate together. They must interact and integrate. Sometimes, as happens in all families, arguments or misunderstandings arise. One family member may demand independence (Mars) in a manner that upsets the family structure (Saturn). Desires are not congruent with reality. Another member may want freedom to explore new horizons (Jupiter), and go about filling this urge in a way that conflicts with another's values (Venus) or still another's urge for emotional safety and security (Moon). One family member may be concerned with the evolution of the total family unit (Pluto), while another fails to understand its concern (Mercury).

Aspects describe the level of cooperation between, and integration of, your various personality "parts." These "parts" may be so divided that, at times, you don't recognize the fact that many conflicts you meet in outer life are reflections of the inner incongruities of your own nature. While some aspects suggest friction, others show parts of your internal "family" that operate together creatively. You might, for example, find a component of yourself that frequently offers another component tools for growth or creative avenues for expression.

Aspects are an interesting study. To fully understand their importance in a chart, however, you must always recognize the condition of the whole family (the whole person), rather than only one member of it (planet). Trying to evaluate a life by viewing aspects as isolated entities is like a physician making an evaluation of a patient's total condition by examining only a toe, a finger, etc. Keep this in mind as you look at aspects in a chart. Always look to the larger picture (the whole chart), and then localize issues within it (aspects).

When considering aspects, keep in mind that the slower moving of the two aspecting planets (the planet most distant from the earth), describes a function of personality that is shaping, and expressing itself through, the function of the faster planet. This concept is particularly important to consider when evaluating the significance of aspects involving planets in, or ruling, intercepted signs. The slower planet is *infusing* its energy into that of the faster. It is challenging the function of the faster planet to operate within its frame of reference.

For example, any aspect between Saturn and Mercury requires a disciplined (Saturn) mind (Mercury). Saturn, the slower moving planet, challenges the Mercury mental processes to operate within the parameters it defines. The aspect itself describes whether this shaping process is comfortable or presents challenges.

If you are not familiar with the various planetary orbits, the following Table should be reviewed.

PLANET	**ORBIT (approx)**
Moon	27 days
Mercury	1 year
Venus	1 year
Sun	1 year
Mars	2 years
Jupiter	12 years
Saturn	28 years
Uranus	84 years
Neptune	165 years
Pluto	230 years

When evaluating the significance of intercepted signs in your chart, particular attention should be placed on aspects to planets in, and ruling, the interceptions. The planetary rulers of intercepted signs represent personal energies that must be developed and utilized in order to bring out the qualities of the intercepted signs. Their aspects indicate opportunities or challenges involving other planetary energies that either help you to, or inhibit you from, tapping into and utilizing intercepted energies that are otherwise difficult to access.

CONJUNCTION (☌) 0 degree aspect: 8 degree orb: Most planets in conjunction with an intercepted planet are also intercepted in the chart, magnifying the potential frustration brought about by the intercepted condition. The functions of these planets are challenged to work together, to merge energies and operate as one. The slower planet (the one most distant from Earth) is attempting to infuse its energy into the function represented by the faster planet. It challenges the faster planet to work within its frame of reference.

Conjunctions can be likened to a celestial "collision" occurring at the time of birth. Two planets have come together in space. From Earth's perspective it appears as though a collision has occurred. Theoretically, this suggests that some kind of merging or integration must take place in order to avoid fragmentation or a shattering of energy. The slower planet controls that space. The faster planet has entered into its territory. Therefore, the faster planet must merge with the slower and operate within the parameters it defines.

For example, Jupiter represents expansion. When conjunct a faster planet, it encourages you to use the energy of the faster planet in an expansive manner ... i.e. expand (Jupiter) knowledge (Mercury), increase (Jupiter) activities (Mars), etc. This urge is not easily facilitated when the planets are intercepted. As you seek outlets for the combined energies, you find difficulty locating facilities that accommodate your urge.

The conjunction is a powerful aspect requiring assertion and suggesting instinctive projection. When two or more planets are conjunct in an intercepted sign, you must first look to the planet ruling the house cusp to provide access to the experiences of the house. Once the door has been opened to the experiences described by the house, you must examine its contents and the placement of the ruler of the intercepted sign. The latter enables you to find other experiences that help you to tap the powers contained within the interception. Other aspects formed to an intercepted conjunction offer assistance in unleashing the power.

The conjunction of intercepted planets offers little assistance regarding the outer expression of the urges represented by the planets involved. It simply intensifies and complexifies the intercepted condition. Look for other planets forming other aspects to this point to find additional resources or strengths to unleash the power of the intercepted conjunction.

SEXTILE (✶) 60 degree aspect: 6 degree orb: The sextile aspect is industrious. Sextiles offer tools for constructive living. Planets in sextile show functions of personality that work productively together. The slower planet, or that most distant from Earth, provides tools that enable you to more successfully use the function of the faster planet. When challenges present themselves, you have access to the skills you need to master them with little stress. For example, how much more efficiently can a mechanic, having access to the tools of his/her trade, repair a malfunctioning automobile than someone having only a hammer or a screwdriver? Likewise, if you have a speedometer in your car, you are less likely to exceed the speed limit. A sextile between Mars and Saturn suggests you have a working "speedometer." A square between these same planets suggests your speedometer doesn't work; you must take extra precautions to avoid exceeding limits. This same analogy can be applied to all avenues of life experience. While life may not always be in working order, if you have proper tools you are in a position to cope with the stresses it sometimes presents. This is the power of the sextile. Of course, having sextiles in your chart does not promise that you will always use the tools they offer, just as having a speedometer in your car is no guarantee that you will not exceed the speed limit.

Planets in sextile describe parts of personality that have learned to work well together. They have established a good working relationship and offer each other tools upon request. For example, a sextile between Moon and Mercury suggests a productive relationship exists between emotion (Moon) and reason (Mercury). You understand how emotions influence thinking. When in an upsetting emotional state, Mercury provides the ability to use reason and logic to help you work through the emotional dilemma.

As with all aspects, the planet having the slower orb represents a function of personality that is shaping (or in the case of a sextile, offers tools for constructive direction of) the faster planet. Saturn, for example, provides discipline and focus for Mars' energy. Jupiter provides expansion and vision to the Mercury mind. Uranus provides originality to all planets faster than itself in orbit. The slower planet in a sextile aspect represents the "oil" that keeps your car running efficiently.

Sextiles involving an intercepted planet provide opportunities to access the interception by using the tools provided, or available, from the planet not captured in an intercepted sign. If the intercepted planet is faster in orb, look to the house containing the slower planet to find experiences and skills that provide tools to help you unlock the potential of your intercepted sign and unleash the energy of the faster planet. The function represented by the slower planet can be used as a tool for constructive expression of the interception.

If, on the other hand, the intercepted planet is the slower of the two, some restrictions apply. At one level, the faster planet is benefiting from the intercepted planet. The insights gained from the intercepted condition of the slower planet is, in itself, an asset. To gain full advantage of the tools available from the intercepted planet, however, you must have some access to the interception. Access can only be obtained by looking beyond what the environment overtly offers with regard to experience. Once you begin to process and integrate your intercepted sign, you find tools for growth regarding the expression, development, and utilization of the faster planet's function.

SQUARE (□) 90 degree aspect: 8 degree orb: Squares set up obstacles and challenges. They represent situations met in life that you have not yet learned to handle. Because you have no positive, well-formed past experiences to call on for direction when confronting squares, you often learn through trial and error.

At one time, it was unacceptable in our society to make mistakes. Squares were considered negative. In today's world, we recognize squares as challenges to develop skills not yet cultivated. Unlike the sextile, that provides constructive tools, squares function with limited resources. In a natal chart, squares indicate where challenges will be met. Once one obstacle has been mastered, a new challenge arises to replace it. Squares are stimulating, provocative, and demanding. They cannot be ignored. Squares challenge you to meet experiences courageously. You never know what's around the next corner because you've never before been on the block. The square is a 90 degree angle and, like turning a corner on a crowded street, you can never be sure what's on the other side.

Squares motivate. They prod. They push you into unexplored territory. When involved with intercepted planets, they often provoke to the point of rebellion. Square warns you that you have no positive experience in your past to call on to help direct your power. You simply have to "wing it." Through crisis, you face the challenge to change your direction and change important facets of your life.

If the intercepted planet is faster in orb than the planet it is squaring, outside crises expose inner powers described by the intercepted planet, challenging you, no matter how naively, to utilize its energy to create change. While frustrating, the square is actually a disguised blessing. It forces issues to a head. It makes you confront environmental limitations (interceptions) and rebel against them in order to unleash your power.

If the intercepted planet is the slower of the two, greater frustration is experienced when unleashing the intercepted sign. The very limitations defined by the intercepted condition may be creating a crisis for the faster planet in its house and sign. As you begin to unleash the intercepted planet, crisis is experienced regarding the expression and direction of the squaring planet. The challenges brought about by the emergence of the intercepted planet creates a domino affect that influences conditions defined by the house containing the faster planet. While the faster planet may not play a role in this emergence, it will be directly influenced by it, and will experience a crisis as a result of it. New skills exposed, once the intercepted planet has been tapped, create a challenge to the faster planet to change its previous way of functioning.

TRINE: (△) 120 degree aspect: 8 degree orb: Trines are flowing, harmonious, easy aspects. They describe functions of personality that work together with no effort required. For this reason, trines can become lazy. Trines indicate natural skills, but do not provide incentive to use them productively.

Trines indicate inborn talents. The ability to harmonize two separate functions of personality (even those that may be very contradictory in nature, such as in the case of Saturn and Mars or Pluto and Moon). The ability to merge these energies is natural and therefore easily taken for granted. Jupiter trine Mercury is broad-minded. Saturn trine Mars provides disciplined energy. Mars trine Venus describes integrated male-female energy. Trines show what *IS* while other aspects describe what *CAN BE.*

When trines involve planets in intercepted signs, they describe a certain complacency regarding environmental limitations. There is little incentive to break free from them. It is easy to work with what already exists because it has no ill affects on the functioning of the planet in trine with it. When interpreting trines, it is important to look to other aspects to these planets to find motivation to use the natural talents, or gifts, they offer.

If the intercepted planet is faster in orb, the slower planet offers ease or relaxation regarding the intercepted condition. In essence, it says: no problem. The environment may not support the functioning of this planet, but that, in itself, has no negative impact.

If the intercepted planet is slower in orb, it provides the faster planet with some special skill. However, in order to utilize this talent, you must first work at accessing the interception to unleash its power.

QUINCUNX (⊼) 150 degree aspect: 4 degree orb: The quincunx brings the challenge to adjust. It puts detours in your path. It forces you to veer away from your conscious destination in order to explore new territory. This is a particularly frustrating aspect because it tends to sneak up on you. With an element of surprise, it forces you to make some hasty adjustments in life.

Things are not always what they appear to be. The future is never so clearly defined. The quincunx is a reminder that there are often forces at work in your life that are greater than ego, more powerful than your personal will. If your mind is set on going from point A to point B taking the most direct route, and quincunxes are met, the will must bend when you discover the direct route has been blocked and you must find an alternative means of reaching your destination.

The quincunx discourages single-mindedness. Sometimes it creates so many distractions in life that no destinations or outcomes are ever reached. This aspect challenges you to adjust and adapt to conditions outside your conscious control without fragmenting, or never reaching any destination or filling any personal needs in life. Can you adjust without losing your focus?

Expect the unexpected is the message of the quincunx. Be prepared to change directions. Yet, don't get lost in the process. It is difficult to remain "centered" when quincunxes are playing in the chart.

When quincunxes involve planets in, or ruling, intercepted signs, you get mixed signals from the world around you. The environment, described by the intercepted planet's house, beckons from a different locale. Can you move from one experience to the next without losing your focus in the process? Look to the slower planet to define the energy creating the distraction in life direction. It challenges you to veer away from your original ideas or behaviors to try something different. If the slower planet is intercepted, internal factors are challenging the faster planet to adjust.

OPPOSITION (☍) 180 degree aspect: 8 degree orb: The opposition is a particularly interesting aspect to observe when it occurs in intercepted signs. Oppositions require what intercepted signs lack. Thus, the dilemma of intercepted signs is intensified when they contain planets in opposition.

Oppositions describe where balance is needed. You attract feedback from others that brings to your attention the need to consider others when acting, and to consider the outcome of potential action prior to initiating new experiences. Be aware of the influence action initiated in one house has on the opposite.

Oppositions deals with laws of karma that state: as above, so below; what goes out comes back. They function like mirrors, reflecting both the beauty and the blemishes of personality. Oppositions show where compromise is required to maintain a balanced life and creative interactions with others. They require a need to always view issues from more than one perspective.

The slower planet challenges the function of the faster planet to approach the issues of its house with objectivity and awareness of the results of perspective action. It provides alternatives that must be considered when making choices pertaining to the area of life described by the house containing the faster planet. Mercury in opposition with the Moon, for example, encourages you to think (Mercury) before acting on emotion (Moon).

While oppositions in intercepted signs intensify frustration, this very magnification enables you to recognize imbalances in your life. And, recognition is the first step in integrating the needs (signs) and energies (planets) that are, to a certain degree, alienated when intercepted. The slower planet wants to express its energy through the function of the faster. However, the intercepted condition creates problems in finding external outlets or facilities for these energies to meet and express themselves as partners.

PHASES AND PLANETARY PAIRS

Just as signs that fall opposite each other in the zodiac must function together as partners, their planetary rulers also share a special relationship. For example, the Aries/Libra polarity is ruled by Mars and Venus. Like their signs, these planets function in polarity. Mars rules masculine, assertive energy while Venus rules feminine receptivity. Each must be operative, and aware of its partner, for life to be well balanced.

Based on sign rulerships, the following are considered natural **Planetary Pairs**.

Mars/Venus
Venus/Pluto
Mercury/Jupiter
Moon/Saturn
Sun/Uranus
Mercury/Neptune

While all planets can be considered in pairs, those ruling sign polarities share a particularly strong relationship. When in aspect, issues are evident in life regarding the polarity they represent. Either the planets work together with exceptional harmony (easy aspects) or there is a particularly challenging relationship between them (harsh aspect). Regardless of whether these planetary partners are in aspect or not, they always interact. This relationship is seen in the phase structure.

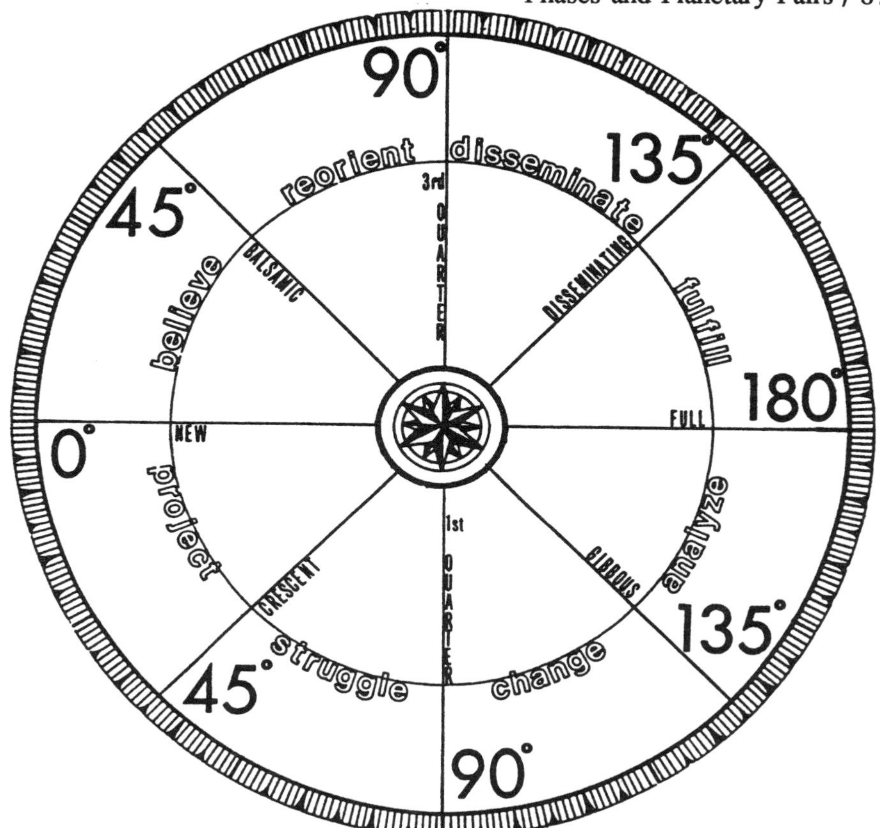

The phase relationship of planetary pairs is always interesting to consider. No planet is ever in a major aspect to all others. There is, however, always a phase relationship formed between them. The following information will give you a basic understanding of the core meanings of each phase.

New Phase: Here we find the faster planet between 0 to 45 degrees ahead of the slower planet. These planets operate together spontaneously. There is considerable instinctive "projection" going on regarding the polarity involved. Like a New Moon, darkness prevails. You are challenged to walk into the darkness with courage. *Action precedes awareness.*

Crescent Phase: Here we find the faster planet between 45 to 90 degrees ahead of the slower planet. These planets operate together with minimal awareness based on lack of past experience. Caution is the keynote. Move slowly and cautiously, but move forward. Like the Crescent Moon in our night skies, minimal light is provided and the shadowy outlines can create eerie anticipation. *Action is qualified by security concerns.*

First Quarter: Here we find the faster planet between 90 to 135 degrees ahead of the slower planet. The slower planet presents a crisis that forces a new direction to be established regarding the function of the faster planet. Frequent changes stimulate movement and growth, or instability. The ever-increasing light of the First Quarter phase brings greater awareness regarding where changes are needed. *Crisis stimulates motivation.*

Gibbous: Here we find the faster planet between 135 to 180 degrees ahead of the slower planet. There is a constant questioning regarding the importance or significance of the life experience. With growing illumination comes a need for frequent adjustments and thorough investigation. *Analysis is the keynote.*

Full: Here we find the faster planet between 180 to 225 degrees ahead of the slower planet. The radiance of the Full Moon illuminates the night time sky. Consider others when making decisions. Turn the lights on before entering a new room in life. Fulfillment or failure depends on the level of objectivity used when expressing these planetary functions. Here you must learn to *think before you act.*

Disseminating: Here we find the faster planet between 225 and 270 degrees ahead of the slower planet. There is a need to share with others the value you have found regarding the larger importance of this planetary pair and its importance in your life. Disseminate, distribute, and share the benefits and insights you have gained through personal experience. *Share wisdom with others.*

Third Quarter: Here, we find the faster planet between 270 and 315 degrees ahead of the slower planet. The faster planet is waning, and awareness that an old cycle is ending begins to penetrate the consciousness. Each learning experience requires reorientation regarding present attitudes. Be prepared and willing to change your mind, or to alter your perspective regarding what has meaning in life. *Crisis in consciousness.*

Balsamic: Here we find the faster planet between 315 to 360 degrees ahead of the slower planet. You are trying to live out an ideal that has not yet become a part of society's consciousness. Use the power of this planetary pair to plant seeds for tomorrow. Realize that the flowers of yesterday will, in time, wilt unless reseeding takes place. The phase cycle is ending so a new one can be formed. *Faith is required.*

MARS/VENUS and PLUTO/VENUS POLARITIES: The partnership of Mars and Venus deals with issues of give and take. Mars represents action based on personal desire. It is the urge to move out to get what you want from life. In itself, Mars rules pure, aggressive, masculine energy, unfettered by personal, social or collective values. Venus represents with the capacity for receptivity. It provides magnetism that allows you to attract substances and relationships that complement your values and concept of worth. Venus represents the part of you that wants to share and to experience social interaction. The Mars/Venus polarity rules all male/female issues ... attraction/aggression, sexuality, reproduction at a physical or artistic level.

Questions posed by the Mars/Venus polarity include: Do you really want what you are so aggressively trying to get? Are your values congruent with your desires? How do you integrate aggressive drives with receptive urges? Passion with love?

This polarity can point to both male and female chauvinism, the separation as well as union of the sexes. It describes the value you place on relationships and how you interact with the opposite sex. This planetary "team" not only rules Aries and Libra, but influences the Taurus/Scorpio polarity due to Mars' co-rulership of Scorpio and Venus' joint rulership of Taurus and Libra. When assessing the Scorpio/Taurus polarity it is important to also consider the role of Pluto.

Pluto exemplifies the profound changes that occur from intimacy of any kind. The Venus/Pluto polarity requires self trust and trust in those who play a significant role in the intimate, private parts of your life. Pluto challenges you, through the major changes it causes in your perspective of life, to re-create your values and concepts of self worth, and to reorganize your desires so that you can play a part in filling social as well as personal desires.

When Venus and Mars/Pluto rule *intercepted signs*, the role modeling you needed regarding integration of self with others was, in some way, not appropriate. The urge to "reproduce" yourself through creativity or procreation does not operate with full consciousness. The houses containing these planets describe fields of activity that may have contributed to the confusion of your intercepted signs. On the same token, they indicate areas of life that hold opportunities to release the Aries/Libra or Taurus/Scorpio polarity into consciousness, and to express the needs of these signs in a unique, individualized manner. The aspect and/or phase between Venus and Mars (Aries) or Pluto (Scorpio) describes how these opposing energies function together and how they can be most creatively integrated.

When this planetary pair rules duplicated signs (or *intercepted houses*) their functions are strongly developed and utilized in the conscious life. You have the capacity to use these energies or powers to direct, influence, or control the environment described by the intercepted house. The aspect and/or phase describes how these energies operate together.

MERCURY/JUPITER POLARITY: The Mercury/Jupiter partnership describes your potential to continually expand your intellect. It encourages you to use your mind to enhance and enlarge your social influence.

Mercury rules the capacity to understand factual data, to ascertain how multiple facts fit together. Mercury provides a desire to accumulate information. Jupiter, on the other hand, rules theory. It wants you to look beyond factual data to explore horizons and avenues of learning beyond those provided in your community. Jupiter encourages you to expand your mind in order to expand your social influence.

Questions posed by the Jupiter/Mercury polarity include: How can I extend my current level of understanding? Where can I look for information to give me a broader frame of reference through which to view my life and better understand others?

This polarity, when not functioning creatively, can indicate intellectual pompousness, excessive communication, or "pie in the sky" thinking. The aspect and/or phase between these "partners" indicates how these urges operate together, how you most characteristically meet new, expansive learning opportunities, and how these separate urges can be most creatively integrated.

When Mercury and Jupiter rule *intercepted signs* in the chart, the environment has not provided the learning experiences you personally need to acquire a broad understanding of life or to acquire information that has meaning to you. The houses containing these planets describe fields of activity that may have contributed to the confusion experienced in the area of life described by the intercepted Gemini and Sagittarius. At the same time, they point to areas of life that hold opportunity to release the Gemini/-Sagittarius interception into consciousness and to express the needs of these signs in a unique, individualized manner.

If Mercury and Jupiter rule duplicated signs (or *intercepted houses*) in your chart, their functions are strongly developed and utilized in your conscious life. You have the ability to use these mental powers to direct, influence or control the environment described by the intercepted houses. The aspect and/or phase describes how these energies operate together.

MOON/SATURN POLARITY: The Moon/Saturn partnership deals with concepts of parenting. The maternal energies of Luna must function as a complement to Saturn's disciplines. This polarity induces an urge to create security at both a personal and social level.

The Moon deals with emotion. It represents the part of you that yearns for security, a feeling of belonging, warmth and nurturing. It functions to protect you by building secure boundaries that promise emotional safety. Saturn, on the other hand, deals with the disciplinarian aspects of parenting. It encourages you to construct boundaries to encompass and protect you when living out your social role. Saturn is the teacher ... the part of you that wants you to function with responsibility and abide by the rules society defines.

These energies must work together to provide a well-balanced emotional life, combined with a sense of security regarding your place in the world. If one planet dominates, you are unable to take care of yourself, emotionally (Moon) or socially (Saturn). Both Moon and Saturn are territory-conscious. Both want security, but each is motivated by different priorities.

Moon and Saturn ruling *intercepted signs* suggest that the environment did not provide role models or security structures you needed to feel secure within your social place. You have been strongly influenced by family in this area of life but you may have difficulty integrating these experiences in a way that provides the security you need. The houses containing both Saturn and the Moon describe areas of life where experiences are met that contribute to this lack of objectivity regarding where you "belong." You need to go inside to find nurturing and self respect rather than looking for outside structures to define where you fit in.

If Saturn and Moon rule duplicated signs (or *intercepted houses*), their functions are strongly developed and utilized in your life. You have the ability to use your "parenting" skills to direct, influence, or control the areas of life ruled by the intercepted houses. The aspect and/or phase between Moon and Saturn describes how these energies operate together.

SUN/URANUS POLARITY: The partnership of Sun and Uranus deals with the process of individuation. The Sun defines your level of consciousness and personal urge for growth. It brings illumination. It represents your "center," your life force.

The Sun shows where (house) personal purpose and a sense of self importance is waiting to be put to use. Its focus is on personal growth, while Uranus, its partner, urges you to become not just "self" centered, but aware of your connection with the universe. Uranus breaks up patterns that limit the individuation of consciousness. It introduces you to collective energies and urges you to develop collective concerns.

These planets must operate in polarity for individuation to occur. The self must be strong (Sun) for Uranus to perform its tasks. Likewise, Uranus must interact with the Sun to keep its erratic energies from fragmenting the consciousness. This partnership represents the relationship between the conscious personality and the unconscious urge to become more than a separate individual ... to become universalized.

When the Sun and Uranus rule *intercepted signs*, their energies do not, at first, operate as partners. You have not been taught, by your environment or its role models, to integrate your urge to be involved with social causes with the part of you that wants approval and reinforcement of your self importance. You could experience difficulty locating external outlets that support your individualistic concerns.

When Sun and Uranus rule duplicated signs (or *intercepted houses*), their functions are strongly developed and utilized in your life. You have the ability to apply progressive ideals and define social causes that both receive vitality from, and contribute to, your personal ego. The aspect and/or phase between Sun and Uranus describes how these energies operate together in your life.

MERCURY/NEPTUNE POLARITY: Mercury represents the conscious mind. Its sole concern is to accumulate and assimilate factual data. It operates as a facilitator, both sending and receiving messages to and from all other parts of personality.

Neptune, on the other hand, operates from outside the consciousness. It calls your attention to beliefs that defy logic. Neptune rules dreams, visions, ideals and faith. How can these opposing energies be seen as partners? Their's is, indeed, an interesting relationship.

Neptune's role, when working with Mercury, is to provide inspiration. When functioning together, this combination can be highly creative, highly imaginative. It carries the potential for genius. If one function dominates the other, however, integration of spiritual and mental energies cannot occur. Neptune sends messages to Mercury that seldom make sense to its logical way of thinking. It challenges Mercury to investigate concepts that go beyond fact, to pursue interests that defy logic, to believe in the value of life's intangibles. If Mercury refuses to heed the Neptunian messages, it remains locked in a linear perspective of life. If, on the other hand, Neptune dominates, and Mercury is obscured, you could easily lose all logical perspective in life and live in a constant state of fantasy or fear.

Mercury and Neptune ruling *intercepted signs* suggest that the environment has not provided the facilities, information, or teachers you needed to learn to blend these opposing energies. It is difficult for you to make sense out of the spiritual or creative messages Neptune transmits. You could waver back and forth between excessive logic and idealism, or allow one function to dominate the opposite. Your spiritual education cannot be filled within the structures of your early environment. You need to "tune in" to a frequency that is unknown to others around you to find your spiritual truths.

If Mercury and Neptune rule duplicated signs (or *intercepted houses*), their functions are strongly developed and utilized in your conscious life. You have the ability to understand (Mercury) the subtle nuances Neptune offers. You have a natural ability to "tune in" to higher truths and make sense out of them. The aspect and/or phase between Neptune and Mercury describes how these energies operate together.

CHAPTER IX

RELOCATION CHARTS

Can relocating to an environment other than the natal location help in the process of accessing intercepted signs? Some astrologers say "yes" while others disagree. In some ways, changing locations and constructing a chart for the new environment rather than the natal place can be likened to a woman changing her name at the time of marriage. Certainly, life changes as result of the marriage, but the major issues she needs to confront in life, her talents, her problems, go with her into the union.

Obviously, relocation can change your life. It will not, however, change your ultimate destiny. While relocating can change the external environment, in early life you are accompanied in relocation by family and its traditions. The basic influences of childhood are not totally altered due to a change in location.

A relocation chart is calculated by using the birth date and constructing the chart based on the latitude and longitude of the new location, after converting the birth time to the time at the new location. Significant changes could occur in the chart once it has been relocated. It is not unusual for intercepted signs to fall on house cusps of relocated charts. Sometimes, signs that are not intercepted in the natal chart become intercepted in the relocated chart. Signs on houses often change, yet planets in signs do not. As the houses of a chart describe areas of life, and the signs on their cusps define your specific approach to these various fields of activity, it isn't surprising to see signs on houses change when relocation charts are constructed. Certainly, you meet new challenges and develop new attitudes and skills in the process of major residential change. You move into a new school system. You have new neighbors. Your home environment changes. Areas of creative opportunity are altered. As adults, the professional environment changes. New associations are formed. Often, new philosophical concepts are introduced. In some cases these changes work to your advantage. In others, they may further inhibit you from actualizing the potentials and meeting the challenges defined by the natal chart.

When considering a relocation chart, always keep in mind that it does not replace the natal chart. It is an extension of it. And, because it is an extension, it often creates further challenges regarding issues of destiny. The natal chart represents the core of who you are. It describes what you need to accomplish in life. It describes the challenges that must be met and the opportunities life will present. These basic issues are not altered by a change in location. You will find, however, that some areas of the globe offer greater ease than others in accessing your talents and confronting challenge. The talents and challenges are shown in the natal chart. Never view the relocation chart as an entity in itself. It must always be considered in relation to the natal chart.

The challenges of intercepted signs will not disappear due to changes of location. The imprint of your life is drawn in the natal chart, just as your finger prints are uniquely your own; they do not change when you marry or move. You could develop new lines in your hands, but your fingerprints will always be your mark of identity, just as the natal chart is your map of destiny.

Certainly, some geographical areas will enable you to more easily access your intercepted signs. Yet, the fact that interceptions are part of your birth challenge does not change. You will still experience the challenges they represent and must still look within to define who you are. A river may change its course, but it still seeks its destination in the ocean. You may change your course, but your ultimate destiny is fixed in the natal chart.

Intercepted signs forced to the surface as a result of a residential move occurring before you are psychologically prepared to confront and integrate their needs could actually be debilitating to growth. In truth, relocating to escape environmental limitations could actually complicate your process of unfoldment. While you can traverse the globe, you can never escape the reality of who you are and what you need to accomplish with your life. The natal chart is the basis from which all other astrological procedures must be considered.

CHAPTER X

TRANSITS AND INTERCEPTIONS

Planets transiting intercepted signs enable you to confront personal needs that are otherwise difficult to access or define. Transits challenge you to address your inner needs and, based on the nature of the transiting planet, to experiment with "parts" of yourself that the environment has not conditioned, educated, or recognized. Transits are the keys that release the powers of your intercepted signs and/or planets. Yet, because you have not had role models to help shape and refine these inner qualities, the initial outer manifestation triggered by transits is often erratic or dis-integrated. Lacking objectivity provided by the sign polarity, the expression of these urges is often imbalanced in some way. Remember, only half of an intercepted polarity is emphasized by a transit. The opposite sign may remain inoperative, unable to provide its balancing role. Like a bull released from his pen, you could demonstrate erratic or excessive behaviors when these signs and planets begin to emerge.

The degree of intensity demonstrated as a result of transiting planets opening intercepted signs is determined by the speed at which the transit moves through them. If you are not familiar with the cycles of planets, refer to the Table in the previous chapter.

The longer a planet takes to transit a house or sign, the greater its intensity or magnitude of impact on your life. The Moon, for example, because it transits each sign in about 2 1/2 days, once every 27 days, will often pass unnoticed. The transiting Moon may stimulate nothing more than an inner "twinge" that tells you there is something more available to you than what has been made obvious by the environment. The slower transits, Saturn, Uranus, Neptune and Pluto will be far more noticeable and intense. Long-term issues are confronted regarding the powers of your intercepted signs during the time they spend in each sign.

This is not to say that transits of the Moon are of less significance that those of the outer planets. The **MOON**, by transit, has a very important function to serve. Transiting Moon's role can be likened to that of a mother's. The Moon moves from house to house in the chart, checking into each "room" of your life, to make sure everything is safe and secure. The Moon brings minor changes to your attention; it elicits an emotional response that calls your attention to the need to adapt or to protect. The Moon does not indicate major traumas, nor does it initiate major change. Memorable experiences are denoted by the slower moving bodies. The Moon's role is to help you maintain a constant fluidity in life as you move from one experience (house) to the next. It helps you adapt to the minor changes of mood and circumstance that are required at a daily level in order to maintain your emotional equilibrium. As the Moon transits intercepted signs and/or planets, you experience an opportunity to access, and to experiment with, inner potentials in minor ways. This prepares you for the time when slower planets bring more powerful urges to the surface.

The transits of **MERCURY, SUN and VENUS** are always tied together. They transit the chart as a trio, staying close together as they move through the zodiac. Their transits point to areas of life (houses) that require attention, and where growth is possible. The Sun illuminates. It lights up the area of life described by the house through which it is transiting. It encourages you to grow in awareness, to find new importance in the experiences ruled by the house through which it is moving. Mercury, the Sun's transiting companion, encourages you to think, to learn, and to communicate. It invites you to intellectualize the experiences enlightened by the Solar transit, and to become more intellectually astute regarding the needs of the sign and the experiences ruled by the house through which it is transiting. Venus operates as a personal magnet. It attracts substances and people into life that cause you to question your values. Venus encourages you to appreciate the value of the experiences available within the house it is transiting.

The Sun, Mercury and Venus move through each sign in about one month, orbiting the entire ecliptic in approximately one year. As they move into intercepted signs, they signal times when you can more easily access the potentials these signs represent. The Sun enlightens you to the fact that you have skills and needs beyond those recognized by your environment. These transits bring an awareness and appreciation of qualities that are otherwise hidden. While they do not provoke, to the extent they demand the externalization of the intercepted signs, they bring awareness and interest.

MARS is more provocative. It urges you to act on the needs represented by the sign through which it is transiting, in the area of life described by its house. Mars transits each sign in approximately 2 months, taking 2 years to orbit the entire chart. While transiting an intercepted sign, it encourages you to act on internal yearnings represented by the sign. This could mark a two month period, occurring once every two years, when you feel compelled to act out needs and urges not supported or guided by your environment. Still, due to the frequency with which this transit occurs, it may go unnoticed other than provoking some dissatisfaction with environmental limitations. You could, as a result, be more irritable than usual during this transit, especially if you feel trapped or unable to find an outlet for the urges and needs represented by the interception. Mars encourages you to dare to initiate action. As you look around your environment, you may feel thwarted due to lack of environmental support, interest, or understanding regarding your desire to take assertive action to get what you want. This could result in rebellious behavior, or it could further suppress personal desires.

JUPITER'S transits encourage expansion. The house through which Jupiter is transiting describes an area of life where you need *more*. Its twelve year cycle is one of growth, distribution and social assimilation. Jupiter remains, by transit, in each sign for approximately one year, encouraging you to grow and expand your level of social influence and exposure regarding the area of life described by its house. When transiting an intercepted sign, tremendous inner expansion takes place. It may, however, be difficult to locate external avenues through which to demonstrate your expansive theories or urge for growth. You want more here. Yet, as you look around, you may find difficulty locating external facilities that provide the expansion you require. You must look beyond the limitations of the environment to acquire what you want. The urge for expansion, promoted by Jupiter, is helpful. It encourages you to explore avenues beyond those available in your environment.

No other planets opens intercepted signs with more force than the transits of Saturn and Uranus. This is particularly the case after having experienced your first Saturn return.

The first 28 years of life are largely spent developing basic skills needed for social integration. Once Saturn makes its first return to its natal place, between ages 28 and 30, opportunity to experience individuation becomes available. This is not to say that it is impossible to begin the process of accessing intercepted signs prior to the Saturn return. However, full awareness of the complexities involving intercepted signs does not come easily, and often comes gradually. Each major pre-Saturn return transit brings out pieces of the puzzle of your life rather than revealing the whole "picture" the pieces make up.

SATURN, by nature, is the great disciplinarian. Saturn wants you to focus, define, and use, in responsible terms, the benefits of its teachings. While transits of Saturn can be restrictive, they also indicate when and where tremendous growth is taking place. Maturity is required to effectively benefit from Saturn's transits.

Saturn "orders" you to focus on the importance of the experiences ruled by the house through which it is passing. It requires responsibility, self discipline and perseverance. You must face realities, focus on, and define, the importance of the experiences ruled by its house. When transiting an intercepted sign, you experience difficulty accessing environmental structures that provide the experiences you need to define your social importance or your social place. Saturn brings an urge for status. When transiting intercepted signs, it is difficult to locate external experiences that encourage this social growth. A dynamic internal growth process is taking place. It is difficult, however, to locate external facilities through which to exemplify your emerging social identity. Responsible rebellion must take place in order to release yourself from the limitations you feel. You will confront personal issues, skills, problems, and needs that have been inhibited prior to this transit. You will try to make sense out of urges that have never been acknowledged before. You will discover a side of yourself that has never before been exposed. This can be considered one of the most powerful growth periods of your life. Throughout the 2 1/2 years Saturn remains in an intercepted sign, you will meet opportunities, difficult though they might be, to develop a part of yourself that has not been previously revealed to you. You will be introduced to significant challenges as you strive to focus and develop personal needs (signs) and urges (planets) that have been obscured due to the lack of role models or educational experiences. Because these needs have not been supported by external conditions, they may surface, at first, as undesirable traits. You have not been taught how to externalize these needs and energies creatively, so, at first, they might be expressed immaturely or erratically. As Saturn moves further into the sign, skills needed for outer expression are refined.

ANY TRANSIT through an intercepted sign brings the potential to uncover and expose needs and urges that are locked within due to lack of environmental tutoring, response, or recognition. By watching transits, you can find optimum periods of life to access "parts" of yourself that need to be recognized and integrated. The slower the transit, the more profound the process of self discovery becomes. If, for example, you pay no attention to Moon transits as it passes through the various sectors of the chart, you will be unprepared for the more dramatic displays brought about by the slower planets.

Transits of Saturn through Pluto simply cannot be ignored. They bring major events and changes to life that will unlock the needs of your interceptions. Whether you use or abuse these experiences is a matter of human choice. You will be exposed to situations that bring the need for integration to your attention.

No other planet brings this need to your attention more abruptly or dramatically than **URANUS**. Uranus brings major changes in its wake. When moving through an intercepted sign, these changes often come more unexpectedly than what is usual with this planet. Uranus transiting intercepted signs often results in an extreme urge to rebel against all social confines. As you become more and more aware of lack of environmental support, you become more and more driven to rebellion. As your intercepted needs are exposed, you experience a dynamic urge to break free of all limitations and expose a part of yourself that others have never fully recognized or supported. The need to free yourself from bondage to the environment takes precedence over all other urges. Those around you may be shocked by your behavior. By rebelling you are exposing personal needs that others have never before recognized.

The house containing the interception describes an area of life where changes must occur. Even though, at first, your choices may seem abrupt and erratic, the outcome of the changes you create at this time in your life enables you to become an integrated being. As you recognize the needs represented by your intercepted sign, and begin to find new outlets for expressing the urges represented by any planets contained within, other areas of life are also affected. Missing links (interceptions) begin to emerge. All areas of life must be reorganized. This is particularly stressed when planets occupy the interceptions. For example, you must look not only to planets in the intercepted signs to find functions of personality emerging in more powerful ways, but to the houses ruled by these planets. The areas of life described by houses ruled by intercepted planets will be powerfully influenced by the release of the intercepted planets' energies. A domino affect begins to occur. Once the barriers of intercepted signs and planets begin to crumble, all aspects of life are redefined and all energies are redirected.

The transits of Neptune and Pluto through intercepted signs are more subtle. It takes **NEPTUNE** approximately 14 years to transit one sign. While its influence is strong, it is deceptively subdued. Uranus, Neptune and Pluto are unconscious planets. As they transit houses of the chart they show where significant unconscious transformation is taking place. Because they deal with unconscious, spiritual unfoldment, it is often difficult to pinpoint specific events that lead to this transforming growth. You know you are changing, but don't know why or how. It is often only retrospectively, after the transit has moved on, that you realize the extent of the transformation that has occurred.

Due to the illusive nature of Neptune, its influence is often one of confusion when transiting intercepted signs. Neptune's role is to dissolve overly rigid structures. Yet, no structures exist with intercepted signs. The transit of Neptune through an intercepted sign may be less outwardly dramatic than that of Saturn or Uranus. Neptune requires faith, while also ruling fear. Neptune is alluring. It challenges you to recognize the power of faith, while also exposing you to the power of fear. Neptune encourages you to face your fears and have faith that you will find safety at the end of your journey into the unknown. When transiting intercepted signs, it brings an inner yearning for an unknown experience. As you look around to find spiritual substance, you realize that the environment does not, and may never, have what you seek. Neptune reveals that nothing is ever completely as it appears. It can free you from attachments to physical dependencies. On the other hand, you may seek escape from realities by abusing the substances ruled by its house.

PLUTO'S movement into an intercepted sign brings out deep, unconscious urges that must be regenerated before they can emerge and integrate with personality. A rebirth is taking place in the area of life described by the house through which it is transiting. When a sign is intercepted in the house, it takes longer than normal to complete the transit. It gives you more time to experience transformation, because it must go deeper into the unconscious than what is necessary when transiting signs are not "captured" in the chart.

Houses containing *intercepted signs* are larger than most others. It always take a planet longer to transit a house containing an intercepted sign than a house that is intercepted by a sign. Due to the complexities involved with the areas of life described by houses containing interceptions, you need more time to explore your personal needs regarding the experiences they rule.

On the other hand, *intercepted houses* describe areas of life that are highly developed. Transits move through intercepted houses quite rapidly. You do not need to focus the same degree of energy on developing intercepted houses. They describe areas of life that are innately well-formed. Transits through these houses simply stimulate the creative potential promised in the natal chart in preparation for their transit into the following house, where you begin to merge the experiences of the intercepted house into the activities described by the following house (the house containing the same sign, but larger degree).

When working with transits, it is important to realize that everyone is experiencing the same transit at the same time. But it impacts a different area of each of our lives according to the house containing the sign through which it is moving. Transits describe opportunities provided by the outside world that stimulate each of us to develop individually in the departments of life described by the house through which they are moving as well as the houses ruled by any planets they aspect while transiting a particular house.

For example, when a transiting planet aspects (particularly a conjunction) an intercepted planet, not only will you experience an urge to explore the area of life described by the house containing the intercepted planet, but the results of this investigation will influence the area of life described by the house ruled by the intercepted planet. As you bring out the energies of the intercepted planet, significant freedom is equally experienced in the house the natal planet rules. Natal planets always seek expression through the experiences of the houses they rule. Planets take up occupancy in a particular house of the chart to acquire experiences needed to fill the requirements of their kingdoms. If, for example, a transiting planet conjuncts an intercepted 5th house planet that rules the 10th house, the creative energy it brings to the surface (5th house) seeks an outlet through career (10th house). Any changes experienced by the intercepted planet will always influence the house that planet rules. It is extremely important to keep this concept in mind when interpreting transits. Many major cycles of opportunity, or times of stress, can be missed when an astrologer fails to consider the connection between planets and their ruling signs.

It is also important to realize that a transiting planet is always attempting to shape and direct the expression of the natal planets being aspected. For example, a transit of Jupiter to natal Mercury encourages expansion (Jupiter) in thinking (Mercury). Saturn transiting Mercury advises you to focus and concentrate (Saturn) on learning (Mercury). The transiting planet wants the natal planet to function according to its rules. Transiting Uranus over the natal Moon encourages you to break up (Uranus) old habits and emotional responses (Moon). Transiting Mars to natal Neptune encourages you to act (Mars) on your beliefs (Neptune). When the natal planet is intercepted, you have no past experience to call on for directing these energies. Your environment, and its role models, have not encouraged or acknowledged the need for their expression.

Transits through intercepted signs, and over planets, begin the process of freeing you from environmental confines and conditioning. This process usually starts out as erratic behavior, because you have not been taught how to direct these energies into outer experience. With time, greater sophistication and integration occurs. In most cases, however, the emergence process of intercepted signs is stressful. Most people feel they are in a time in their lives when they are somewhat out of control and lack direction. Yet, especially if Saturn or Uranus are the instigators, there is a compelling need to release the pent-up energy defined by the interceptions.

CHAPTER XI

ENVIRONMENT VS DESTINY CHARTS

Have you ever wondered who you might have been if raised in a different family, brought up in a different environment, exposed to different values? Or, have you ever wondered who you might be had you allowed the environment, your family, the system, to dominate your life? Obviously, had you been born into different circumstances, life would have led you on a course very different from the one you have taken. How much has your environment influenced your destiny? And, how much has your destiny influenced the choices you have made? How much has destiny directed your life in ways other than what your environment expected for you?

In earlier times, and in other cultures, people grew up assuming that they would remain in their specific social "class" throughout their entire lives. They would take over the family business, maintain the family estate, and stay centered in the security or confines of their heritage. A pauper's son would be a pauper. The mother's daughter would become a mother and a wife. The doctor's son would join his father in medical practice. The world has changed. And, our approach to astrology has had to change with it.

Many cultures still hold on to old traditions. The caste system is still used throughout many locations on our globe. People who break away from the family mold, who rebel against the systems that classify them based on their heritage, financial status, and so on, are viewed as outcasts rather than individuals. In these conservative societies, the Equal House chart is widely used, while in more liberal cultures few astrologers use the Equal House method of chart construction.

The Equal House chart is designed by finding the ascendant sign and degree and placing all other signs in their natural order around the chart, using the same degree for each house cusp. Obviously, no intercepted signs could exist in this house division. It is my belief that the Equal House chart describes an individual's life as it would be had s/he followed the path of life defined by the environment, never questioning issues of destiny, but rather accepting the concept of "fate." In some cases, the Equal House division will only slightly vary from a chart calculated for the Placidus house system or another method of house division using unequal houses. In other cases, significant changes occur. Often, the sign on the tenth house cusp is different in the Equal House chart from that found using any other house system. (Many advocates of the Equal House division insert the Midheaven into the chart, but do not consider it the tenth house significator.)

It has been my observation that people who have lived their lives exactly as they have been taught are manifesting their Equal House charts. When major changes occur between the Equal House chart and charts using unequal houses there are major contradictions between how they have been taught to function in the world and what their inner selves want them to become. The Equal House chart defines the "conditioned life," while the chart having unequal house divisions defines how the individual can fulfill his, or her, unique destiny within the environment s/he is living. I call the Equal House chart the **Environmental Chart.**

On the other hand, an Equal House chart can also be constructed using the Midheaven as a starting point, placing it on the tenth house cusp and inserting the signs sequentially around the rest of the chart. The same degree as that of the Midheaven is used for each cusp. This chart will differ from both of those previously mentioned.

The Midheaven represents the highest rung on your ladder of success. It is the point of conscious social attainment. It is the point of social destiny. I call this Equal House chart the **Destiny Chart.** It shows what route would most easily lead you to your social destiny. However, because you were born into a specific environment, family, and social structure, certain compromises must be made to reach this destiny. Compromises required to integrate your destiny with environmental realities are described by the chart calculated with uneven house cusps.

In some way, you could say that the Destiny Chart reveals your ideal path. The Environment Chart defines the conditioned or taught route. The Unequal House Chart blends both of the above, making it possible to

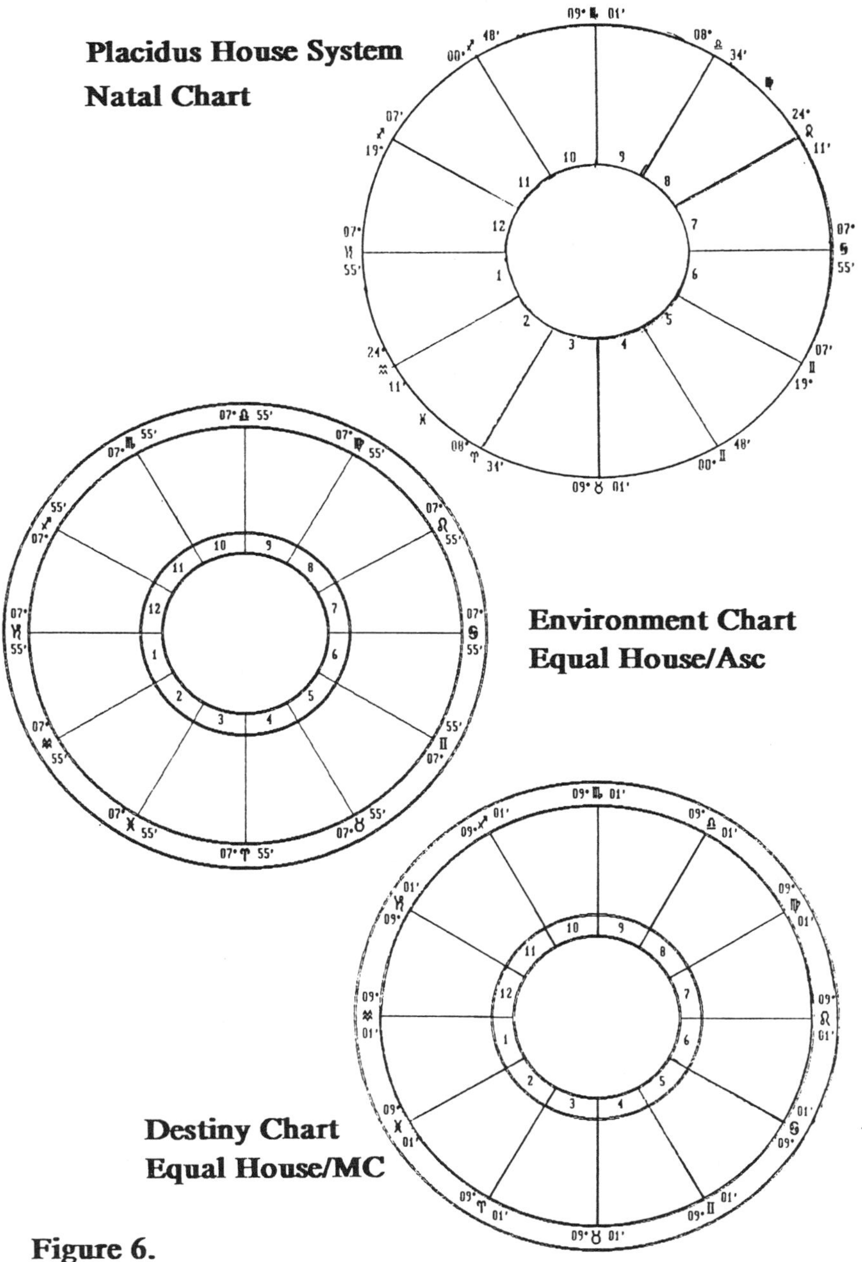
Placidus House System
Natal Chart
Environment Chart
Equal House/Asc
Destiny Chart
Equal House/MC

Figure 6.

reach your destiny within your environment by making certain compromises or adjustments.

When viewing the Destiny Chart, it is not unusual to find a sign on the first house cusp that differs from the calculated Ascendant. Likewise, other important factors could change. When the first house sign (ascendant) changes, we find individuals who have had to learn to wear a mask (first house) different from what would be consistent with their life mission (Midheaven). Making this adjustment enables them to fulfill their destinies and still conform to, and survive within, the environment.

For example, a Destiny Chart having Scorpio on the 10th house cusp would naturally have an Aquarius ascendant ... the sign falling at a 90 degree angle to the Midheaven. However, when a chart has been calculated using unequal houses, it is not unusual to find a Capricorn Ascendant. These individuals all share a common mission (MC). They need a profession or advocation that encourages them to invest intense emotional energy. They need to feel that, through their professional endeavors, some kind of change in old patterns, systems, methods, will occur. The most comfortable persona (first house) enabling them to participate in "change work" (Scorpio) is described by Aquarius, the first house sign of the Destiny Chart. However, due to environmental factors, those having Capricorn rising have had to present themselves to the world wearing a more conservative mask. Had it not been for environmental conditioning, Aquarius would have been the natural mode of self projection.

I have interviewed numerous people sharing this particular combination of Ascendant/Midheaven in their natal charts. All professed to being frustrated Aquarian's. All testified to having been raised in an environment that required them to abide by its rules, to be responsible, and to always be concerned with their reputations (Capricorn rising). While this environmental infusion created limitations regarding their inner urge to reform (Aquarius), the process of wearing a conservative masks made it possible for them to function in a world that would not accept their true Aquarian perspective of life. Excerpts from these interviews follow:

Steven: "I was very artistic as a child. I think my parents assumed I would pursue a career in graphic arts, advertising or some other artistic field (Libra on 10th house of Environment Chart). They encouraged me in this area, but it never felt quite right. Something was missing.

"I am presently involved in a vocation that enables me to use my artistic talents, but offers more in-depth involvement and utilizes more psychology.

I am interested in what goes on under the surface of people, so I have been drawn to psychology (Scorpio MC on Destiny Chart)."

Ruth: "In youth, I was musically inclined. I came from a strict, religious family and was encouraged to develop my musical talents for work in the church. I don't think my family really encouraged me to pursue a career. They assumed I would marry and mold my life around my mate. I am now a professional therapist."

Ruth has Capricorn rising. In the Destiny Chart, however, Aquarius is at the horizon. Ruth never felt she "fit in" with others in her conservative family/environment. In the Destiny Chart Scorpio is on the MC, while in the Environment Chart Libra occupies the 10th house cusp. In the latter chart, the Venus-ruled 10th cusp suggests a career in the arts, or in Ruth's case, success through marriage. This was not enough for Ruth. The Scorpio MC attests to a strong need to make a difference in the world by merging with others to produce needed change.

Nancy: "As a child, I played the flute and took extensive lessons in dance (Libra on Environment Chart 10th cusp). I always thought my family wanted me to teach dance as a vocation. I couldn't conform to their expectations. I turned to astrology and metaphysics instead."

Stephanie: "I am presently involved in medical research. Uncovering mysteries is exciting to me. As a child, I came from a very strict family. My mother was very creative and excellent in interior design. While I'm sure she would have liked me to follow in her footsteps, it lacked the depth I needed (Scorpio on MC of Destiny Chart)."

Another example is seen in the chart of the woman discussed in Chapter III. She has an Aquarius Midheaven with Gemini on the Ascendant. Her Environment Chart, based on her Ascendant, gives Pisces on the 10th house cusp, while the Destiny Chart changes the Ascendant from Gemini to Taurus.

This woman learned at an early age to wear a mask described by Gemini ... to be flexible, appear curious, and present herself as naive. Under her surface, however, a Taurus urge was strongly felt. While taught to be detached and cerebral in her outlook on life, her most natural approach with regard to her destiny was defined by Taurus. She is a strongly sensual individual who, due to environmental conditions, was challenged to put aside her sensuality and appreciation for the physical world and make choices on the basis of intellect rather than substance. Notice that Taurus is intercepted in the horoscope calculated in the Placidus house system.

When intercepted signs interfere with the natural sequence of signs on houses there is always a conflict between what you were brought up to be, or believe, and what your inner self wants you to become. When this interference in synchronicity influences the natural relationship between the Ascendant and Midheaven the resulting dilemma requires you to meet the world (Ascendant) in a manner that may feel artificial to you. Or, you could identify with the socially conditioned persona (Ascendant) to the degree you fail to recognize and pursue your destiny (Midheaven). Considering these Equal House charts will help you clarify what parts of yourself are truly yours (Destiny Chart) and what parts have been conditioned by environmental factors (Environment Chart).

It is important to realize that in order to fulfill your social destiny (Midheaven) you must adapt to your environment. Neither the Environment nor the Destiny Chart define how these two, often contradictory, forces can be integrated. By calculating the horoscope using unequal houses you are finding your most effective way of reaching your social destiny within the system of which you are a part. Sometimes, concessions must be made. Sometimes major adjustments and detours are experienced. When intercepted signs are found in the natal chart, the adjustments can seem more strenuous than when the Destiny Chart and the Environment Chart have few differences.

We are all products of the environment. Therefore, we must learn to adjust in order to function within it. Astrology offers tools for understanding the dilemmas involved with the integrative process. It need not take a lifetime of struggle to manifest your whole self. It may, however, take a life time to find your true self if you have no keys to help you unlock and disclose your mysteries and complexities. Astrology offers these keys. It provides tools for helping people access those keys. The horoscope describes one's true potential and discloses techniques that can be used to manifest destiny in a manner that society accepts. The Destiny Chart, the Environment Chart and the Unequal House Chart define the total process.

CHAPTER XII

INTERCEPTIONS IN REVIEW

Intercepted signs require you to find answers to life's questions from sources beyond those available in your immediate environment. They require you to, in some cases, defy the restrictions of your environment, or society, in order to find yourself. Your needs, and your perceptions, are different from what is normal to your environment. As the environment does not provide what you need for growth, you must find tools for development in more obscured areas. This leads to extensive self examination. It also leads you to investigate aspects of life not yet recognized by your environment. Are these not the very skills used by the inventors and genius' of our world?

Intercepted signs, once acknowledged and put to work, produce amazing outcomes. The outer expression of these signs, once brought to the surface, end up being very unique and individualized. They have not been conditioned by environmental factors. How can the environment shape what it doesn't know exists?

For example, with Gemini or its partner, Mercury, intercepted in the chart, your curiosity and thirst for knowledge can only be quenched by seeking information not available in the confines of your particular environment. The questions you ask are not fully or adequately answered by the educational facilities readily available. This ultimately challenges you to investigate, to seek information independently, or to go outside normal educational channels to find the answers you seek. Unless you allow the environment to swallow you up and obscure the needs represented by the interception, you will find that the knowledge you finally acquire will be uniquely your own. This is the power that can come from intercepted signs and planets in the horoscope. This is the blessing that can result from not "fitting in."

Earlier in the book I mentioned the limitations evident to those living in extreme northern or southern latitudes. The weather, for example, prohibits "normal" activities. Food products are not easily available and must be shipped in from "foreign" territory. It takes originality to survive in a climate that denies so many normal outlets of activity. Those who look beyond what the environment offers discover unique resources and systems that enable them to overcome the limitations. They flourish as a result. Because your intercepted signs and planets show aspects of personality that have not been conditioned or programmed by outside sources, their resulting expression is uniquely your own. These qualities, when they do emerge, are stamped with your identity.

PART TWO

RETROGRADE PLANETS: A Different Perspective

INTRODUCTION TO RETROGRADE PLANETS

When planets retrograde, they appear to move backward through the signs of the zodiac. This reversed motion is only a visual illusion. Like a train passing a moving automobile, passengers in the train experience the illusion that the car is moving backward due to the speed at which the train is moving.

Retrogradation is a geocentric, or earth centered, phenomenon. When viewing the solar system from a heliocentric (Sun centered) perspective, no retrogrades could occur. However, while standing on the surface of the Earth, watching planets move through their orbits, while our planet also moves through space, planets retrograde with regularity. Their retrogradation represents a time of transition ... a change from one cycle to another.

Some of our older literature suggests that retrograde planets do not operate with full strength. Retrogradation has been blamed for weaknesses in character on one hand, and violence on the other. While repression or insecurity could manifest when planets are retrograde in a natal chart, their functions cannot be considered either malefic or weak. In fact, retrograde planets operate with powerful intensity.

It is important to realize that a planet, when retrograde, is nearer to Earth than at any other time in its orbit. How can a retrograde planet function weakly when it is closer to our planet than when it is direct? The power of the planet, because of its close proximity to Earth, can create confusion that leads to repression of its energy.

Retrogrades function as powerful urges that must be accepted and integrated into consciousness. Rather than viewing retrograde planets as weaknesses, consider the following possibility. Could it be possible, because retrograde planets are closer to Earth than at any other time in their cycles, that their energies are intensified? If so, doesn't it make sense that their strengths, rather than their weaknesses, create potential difficulty in directing their energies and integrating their functions?

For example, a mind (Mercury) that works overtime is easily subjected to "burn out" or over-extension. When the mind operates with greater intensity than the consciousness (Sun) can assimilate, confusion results. Or, when the urge to have structures and boundaries in life is more intense than "normal," is it not likely that people will face constant challenges that lead them to question the
limits or boundaries they have set, or have allowed to be imposed on them (Saturn)? In the following chapters, these and other ideas will be addressed.

The astronomical and interpretive facts upon which the entire body of the remainder of this book are based are provided in Chapters XIII and XV. For this reason, it is important to read these chapters carefully. Illustrations are available to clarify the astronomical events that create retrogradation.

CHAPTER XIII

HOW PLANETS RETROGRADE

To fully comprehend the significance of retrograde planets in chart interpretation, it is important to understand the astronomical features that create them. To do so, consider figure 7 on the following page.

The planets are shown according to their *heliocentric* orbits around the Sun (A). The Sun is at the center of the diagram, representing the center of our solar system. Because the Sun is not a planet, but the star around which all other planets in the solar system orbit, it can never retrograde. The Moon is a satellite of the Earth. It orbits Earth rather than the Sun and it never retrogrades.

Notice that Mercury and Venus orbit the Sun *inside* Earth's pathway. In *geocentric* (B) astrology, they are always near to the Sun in the natal chart. Mercury, for example, is never more than 28 degrees ahead or behind the Sun. Venus is always within 48 degrees of the Sun.

When viewing Mercury and Venus from a Sun-centered (heliocentric) perspective, we see the full circle both planets make around the Sun. Mercury orbits the Sun in about 88 days; Venus in 225 days. The Earth orbits the Sun in one year. Its cycle is the basis of our calendar. It defines our seasonal changes and establishes the basic structure for the horoscope.

Heliocentric Mercury orbits the Sun three times in a little less than one year. During any year's period, it conjuncts the Sun six times. This is why it retrogrades, from a geocentric (Earth centered) perspective, more frequently than any other planet. When Mercury is at its closest point to Earth, and aligned with (conjunct) the Sun, it is at the midpoint, or peak, of its geocentric (Earth centered) retrograde phase. This occurs three times each year. This particular conjunction is called an *inferior conjunction*. Mercury is always retrograde at its inferior Solar conjunction.

As you examine figure 8, imagine yourself standing on the Earth's surface looking toward the Sun. Notice that Mercury and Sun align with the Earth

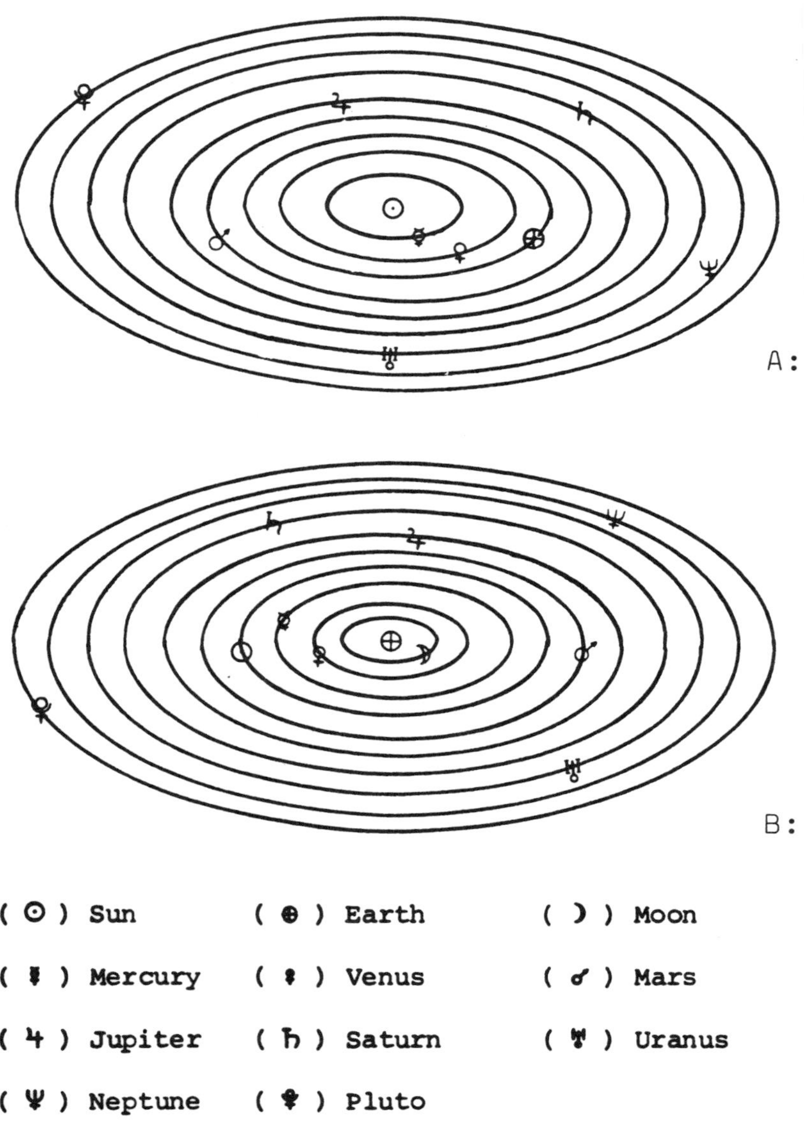

Figure 7:

A: Heliocentric or Sun-centered.

B: Geocentric or Earth-centered.

at two points (A and B). From Earth's perspective, a conjunction of Mercury and the Sun occurs at both of these points. Also, notice how close Mercury is to Earth during its inferior, or retrograde, conjunction (A).

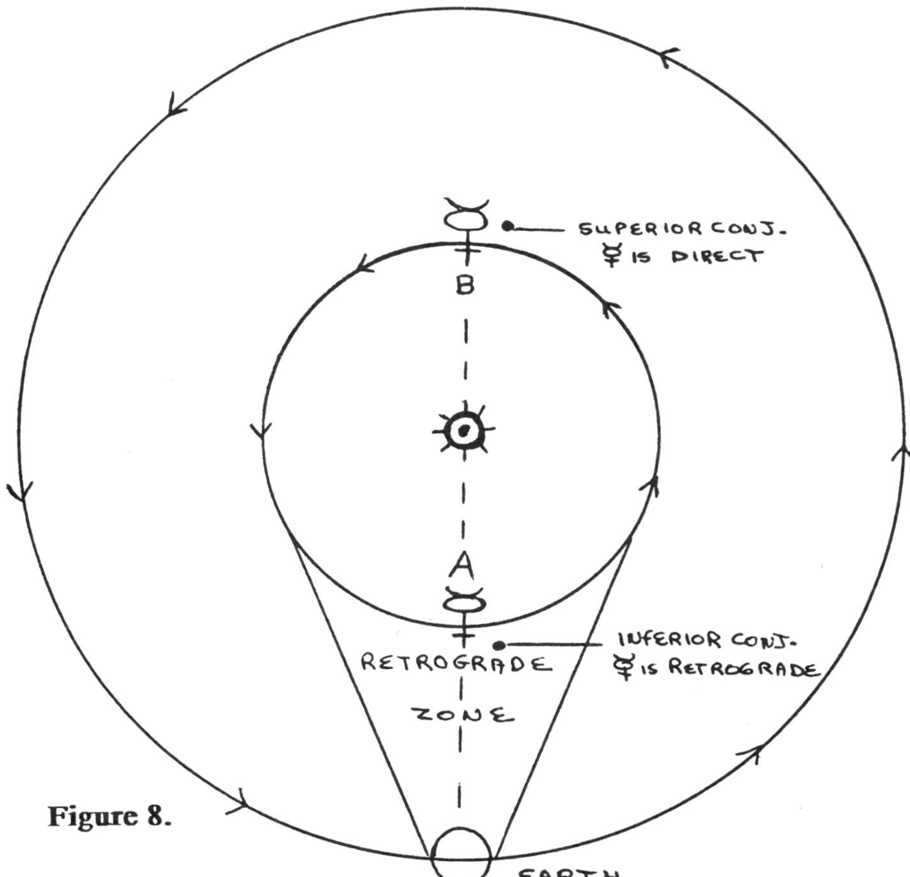

Figure 8.

The Mercury/Sun conjunction occurring at Mercury's farthest point from Earth (B) is called its superior conjunction. At this point, the Sun is between Earth and Mercury. Heliocentrically, Mercury and Earth are in an opposition. Still, from Earth's perspective, a conjunction is occurring. Mercury and the Sun are aligned in space. Mercury is always direct during its superior conjunction. The interpretive significance of the superior and inferior Solar conjunctions will be explained in later chapters.

As Venus also orbits between Sun and Earth, it is never seen in opposition to the Sun in a natal chart. Venus also forms superior and inferior Solar conjunctions. When visible from Earth, Venus is at its peak of brightness during the retrograde conjunction because it is at its closest point to our planet.

Our Earthly perspective of the orbits of Mercury and Venus is distorted because of the movement of our own planet. While we visually observe the planets outside Earth's orbit transiting the full 360 degrees of the zodiac independently from the Sun, this is not the case with Mercury and Venus.

From Earth's perspective, this complete orbit is obscure due to our own planetary movement. We see Mercury and Venus "swinging" back and forth within a limited territory. Figure 8 shows why this appears as it does from Earth.

Realize that the Earth is also in the process of orbiting the Sun, even though not evident in this figure. Viewing these planets in this light provides another dimension to the retrograde condition.

We see Mercury move from a Solar conjunction to a maximum of 28 degrees ahead of the Sun. It then retrogrades back to the conjunction and continues to retrograde a near equal number of degrees behind the Sun before turning direct to again conjoin the Sun. This entire process equates to one complete solar orbit of Mercury.

In figure 9, the orbit of Mercury is shown from still another perspective. It plots Mercury's cycles over a one year period. While technically not the starting point of Mercury's orbit, I have picked a beginning point for the sake of illustration. It begins at Mercury's retrograde station at 25 degrees of Capricorn on December 30, 1990. Notice that Mercury, in its process of moving backward through the degrees of the zodiac, makes an inferior conjunction to the Sun at 18 degrees Capricorn and continues to move backward until it turns stationary direct at 9 degrees of Capricorn. At this point, Mercury moves ahead in direct motion. Its next solar conjunction occurs at 27 degrees Pisces. This is a superior conjunction. Mercury is at its farthest point from Earth at 27 degrees Virgo. As Mercury continues to move, it reaches its next retrograde station at 17 degrees Taurus. It then begins its backward transit to make its next inferior conjunction to the Sun at 13 degrees of Taurus. It finally reaches its direct station at 07 degrees of Taurus. Follow its movement throughout the whole cycle to where it ends at the same degree and sign of its first stationary direct point.

As you watch each leg of Mercury's journey over a one year period, note that it has made a total of six conjunctions with the Sun ... three inferior (or retrograde) conjunctions and three superior (or direct). This illustration represents three complete cycles of Mercury around the Sun. Also, note that during this one year period, Mercury has retrograded in the Earth signs.

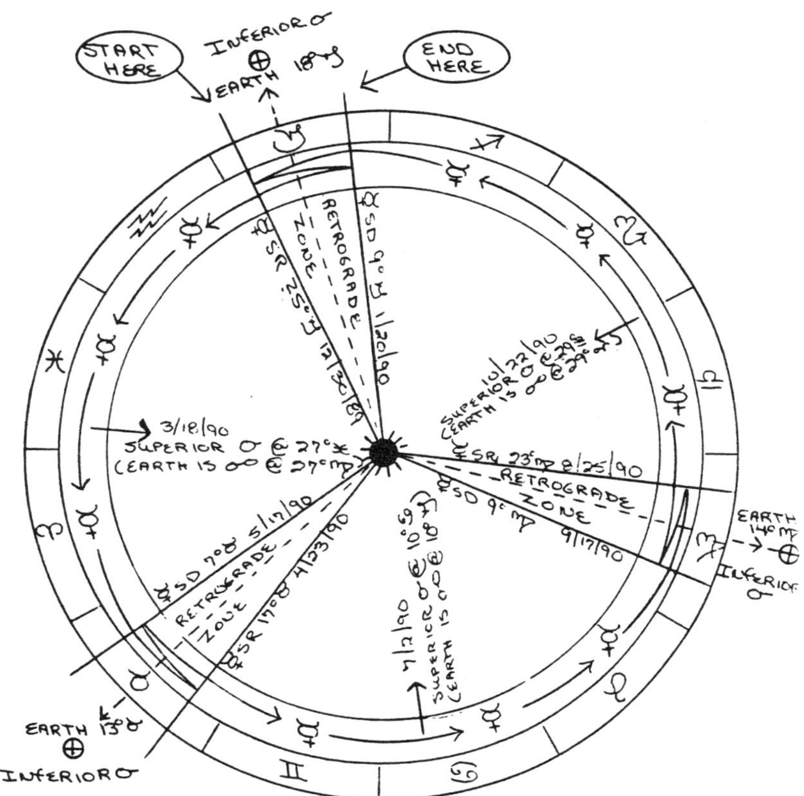

Figure 9.

From an interpretive perspective, the Element emphasized each year by Mercury's retrograde territory is significant. In a later chapter, we will examine Mercury's transiting cycle from an interpretive perspective. At this point, simply appreciate the complexity and symmetry of the cyclic unfoldment.

Venus' cycle operates similarly. However, Venus will venture up to 48 degrees ahead or behind the Sun when viewed from a geocentric perspective. Each "swing" Venus makes represents one complete Solar orbit. While Mercury retrogrades 3 times each year, Venus retrogrades only once in approximately 1 1/2 years. During this span, it makes one inferior (retrograde) and one superior (direct) Solar conjunction.

Mars through Pluto lie beyond the Earth's orbit. These planets, like Mercury and Venus, reach their closest point to our planet at the midpoint of their retrograde phases. We see this, in the Ephemeris, as an opposition between the planet and the Sun.

Mars is the first planet lying outside the Earth's orbit. To understand how Mars (and all planets beyond) experiences retrogradation, refer to figure 10 and imagine yourself standing on the surface of Earth, looking out into space. Notice the proximity of Mars to Earth during the time it is retrograde (A). As with all planets, Mars reaches it closest point to Earth at the midpoint of its retrogradation. If standing on our planet, observing Mars in the sky, you would be looking away from the Sun when Mars is retrograde. The Earth is between the Sun and Mars. In the natal chart, this phenomenon is noted as a Sun/Mars opposition. From a Sun-centered perspective, it is a Mars/Earth conjunction.

It is important to realize that Mars through Pluto move slower than the Sun in their geocentric, or Earth-centered, orbits. The Sun, therefore, is always applying to, or moving away from, aspects to these planets. When Mars and Sun are aligned, from Earth's perspective we find a Sun/Mars conjunction (B). Mars, at this point, is at its greatest distance from Earth, with the Sun found between it and our planet (B).

Mars, as it orbits through space, is approached by the Sun and Earth. Mars turns retrograde after it has moved beyond the degree at which it later aligns with Earth and is opposed by the Sun. Once this occurs, Mars appears to stop its forward motion and begins to retrograde. While retrograde, it conjoins Earth and forms an opposition with the Sun. It continues to retrograde a considerable distance behind the Earth, or before the point of its Solar opposition. Another station is made as it prepares to move forward through the zodiac. This same pattern is followed by all planets beyond the orbit of Mars.

Mars enters the *retrograde zone* prior to its actual retrogradation. This zone is determined by finding the total retrograde arc. The arc begins at the point where Mars later makes its direct station. It ends at the degree it makes it retrograde station. Between the time Mars transits the earlier degree, or the point at which it eventually turns stationary direct, while moving ahead in the zodiac, up to the time it actually turns retrograde, the planet is considered to have gone *beyond* the realm of existing consciousness (Sun). In some way, the energies represented by Mars have been overextended. They have gone beyond the limits or structures society has defined. People born during this pre-retrograde period often demonstrate this principle in their behaviors. While more information will be provided on the interpretive significance of

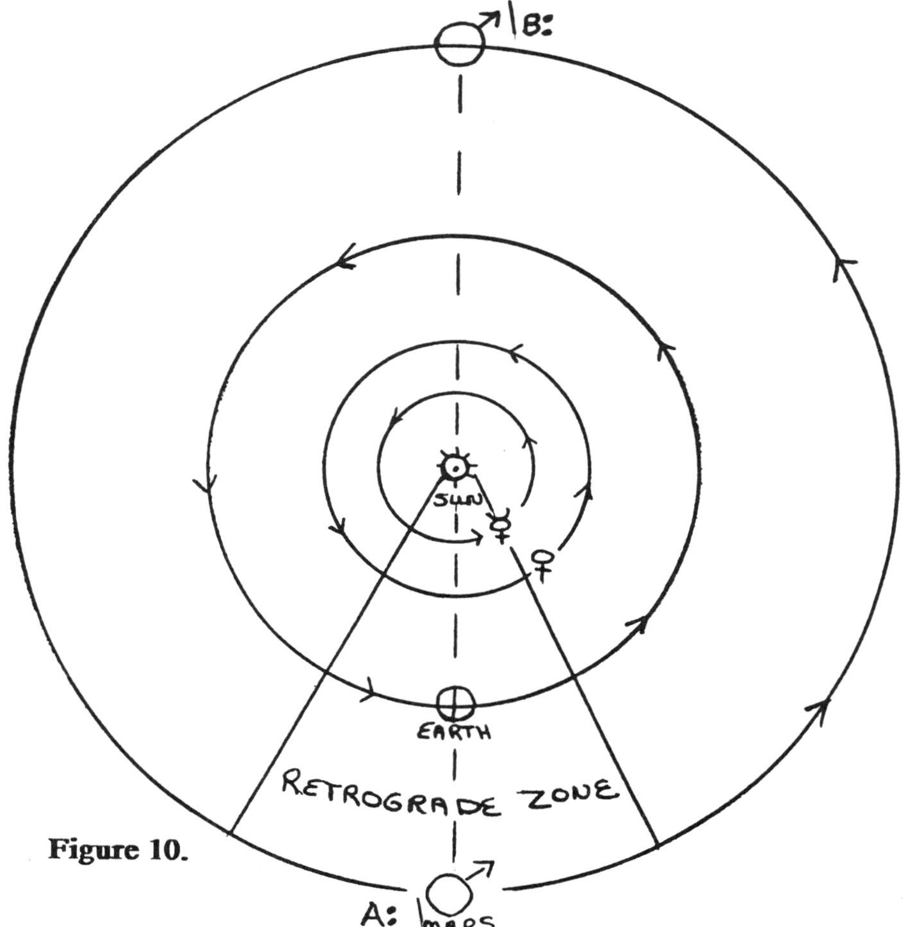

Figure 10.

the pre-retrograde phase of planets later in the book, you should note that the energies of any planet, once entering the retrograde zone, before its retrogradation, often operate beyond the conscious realms.

It is important to realize that retrogradation occurs due to a planet's physical relationship to the Sun and Earth. The Sun provides consciousness to all functions of personality. When, because of the Earth's relationship to a planet, retrogradation occurs, significant shifts in consciousness take place.

Each process experienced throughout a planet's complete orbit is very important to consider in order to get a total view of its interpretive importance when both direct and retrograde. In Chapter XVI, the interpretive implications of these cyclic stages will be addressed.

CHAPTER XIV

THE RETROGRADE DILEMMA

Any planet, when retrograde, represents a function of personality operating against the normal tide of social trends. Retrogrades often manifest in personality as feelings of not "fitting in" with society's mainstream. If you have retrograde planets in your chart, you were born at a time soon after society, as a whole, had over extended safe or productive boundaries. Caught up, in the moment of birth, in this confrontational cycle with the past, you personify the need for change in social action and/or perspective.

It is interesting to study the history behind your retrograde planets by researching social issues of import at the time of your birth. Find how the need for transition was manifesting in the news. For example, during transiting retrogradation, discoveries are often made that change the course of history at some level.

Retrograde planets imply a need to slow down, back up, and research (re-search). People born with retrograde planets realize there is more to any situation than what is apparent on the surface. This leads to introspection and investigation.

Your retrograde planets describe "parts" of you that are special in some way. A part of you, represented by the retrograde planet, cannot conform to the basic ideas (Mercury), values (Venus), physical drives (Mars), aspirations (Jupiter) or rules (Saturn) of your society. The normal means by which people develop these energies do not work for you. How you manifest these planetary functions could exemplify future social trends. (The non-conforming issues brought to play by retrograde Uranus, Neptune or Pluto are more obscure. As these planets do not operate at a conscious level, you may never recognize, through objective experience, how their retrogradation shapes your life.)

Retrograde planets are planets in transition. They represent parts of personality that do not find comfort in pursuing society's conventional directions. They bring to peoples' attentions things, attitudes, or behaviors that simply won't work anymore. In the natal chart, retrograde planets represent parts of you that want something more for you than what the masses consider normal. They want you to go inside to find your own reality, your own center, and then make outer choices based on your internal truths.

Retrograde planets process experiences and information by going into the unconscious, where they go through some kind of metamorphosis before finding creative external outlets for expression. Rudhyar suggested that these planetary energies ultimately find outer expression by joining with functions of the unconscious (Uranus, Neptune and Pluto). This implies that a retrograde planet's potential for unique, creative expression is powerful. However, frustration is encountered in the process of the transition ... before the retrograde function is able to define is own truth apart from what society defines as important.

Sometimes people simply give up before allowing the internalizing process to be completed. This can result in personal feelings of inadequacy concerning the retrograde planet's function. It is important to realize that spontaneous action supported by society is not appropriate for you. It results in premature action for a retrograde function.

For example, pressure to communicate spontaneously (Mercury) results in misunderstandings; pressure to act spontaneously (Mars) results in misplaced energy; pressure to define values (Venus) results in lack of self esteem or failed relationships. Yet, the nature of the "human beast," in its attempt to survive in a "foreign land" is to try to become the foreigner, only to alienate him/herself from his/her own individuality. This leads one to act prematurely, only to have to repeat the action in order to acquire missing pieces and realign oneself with one's own center. This is a particular problem for retrograde Mercury, Venus or Mars.

Because retrograde planets describe functions of personality that operate against the normal flow of human nature ... the drive to move ahead, to create new experiences, to integrate with the mainstream of society ... they require a certain detachment. Retrogrades do not imply inhibitions of social interaction, but a need to evaluate the meaning or significance of all outer affairs. You need a strong internal security in who you are as separate from others. You need to develop inner strength to demonstrate characteristics, behaviors, or ideas that are considered unusual or abnormal by the majority.

Your behaviors may show both what is not working in society and what normal, or expected, behaviors will not work for you. You need to detach from the mainstream. You need to reevaluate taught concepts in order to see them in a new light. In extreme cases, retrograde planets can point to deviant behaviors. However, that tendency is the exception, not the rule.

As mentioned in the section on Intercepted Signs, objectivity is the basis of all oppositions in a chart. All Solar oppositions occur at the midpoint of a planet's retrograde phase. Detachment occurs in the first half of a planet's retrograde period. This leads to objectivity at the midpoint of the cycle when the Solar opposition occurs. Rather than moving forward with the progressive flow of society, you need to stand back and observe where society is headed when planets are retrograde in the chart.

The detachment required of retrograde planets can result in difficulty interacting with others. While in the process of internalizing and digesting experiences, others may perceive you as inattentive or aloof. This is especially the case with a retrograde Mercury or Venus. In some way, you must separate yourself from external stimuli to evaluate and internalize. In the process of doing so, others are aware of your "distance" and could interpret this moment of introspection or digestion as lack of interest. In reality, you are so involved that you need to take a moment to savor or relive the experience before moving on with the mainstream of what is taking place around you. While contemplating, you may have missed your next "cue."

Another interesting phenomenon attributable to retrogradation involves planetary rulership. While a direct planet operates to first fill the needs of its primary ruling sign, and then moves on to handle the affairs of its secondary ruling sign, retrograde planets, because of their apparent backward motion, must function in reverse. A retrograde planet functions first as representative of its secondary sign before finding expression through its primary sign. This process discloses another reason that retrograde planets are sometimes delayed in finding outlets for expression. While each planet will be addressed in depth in later chapters, the following examples of how retrograde planets operate "backward" through their ruling signs should be noted.

MERCURY rules both Gemini and Virgo. When direct, Mercury goes about the process of filling its intellectual yearnings by acquiring information from a variety of sources. This is shown by its rulership of Gemini. Gemini is curious, needs variety, and thrives on communication. The data Mercury gathers is first processed through Gemini. It is subsequently fed into the Virgo experience where it is sorted, analyzed, processed and digested. Virgo's role, in relation to its ruler Mercury, is to define a useful application for the information Mercury acquires.

When Mercury is retrograde, this natural process is reversed. Before information can be accepted and communicated effectively, via the Gemini experience, it must be internalized, analyzed and digested. The latter is a Virgo process. Only after Mercury's input has been put through Virgo's thorough digestive process are effective communication skills developed.

If you have Mercury retrograde, and you do not allow yourself sufficient time to process each piece of data your mind acquires, to internalize information, you could have problems communicating in a manner others comprehend. Information must be internalized, understood with regard to your own personal life, before a creative response can be given. As a result of this analytical process, the post-processed information takes on new meaning and is communicated, through your Gemini activities, with a different perspective from what was originally ingested.

VENUS rules both Taurus and Libra. When direct, Venus operates first through Taurus to acquire experiences and substances that validate your personal worth. Venus, in partnership with Taurus, describes what you want from life. It encourages you to appreciate your value as an individual and the pleasures life can offer. Then Venus brings its energy to the Libra experience, where relationships are formed. Through its rulership of Libra, you learn to interact with others and find value in relating. If Venus is direct, self love leads to love of others. You attract others according to your level of self worth.

When retrograde, this process is reversed. If you have Venus retrograde you are unable to fully appreciate your own worth until you evaluate your life in relation to others. Self love comes as a result of comparison. You must interact with others (Libra) in order to define your own worth (Taurus).

MARS, when direct, uses its aggressive drive to initiate action that leads to an awareness of your separateness. Mars automatically feeds the results of the activity it initiates, or provokes, to Aries. Independence and an awareness of the *I AM* are developed. Mars provides motivation that stimulates action. It provides courage to go into the world to get what you want from it. Then Mars moves to Scorpio, where personal desires are controlled and recycled into desire for involvement or intimacy. Excessive or selfish desires are regenerated through the Scorpio experience.

Issues of control are evident when Mars is retrograde in the chart. Like Mercury and Venus, Mars retrograde functions through its secondary sign, Scorpio, before finding release through its primary sign, Aries.

Mars retrograde operates with great intensity. Powerful desires are evident that must be directed to Scorpio before finding an outlet through Aries. The *I AM* is suppressed until confrontation with your own power is experienced.

The energies of Mars are laid bare when retrograde. A sense of vulnerability is evident. This is due to the regeneration required by its Scorpio rulership. You must examine the core sources of your desires (Scorpio) before finding, and appreciating your separateness from others (Aries).

JUPITER: While Mars provides the courage to step into the world of society, Jupiter begins the process of socialization. Through its rulership of Sagittarius, Jupiter introduces you to social principles, ethics, and the basic morals of society. It provides incentive to expand through social participation. Once Jupiter opens the door to social expansion, it carries the results of its social exposure (Sagittarius) to the area of life ruled by Pisces, its secondary ruling sign. Through its Piscean connection, Jupiter helps you to integrate outer experiences with your spiritual life. You realize your connection not just with your particular society, but to the collective of mankind.

When Jupiter is retrograde, you must develop these Piscean principles before it finds release through normal Sagittarian outlets. You must come to terms with your inner spirituality, beliefs and ideals (Pisces) before socially accepted principles, religions and morals (Sagittarius) make sense to you. Experiences outside consciousness (psychic visions, etc.) cause you to reevaluate society's established religions, ethical standards, and social influences.

SATURN enforces the rules that Jupiter exposes in its quest to expand in the world of society. When direct, Saturn functions first though its primary sign, Capricorn. Here, Saturn provides discipline and presents responsibilities that must be confronted in order to establish a place for yourself in the social arena (Capricorn). Once the rules of society have been defined, Saturn moves to its secondary sign, Aquarius, where the rules are updated when found no longer applicable to our ever-evolving planet. Through Aquarius, Saturn functions to find responsible modes of rebellion. It challenges you to break out of systems that no longer adequately support the future you want for yourself or for humanity. Saturn direct must know where it belongs in the social system (Capricorn) before it is able to free itself from it (Aquarius).

When Saturn is retrograde, it is difficult to define where you fit within the existing structure of society (Capricorn). Before finding your place, you must first break free (Aquarius) from socially conditioned attitudes regarding where you "belong." Saturn must function through its secondary sign, Aquarius, before authority will be given within the Capricorn experiences. You won't find your "place" in life's puzzle (Capricorn) until after you detach (Aquarius) from society's mainstream.

While the collective planets, Uranus, Neptune and Pluto, have singular rulerships, it is interesting to consider them as "quasi" rulers of the signs that Mars, Jupiter and Saturn rule.

URANUS, as ruler of Aquarius, functions to break up crystallized structures or life patterns that have become obsolete. These structures are defined by Saturn. When direct, Uranus goes about its business of reform with no obstacles placed in its path. When retrograde, Uranus must first learn to work within Capricorn structures before finding opportunity to provoke creative change. Rather than tearing down obsolete structures, or shattering old belief systems that bind people to the past, Uranus, when retrograde, must enter the system (Capricorn) and reform it from within. Rather than tearing down the old in order to build anew, Uranus retrograde renovates what already exists. Its message is: reform within the system rather than rebelling totally against it. This requires the Uranus function to operate with greater objectivity or awareness than what is necessary for Uranus direct.

NEPTUNE rules vision and idealism. When direct, Neptune promotes blind faith in your inner commitments. Neptune rules all that is vague and has no definition. It represents the inner voice that calls you into the unknown to pursue your ideals and dreams with no questions or doubts.

Just as Jupiter rules both Sagittarius and Pisces, Neptune can be considered, for the sake of clarifying how it functions when retrograde, as a "quasi" ruler of Sagittarius. When Neptune is retrograde, you are challenged to use knowledge available to uncover life's mysteries. Rather than accepting on blind faith, Neptune retrograde challenges you to explore (Sagittarius) the vast possibilities that lie beneath all Piscean abstractions. Faith results from the Sagittarius exploration. While Neptune retrograde can intensify your doubts, it also provides an ability to unveil life's mysteries by finding a philosophical basis for your beliefs.

PLUTO'S rulership of Scorpio is questioned by some astrologers. Some feel that Pluto rules both Scorpio and Aries. The joint rulership makes sense. Consider Scorpio as Pluto's primary sign and Aries as the secondary. The *I AM* of Aries becomes the *I AM REBORN* once Pluto is activated in life.

Pluto, when direct, works through its primary sign, Scorpio, to introduce the fact that the individual ego cannot always control life around itself. To be a part of any system (social or collective), certain personal sacrifices are required. Pluto shows your role within the masses. It teaches concern for collective issues that extend beyond ego. As Pluto is an unconscious planet, most people are unaware of its full influence in their lives. Some never make the connection between what is going on at a global level and what is taking place in their personal lives. Once this connection is made, a new identity (Aries) emerges.

When Pluto is retrograde, it operates through Aries before finding an outlet in Scorpio. Before a commitment to some social or universal cause can be defined, inner changes in your sense of identity must occur. Pluto's regenerative energy must be internalized before freedom is given to contribute to the regeneration of the planet. The strong identification (Aries) with collective forces leads to an urge to contribute to external social change.

CHAPTER XV

THE EIGHT STAGES OF CYCLIC UNFOLDMENT

There are eight basic stages to all planetary cycles that must be considered to fully understand the significance of retrograde planets. Six of these stages fall into the retrograde zone. These stages include:

1) Solar Conjunction (Superior) to Retrograde Zone
2) Pre-Retrograde to Retrograde Station
3) Retrograde Station
4) First Half of Retrograde Phase
5) The Solar Opposition or Inferior Conjunction
6) Second Half of Retrograde Phase
7) Stationary Direct
8) Stationary Direct to Solar (Superior) Conjunction

The stage at which a planet was operative at the time of birth, defines in very specific terms how the planet functions in your life. For example, approximately one in every twelve people have Mars in the same sign. The interpretive significance of its sign placement is well documented. However, little work has been done to refine its interpretation based on where Mars was in its Solar cycle. An individual born with Mars in its pre-retrograde stage expresses different characteristics than one born at the time of its Solar conjunction, even though Mars is direct during both of these stages. Likewise, if Mercury is retrograde at birth, its retrograde condition should be noted along with the stage of its retrogradation. By understanding the significance of the whole cycle, you will refine all interpretations of natal and transiting planets. You will begin to see that both the retrograde and direct planets in your chart represent natural forces, designed by nature, that play a very important part in shaping your life urges and behaviors.

Because Mercury and Venus lie between the Earth and Sun, their cycles must be viewed differently from those of planets that orbit beyond Earth. Figure 9, provided in Chapter XIII, shows the cycle of Mercury over a one year period. The eight stages of its cycle are clearly shown. Each planet has a pre-retrograde phase, a stationary retrograde stage, and so on. What is unique to Mercury is that this process is repeated three times each year.

In all cases, the midpoint of a planet's retrogradation occurs at the time it reaches it closest point to Earth. In the Ephemeris, this is seen as a Solar opposition when viewing Mars through Pluto. In the cases of Mercury and Venus, it is an inferior conjunction to the Sun.

In later chapters, each planet will be evaluated individually. But first, the significance of the eight stages of unfoldment from a "generic" perspective must be addressed.

An APPENDIX is provided at the back of the book that provides Tables to help you determine the stages in which your natal planets fall. I have not included Uranus, Neptune and Pluto because these planets are always in their retrograde zones. Any Ephemeris that lists planets for the date of your birth will tell you whether Uranus, Neptune or Pluto were retrograde on your date of birth. The Tables in the Appendix can be used to help with natal analysis as well as transits. They cover years from 1920 to 2000.

STAGE I: Solar Conjunction (Superior) To Retrograde Zone. A planet moves into stage I as it conjoins the Sun. In the cases of Mercury and Venus, stage I begins at the superior conjunction. Realize, when a planet has reached this point, it has already been direct for half of its direct transit. Once the Solar conjunction occurs, the Sun begins to move away from planets that orbit outside Earth's path. The focus gradually changes from personal growth (Sun) to greater concern for your social role at the point of opposition.

In the case of Mars through Pluto, the Solar conjunction marks a time of spontaneous projection. As the Sun enters its new phase with these planets it marks a time of rebirth. It begins a process of discovery, marking a time when you naturally seek new experiences and new knowledge around which your future will be built. During this stage of its cycle, the planet is direct in motion. No obvious obstacles are placed in its progressive path. Much like the new-moon personality, the function of this planet operates instinctively, spontaneously, dramatically.

If you are familiar with the concepts of the Lunation Cycle, this stage of a planet's orbit is experienced similarity to the New Moon. The planet is moving from a new phase toward the full (Stage 5), at which time the new experiences accumulated during stage I become an integrated part of consciousness.

The conjunction of the Sun with Mars through Pluto infuses, or revitalizes, the energy of the planet. Yet, because the planet is at its maximum distance from Earth, full awareness of the purpose of this infusion is not available. The planet's energy is projected instinctively, with no clear perception of what the future has in store with regard to its expression. While objectivity is blinded by the Solar radiance, courage and motivation are strong. As the Sun and planet separate, greater awareness and objectivity is evident. In time, it moves into the retrograde zone and the pre-retrograde stage begins.

Because Mercury and Venus lie within the orbit of Earth, they are never far from the Sun in a natal chart. Therefore, their stage I development must be viewed from a different perspective. Mercury and Venus are considered to be in a "quasi-full phase at their superior Solar conjunction. From a heliocentric perspective, the Earth and Mercury are in opposition. This marks a time when the thinking function of Mercury becomes more deliberate and concerned with social protocol. The superior conjunction marks a point at which both Mercury and Venus switch from rising before the Sun to rising after the Sun. Both Marc Edmond Jones and Dane Rudhyar noted the significance of this phenomenon in their writings. More will be provided on its interpretive value later in the book.

From this point until they enter the retrograde zone, Mercury and Venus function with few restrictions placed on their urges for social integration.

Planets, in continuing their orbits, are separated from the Solar (superior) conjunction to be eventually stopped at their retrograde stations. This station is considerably beyond the degree at which the Solar opposition (Mars through Pluto), or inferior conjunction (Mercury and Venus), will later occur. Prior to retrogradation, the planet enters the retrograde zone. This initiates the pre-retrograde stage of its cycle, marking a critical point in any planet's cycle.

STAGE II: Pre-Retrograde Stage. The pre-retrograde stage begins when a planet enters the retrograde zone, i.e.: the total arc over which the planet will later retrograde.. In the case of Mercury, this occurs approximately two weeks before its actual retrogradation. Mars, on the other hand, enters its retrograde arc just short of two months before turning retrograde. The retrograde zone begins at the zodiacal degree at which the planet will eventually make its direct station.

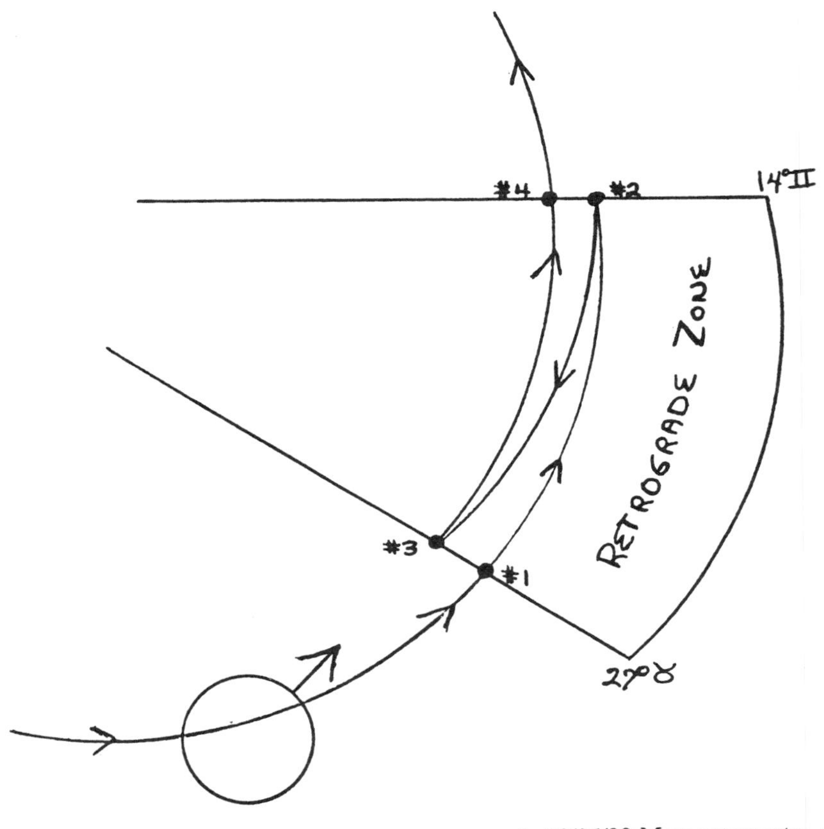

Figure 11.

1: 08/26/90 Mars enters retro. zone.
2: 10/20/90 Stationary retrograde.
3: 01/02/92 Stationary direct.
4: 01/22/91 Leaves retro. zone.

For example, refer to figure 11. On October 20, 1990, Mars turned stationary retrograde at 14 degrees Gemini. It retrograded to 27 degrees Taurus on January 2, 1991. It entered its retrograde zone August 26, 1990 when it first transits 27 degrees Taurus. Once Mars made its first pass over 27 degrees Taurus in August of 1990, it entered its retrograde zone, even though it had not yet turned retrograde. This transit introduced the pre-retrograde stage of its two year cycle.

When a planet moves into its retrograde zone, old patterns begin to break down. Yet, an urge to hold firm to the old, and continue to forge ahead, is strong. The planet, particularly once it moves to the degree at which it later conjuncts Earth, or opposes the Sun is functioning *beyond its ability to integrate experience*. The function of personality, represented by the planet, tends to get ahead of itself. In some way, it has gone beyond the normal limits set by our socio-cultural standards. There is an urge to continue initiating new experiences and force issues to proceed. However, there is a tendency to initiate action without full awareness of the potential results or ramifications. If you were born with a planet at this stage of its cycle, you may often feel compelled to go beyond "normal" limits set by society. This can be demonstrated, through personality, as rash behavior, a sometimes frantic urge to keep moving ahead at all costs. Or, it can manifest as an urge to promote goals for the future that are not yet recognized as valid by the majority. You are striving to create something new, but may leave unfinished business from the past and overlook important details in your desire to forge ahead. Visions or ideals are powerful, but vehicles for constructive application are not always available. In theory, the planet has over-extended itself, or over-shot its desired destination (Solar opposition). It has become lost in its own energy. Disintegration can easily be experienced.

As the planet moves to its farthest point in the retrograde zone, in its direct motion, it is finally stopped by retrogradation. This brings us to the next stage of cyclic unfoldment.

It is interesting to note that Neptune and Pluto are always in their retrograde zones. Their cycles overlap. They enter the retrograde zones of their new solar cycle before leaving the retrograde zone of the previous cycle. Uranus is free from its retrograde zone for less than one day in its Solar cycle. This phenomenon is not surprising, because Uranus, Neptune, and Pluto always operate outside consciousness.

STAGE III: Stationary Retrograde Stage. Once a direct planet reaches its farthest point from where its conjunction to Earth later occurs, it is stopped. It becomes stationary in preparation for retrogradation. While Earth moves ahead in its orbit around the Sun, it appears as if the Sun is moving forward through the signs. The retrograde planet appears to move backward to join it. Any planet having reached this point in its cycle is stopped.

While it has been forging ahead, it has left unfinished business in its wake. It must now return to its source to become re-energized by Solar power and digest the experiences it has thus far ingested. Like running into an invisible wall, the planet is forced to a complete halt. It can no longer move forward until it examines the value of what it has thus-far experienced or created.

If you were born when a planet was stationary retrograde, you are retrospective and need to understand the importance of the past (personal, social, collective) is extremely important. Intensity is the keynote. You are aware of limitations. You are constantly challenged to define why you exist. As the planet is stationary, neither moving forward nor backward in its cycle, it possesses dynamic strength and power of endurance. This can indicate unbending behavior. It suggests a tendency to get stuck in ruts that immobilize. From a positive level, it describes acute awareness, and an ability for in-depth perception. This stage reminds us that we are always able to see greater detail, with greater clarity, when we stop the vehicle transporting us to truly look at the scenery.

STAGE IV: First Half of Retrograde Stage. During the first half of its retrograde period, a planet appears to move backward to meet the Earth. In essence, it is bringing the results of its experiences home, to our planet, to be confronted and integrated into consciousness. This first half of the retrograde stage is critical. If you were born with a planet in the first half of its retrograde stage, you probably feel out of touch with the natural movements going on around you. What others take for granted, you must examine to find some personal meaning. You may feel set apart from the mainstream.

It is important to realize that this planet functions powerfully within the personality. It is now very close to Earth. The function represented by this planet is a powerful part of your psyche ... so strong, in fact, that it may overpower the functions of other planets in the chart. The needs of retrograde planets are so dynamic that concern for fulfilling and utilizing their potentials can often seem overwhelming. At this Stage, there is the need to have more knowledge (Mercury), greater understanding (Jupiter), more control over desires (Mars), more out of personal relationships (Venus), stronger structures (Saturn) and so on. These urges are experienced because you sense a significant lack in your ability to use the energy of the Stage IV planet.

As the planet retrogrades to meet Earth, the concern intensifies. You are challenged to be more aware of the workings of the retrograde planet in you personal life. The need to internalize experience, and to face the future with a good grasp of a past that is in some way incomplete, due to the planets previous movement into "out-of-bounds" territory, remains a strong issue throughout the first half of the retrograde stage.

STAGE V: The Solar Opposition or Inferior Conjunction. At the midpoint of their retrogradation, planets orbiting outside Earth's path (Mars through Pluto) are opposed by the Sun. Mercury and Venus form their inferior Solar conjunctions. This marks a critical point in the retrograde process. To fully comprehend the importance of this stage, you must understand the nature of the opposition aspect.

The opposition of the Sun with planets outside Earth's orbit cultivates awareness. It defines the point in any cycle where fulfillment is reached and outcomes become evident. Responses or reactions from others are experienced that provide greater objectivity regarding how the planet's energy is being used. The opposition requires you to stand back and view life through others' eyes.

Self awareness can only be acquired via relationships or confrontation with the "not-self." The opposition represents the point in any cycle where either fulfillment or breakdown occurs. When the Sun is opposed to any planet, you must evaluate the purpose or importance of your life. You must objectively evaluate who you are. This can only be done by comparing your life with the lives of others. Any planet in opposition to the Sun is retrograde.

Retrograde planets challenge you to look within to find answers that do not always conform to the status quo. If you were born with a planet at this Stage of its retrograde cycle, you must take personal responsibility for the expression of the planetary energy.

Planets cross the degree at which the Solar opposition (or inferior conjunction) occurs three times in each Solar cycle ... once when they move into the retrograde zone, once when retrograde, and again as they moves ahead into their next full cycles. The retrograde transit is the only time when a Solar opposition (or inferior conjunction) occurs. At this point, the Earth and Sun have moved into alignment with the retrograde planet.

When viewing Mercury and Venus, this marks the time of an inferior Solar conjunction. Mercury and Venus switch places with the Sun. Until the next Solar conjunction, these planets will rise before the Sun. Prior to this time, they rose after the Sun.

While planets outside Earth's pathway are in full phase with the Sun at the midpoint of their retrograde stage, the inferior conjunction of Mercury and Venus begins their "quasi" new phase transition. Mercury and Venus, hereafter, operate with greater spontaneity and less concern for social protocol. The significance of this transition will be explained more thoroughly in the following chapter.

The Solar opposition marks a period when you become aware (Sun) that some change is in order. Everything relating to the planet's function must be taken personally. Confrontation is taking place. The search for meaning in your life has reached its peak.

The planet, being at its closest point to Earth, operates with extreme intensity. The Solar opposition occurring with planets outside Earth's orbit provides illumination. This is one of the most powerful stage of any planetary cycle. Transition is the keynote.

Aware of the fact that "normal" behaviors (personal or social) are no longer adequate to fill personal needs, you are urged to walk away from (retrograde) the mainstream to become enlightened (Sun). Because of this, if you were born when a planet is in Stage V, you demonstrate acute objectivity, and often detachment. There is a need to define your own reality apart from what is considered "normal."

Certainly, confusion can be experienced at this stage of unfoldment.. Social expectations, or norms, pull you in one direction, while the self pulls you in the opposite. Once you come to terms with your unique life processes, confusion is transformed into enlightenment.

STAGE VI: Second Half of the Retrograde Zone. As a planet retrogrades away from the Solar degree, it enters the second half of the retrograde zone. While still functioning against the "normal" flow, an awareness has been reached regarding the personality urges it represents.

This is a time of continued internal development. It is a time of preparation for a new direction once the planet turns direct by transit. It is important to take care of unfinished business, gather information, and acquire new psychological tools in preparation for the new burst of energy that will be experienced once the planet turns direct.

If you were born when a planet had reached this stage in its cycle you are challenged to not only recognize (Stage V) the uniqueness of your personal needs and energies, but to explore social avenues through which to live out, or manifest, the unique behaviors associated with the retrograde planet. There is a strong desire to live out a belief, an ideal, or new behavior patterns that the world, in general, does not understand or accept as valid. You may be living prophet of issues society has not yet, but will soon need to, address.

STAGE VII: Stationary Direct. Upon turning stationary direct, a planet operates dynamically. Here, we find a function of personality that has previously been inhibited, by social factors, from expressing itself fully. Now restrictions are lifted. A sense of freedom is experienced.

At this stage in its cycle, a planet is given the "go sign" by the outside world. The stationary direct planet, due to its previous retrograde restrictions, is now ready to overtly function with full power. Like a tiger let out of a cage, this planet exemplifies freedom in all actions it promotes. There is sometimes a frantic urge to move forward to experience more from life. The stationary direct planet represents a part of you that feels it has a lot to catch up with. A stationary direct planet always functions powerfully in its urge to move forward into new experiences.

STAGE VIII: Stationary Direct to the Solar (Superior) Conjunction. This stage can actually be broken into 2 steps; the first sub-stage occurring between the time the planet moves from its direct station to the time it moves out of the retrograde zone. During this phase, the planet goes through the "gears" necessary to reach "overdrive" in its forward travels. It is in the process of "catching up." The planet functions powerfully to cover new territory and acquire new experiences that catapult it into the new cycle. (The pre and post retrograde stages of Uranus through Pluto always overlap. Therefore, from an interpretive perspective, their post retrograde Stage is less dramatic than those of Mercury through Saturn.)

Once having moved out of the retrograde zone, the planet experiences no further pressure. It moves ahead in its cycle unfettered by the past or by non-conformism. Socialization is occurring. These planets now operate with full power to accumulate social experiences that eventually lead to another new "birth" as they approach their next conjunction with the Sun. Once these planets move out of the retrograde zone, there is no further need to focus on introspection, no further need to define your life energies as unique from the norm.

In the following chapters, the planets are addressed individually to show how they are shaped by their stage of cyclic unfoldment at the time of birth. The importance of their transiting cycles will also be addressed. Refer to the Tables provided in the Appendix that list each planet's retrograde cycle from the years 1920 to 2000.

CHAPTER XVI

THE PLANETS

While you may have no retrograde planets in your natal chart, you will experience their energies when they retrograde in transit. For this reason, it is recommended that you read the following sections pertaining to both natal and transiting planets when retrograde. Doing so will give you a broader understanding of the cyclic unfoldment of all planetary cycles.

The retrogradation of Mercury, Venus, and Mars function more obviously in daily life than those of the social and collective planets. Realize that retrogradation occurs out of the relationship planets make with the Sun and Earth. The retrograde phenomenon is Earth centered, and therefore, very personal.

Many astrologers cringe at the thought of planets turning retrograde by transit, knowing their tendencies to create confusion and incongruity in life. If the truth be known, these special stages of planetary cycles can be used as times of personal growth, reorganization, reflection and integration. They should be viewed as necessary and desirable occurrences. Once you learn to use your natal and transiting retrograde planets, your life will begin to function smoothly, productively and creatively. You will develop skills in objectivity. By recognizing the importance of retrogradation, retroaction and reevaluation, you come to value the retrograde moments of life.

MERCURY

Mercury, the planet closest to our Sun, closest to our "center," represents the link that connects all functions of personality (planets) to consciousness (Sun). Its role is that of a facilitator. Mercury acquires and transmits information that keeps our various "parts" connected and keeps us on frequency with others.

In a natal chart, Mercury represents the mind. Its sign shows how you process information. Its house describes where information is accessible that keeps you "on line."

Mercury's energy is considered neutral; in itself, it is non-judgmental. Its role is to acquire and distribute information. Other planets, in their phase and aspect with Mercury, describe how that information is interpreted and put to use. Mercury can be likened to a universal telephone system. A telephone is neutral. It places no judgement on communications sent or received. The FCC (Saturn) outlines the rules that apply to its use. Jupiter shows the extent of its use. It provides the "long distance lines" for communication. Mercury provides the language. Other planetary energies determine how the language is interpreted.

While Mercury's sign, house, and aspects are important to consider, and certainly provide extensive information on the workings of the mind, to fully understand Mercury's role in a birth chart, several other factors should be considered.For example, the speed at which Mercury was moving at the time of birth suggests the rate at which you process information. If Mercury was accelerating in speed at the time of your birth, it will function differently than if Mercury was decelerating. If Mercury rose before the Sun on the date of your birth, your mind functions differently from those who were born when Mercury rose after the Sun. If Mercury was combust the Sun (within a 3 degree conjunction) it functions differently than if it was at its maximum distance (28 degrees) from the Sun. And, of course, if Mercury was retrograde, or in its retrograde zone, on your date of birth, your mind functions differently from those born when Mercury was direct and outside of the retrograde arc. All of these factors are important to consider when evaluating the mental processes via the natal chart. The stage at which Mercury was operative in its Solar cycle discerns which of these variables was active at the time of your birth.

While the average daily motion of Mercury is 1 degree 23 minutes, it accelerates to over 2 degrees per day when nearing its superior, or direct, conjunction with the Sun. It then begins to decelerate to 0 degrees of motion at its retrograde station.

Mercury accelerates in speed when rising before the Sun. In the natal chart, Mercury is found in an earlier degree, or sign, than the Sun. For example, Mercury at 25 degrees Cancer rises before the Sun at 5 degrees Leo. The Sun is at a greater longitude than Mercury. Marc Edmond Jones called Mercury, when rising before the Sun, an *evening star*. When rising after the Sun, he called Mercury a *morning star* (see figure 12 on the following page). Another term for an accelerating Mercury, or Mercury rising before the Sun, is *Prometheus*, a word of Greek distraction meaning progressive or forward moving. Prometheus, in Greek mythology, was the "carrier of the flame."

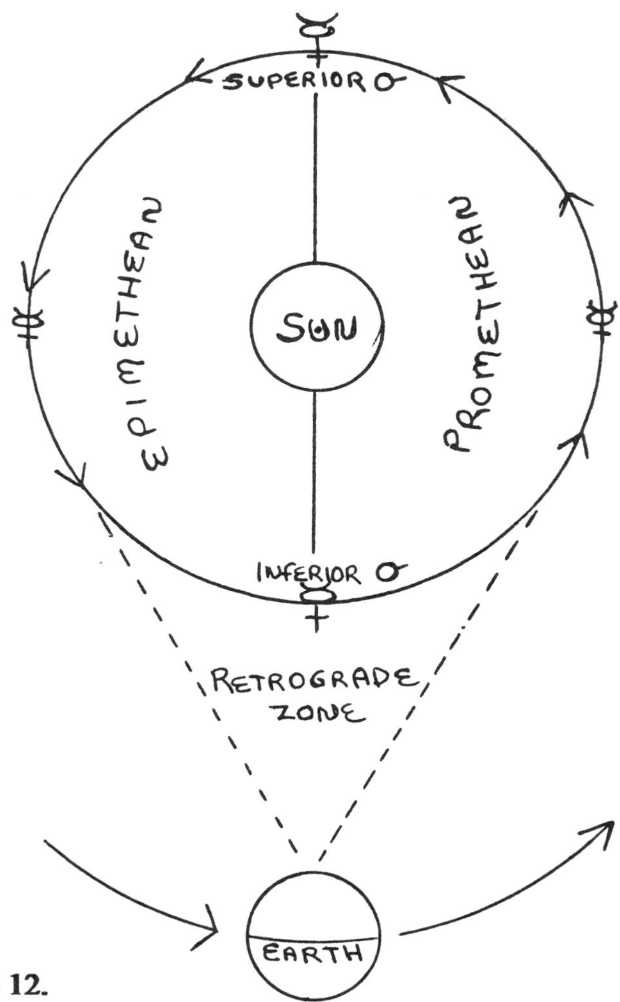

Figure 12.

Mercury becomes Prometheus at the time of its inferior conjunction to the Sun. This marks the birth of a new cycle. Mercury is half way through its retrograde stage at the inferior Solar conjunction. Rudhyar describes an individual born during the Prometheus stage of retrogradation as one who is eager to free him/herself from custom, but often bound by the very things s/he wishes to forget. There is a strong urge to break from conditioned attitudes. Yet, the retrograde condition infers a need to first reevaluate the past's significance. The Prometheus direct Mercury concerns itself not with the past, but the future. There can be a strong mental restlessness and impulsiveness, an urge to investigate new knowledge, to look ahead to the future rather than accepting only knowledge based on historical fact. The Prometheus retrograde mind wants to investigate future possibilities, but always finds something lacking in the information it gathers, if in no other way than lack of social agreement or acceptance. This leads to extensive analysis and a need to detach from the mainstream.

The Promethean retrograde Mercury describes a mind that can easily get ahead of itself. There is a thirst for greater understanding and new sources of information. If your natal Mercury is retrograde and Prometheus, your mind looks ahead toward a future way of life that others have not yet perceived. You are a living "prophet" of what could be in the future. Information provided by the past (personal and social) does not sufficiently answer your questions and concerns.

Realize that the retrograde Mercury is strong. Mercury is close to Earth at this stage of its cycle. The mind is by no means weakened because of Mercury's retrograde condition. It is, in fact, intensified. The retrograde mind must go through extensive analysis before accepting or rejecting information. This slows the learning process only because of the internalization involved with all retrograde planets.

Our public schools are designed to fill the needs of the "norm," often at the expense of considering the unique academic needs of the retrograde Mercury child. The intellectual potential, or ability to learn, is not determined by whether Mercury is direct or retrograde at birth. Throughout history, many brilliant people have been born with Mercury retrograde. But, the *way* a child perceives and digests information is quite different for a retrograde Mercury child than one born when Mercury was direct.

If your Mercury is retrograde, you must learn to take whatever time you need to internalize data. Public schools are not designed to approach learning experiences with such depth. This can lead to "hang ups" in early life when you first realize that you are not intellectually functioning on the same "wave length" as others.

One of the greatest dilemmas experienced by the Prometheus retrograde Mercury involves impatience. Mercury is in the process of rebirth, entering a new Solar cycle. Yet, due to its initial retrograde condition, it is unable to move into the new cycle unfettered by the past or social stigmas. You may feel you are always fighting the world around you ... always mentally either one step ahead or behind the norm. You may try to ingest more than you can intellectually digest. Your mind, while working against the mainstream, trying to free itself from old attitudes, is stuck in social patterns that inhibit progress. Knowledge provided by society must be reevaluated and viewed from a new perspective. The information you accumulate, once processed, is eventually interpreted in a whole new context, differently from how it was presented.

The Promethean retrograde Mercury is always in want of more information than what is available from the system. You are aware of significant lacks in all information you receive. You innately realize that a positive future (personal and social) requires more information than what is presently available. From a personal level, you question the value of your knowledge. You are never satisfied with the answers provided by the mainstream. You may need to turn your back on society's educational programs to seek answers to your complex questions through personal experience or aesthetic pursuits. You must take frequent "time outs" to evaluate information presented by others. Yet, society does not always provide the time you need to examine what it has offered. It interprets your reflective moments as slowness or inattention. Your answers must come directly from your "source" (Sun) rather than through customary channels.

At the time of Mercury's inferior Solar conjunction, Mercury lies directly between Earth and the Sun. It is a direct link between the Source (Sun) and life on our planet. Retrograde Prometheus Mercury strives to acquire information directly from this source rather than relying on social opinion and historic fact.

The Sun represents the "part" of you that wants you to be "all that you can be." It is your inner light, your spirit. While it wants you to participate in the larger social arena, it also wants you to recognize your personal power and creative potential. Retrograde Mercury provides a channel, or frequency, that enables you to communicate with your source. By doing so, you discover that some of the information you receive, or have been taught, via the collective system, is not in harmony with your inner reality of truth. William Lilly, Alfred Adler, Paul McCartney, and Howard Hughes had Mercury in its Promethean retrograde phase.

You want more from society's educational facilities. You want more from conversations shared with others. You want more information than what the outside world provides. You are frustrated because you truly need more information to make sense out of life. This can lead to several outcomes. At one level, you could read more into conversations shared with others, books, lessons, etc., than what is intended. This can promote neurosis on one hand, and genius on the other. At another level, your sense of timing might be off center from the rest of the world. You might, in your attempt to "fit in," feel pressured to initiate experiences, topics of conversation, or make significant purchases, and so on, at the wrong time, later to find it necessary to return to your "source" and try again.

You were caught up, at the moment of birth, in social transition. Society was being forced to recognize procedures that were no longer working effectively. Communications were breaking down. The "universal" phone lines were jammed. An overload was taking place. You demonstrate this dilemma in your communications with others and how you process information.

For example, Mercury retrograde suggests frustrations in communication. Communication lines get crossed. While you are looking for meaning in information presented to you by others, they have moved on to a new topic of interest. When, at last, you respond to the original questions or comments, the focus of general conversation amongst others has shifted. You feel out of synch. When attempting to keep "on line" with the mainstream, without taking time to internally experience, or savor, each moment, you may speak out of turn or respond inappropriately. When you do not take time to thoroughly digest the content of conversations, you tend to either be ahead of, or behind, the mainstream.

Prometheus retrograde Mercury cannot accept information presented by others as final, or as truth. Your perceptions are different from those of others. You need to find comfort in the uniqueness of your perspective rather than seeking conformity.

The retrograde mind operates against the mainstream. It is not a conformist. Yet, due to the stress society places on its participants to conform to its perceptions, to always respond on the cues it gives, you could feel out of place, intellectually inferior, or in a state of perpetual confusion. You are an idealist, mentally tuned to what the future could be, looking for answers beyond those in evidence.

Because the inferior Solar conjunction of Mercury marks the birth of its promethean stage, the progressive, instinctive patterns of the promethean energy are new and somewhat naive. This potential intellectual naivety is particularly strong at the conjunction point. At this time, Mercury is *combust* the Sun.

In our older literature, any planet combust the Sun (conjunct within 3 degrees) was considered detrimental. It was said that the power of the Sun "burns out" the energies represented by the planet. In truth, any close conjunction does not provide much objectivity. Any planet combust the Sun is entering a new Solar cycle and consciousness is minimal. Instinct plays a strong part in any new phase experience. If Mercury is combust the Sun, you may not be conscious of the power of your intellect. The logical mind (Mercury) seems blotted out by the Solar radiance. You are instinctively projecting, through communication and orientation to knowledge, a new way of thinking, a new way of perceiving future possibilities. Yet, you may be unaware of the significance, or meaning, of this projection. Unconscious residue surfaces through communication and thought processes.

Between the time Mercury experiences its inferior and superior Solar conjunctions, it turns stationary in preparation to move direct. The direct station of Mercury always occurs in the Promethean half of its cycle.

If you were born when Mercury was at its direct station, you demonstrate strong mental determination. Your mind is set on what it wants. You are determined to reach your mental goals. As you were born at the end of Mercury's retrogradation, you could exhibit an almost frantic urge for mental freedom. You sense a new direction for investigation and experimentation, and you have a dogged persistence to move ahead with your ideas at all costs.

A stationary direct Mercury shows mental stability in the extreme, often resulting in overly fixed attitudes regarding how the future *should* unfold. This is accompanied by a sense of anticipation or apprehension. While a certain lack of mental flexibility is evident at either station, because Mercury is "frozen" in space, it finds compensation in its capacity to focus on specifics. Only by standing still can one clearly see what lies ahead.

A few days after Mercury's direct station, it begins to accelerate in its race to conjunct the Sun on the opposite side from Earth. It reaches its farthest point from the Sun while still in the retrograde zone, moving toward its next superior Solar conjunction. The mind becomes more visionary and aware of the significance of symbolism.

In the words of Dane Rudhyar, the Prometheus direct Mercury "eagerly reaches toward the future and seeks to convey the rhythm of tomorrow to the ego." If you were born with Mercury Prometheus and direct, your mind follows inner guidelines rather than social rules. You are eager to learn, eager to meet new mental challenges not yet solved by society. You are a mental pioneer. Your mind functions on instinct rather than logic ... on ideals rather than known realities. There is a tendency to mentally live in the future at the expense of meeting conservative requirements of today.

Intuition regarding the future is strong. Prometheus direct Mercury bets on hunches over historical sequence. It seeks out knowledge that influences the future rather than information that clarifies, or conforms to, the past. History is only useful when referenced with where it is leading.

As Mercury increases in speed, mental enthusiasm also increases. Mercury takes on the pure characteristics of Prometheus. If you were born when Mercury was moving faster than its average daily motion of 1 degree 23 minutes, you process information rapidly. You may find it frustrating to communicate with people (such as those having Mercury retrograde) who are more deliberate or introspective. Your mind moves swiftly from one thought to another. You are quick to respond and may, at times, finish other peoples' sentences to get to the next line. Your mind is always thirsty, always restless. A disadvantage of a "fast" Mercury is its tendency to keep the mind racing long after the physical body has called for time out. Some examples of people born with a "fast" Mercury that had reached its maximum distance from the Sun are Dane Rudhyar, Shakespeare, Washington Irving, George Washington, Michelangelo, Alan Arkin.

As Mercury continues its direct movement, it soon moves to its superior Solar conjunction. At this time, it changes places with the Sun, hereafter to rise after the Sun. This is evident, in the natal chart, when Mercury is at a later zodiacal degree, or sign, than the Sun. For example, if Mercury is at 14 degrees Sagittarius, while the Sun is at 28 degrees Scorpio, Mercury rises after the Sun. Mercury is no longer an evening star, but a morning star. It is no longer considered Promethean, but *Epimethean* in nature. (Epimetheus was the brother of Prometheus. Epimetheus demonstrated the opposite qualities of his impetuous brother. His name, Epimetheus, means afterthought.)

Once Mercury has entered its Epimethean phase with the Sun, it functions less liberally and more conservatively. This transition occurs at the superior Solar conjunction.

At the exact time of the superior conjunction, Mercury is again combust the Sun. A crisis in thinking occurs at this stage of its cycle. The mind is challenged to cease functioning on instinct only. It must begin to evaluate information on the basis of its current social significance. This represents the quasi-full phase of Mercury's cycle. The mind switches from being introverted to extroverted, from its concern for exploration into the unknown to concern for preservation of what already exists. When combust, confusion is experienced due to the transition taking place.

At the superior conjunction, the Sun is between Mercury and the Earth. The mind is literally in opposition to, or at odds with, Earthly matters. It must become aware (full phase) of its need to integrate and become a part of the existing social structure. Mercury is moving rapidly at the time of its superior Solar conjunction. It is only combust the Sun for a short period of time. If you were born with Mercury direct and within 3 degrees of the Sun, you were born during this superior combust stage. You demonstrate, through communication and approach to learning, the confusion Mercury must now face ... the need to adjust from an impetuous way of thinking to a deliberate, conservative, "prove it" mode.

The Epimetheus Mercury mind wants to get results for information acquired. If you were born with Mercury rising after the Sun, you make intellectual judgments based on precedent. Once Mercury forms its superior Solar conjunction, it begins to decelerate in speed. You learn by referring to previous experience (personal and historical), and make choices based on what has been rather than what could be.

You are objective, while the Promethean mind is subjective. You evaluate facts, while the Promethean mind forms images of what the future holds. Your mind operates more methodically than the Prometheus mind; it functions with greater thoroughness, maturity, and concern for maintaining stability and constant growth.

Rudhyar points out that the Epimethean mind makes decisions based on historical data. This is not a risk-taking mind, but one concerned with maintaining safe boundaries. You are "on line" with society, in "synch" with social trends, aware of the need to integrate with the world around you in order to benefit from, and contribute to, its knowledge. While the Prometheus Mercury has little regard for social protocol, you are aware of the importance of maintaining a strong intellectual connection, or link, to the world at large. The urge to play an important part in social development is intense when Mercury reaches its greatest distance from the Sun in its Epimethean direct Stage. People such as Socrates, Madam Curie, Leon Uris and Marc Edmond Jones all share this Mercury/Sun Stage. The Epimethean Mercury provides the kind of mind necessary to succeed within society's systems. It is able to integrate, while the Promethean Mercury seeks to disassociate from the mainstream to investigate the unknown.

It is said that the Epimethean Mercury provides good business sense, while the Promethean Mercury breeds the mind of the artist or nonconformist. The Epimethean Mercury wants to get results, and hops on the social band wagon to use society as a vehicle for success.

As Mercury continues to decelerate in speed, it eventually moves into its retrograde *zone*. It crosses the degree at which it will make its direct station after its retrogradation. If you have Mercury direct in its Epimethean stage, and in its retrograde zone (the arc over which it will retrograde after your birth), you were born during a critical stage of its cyclic unfoldment.

The mind, in its attempt to produce and integrate with the mainstream, begins to lose touch with its true "source." It is easy to get caught up in society's mainstream to find, in time, that you have exceeded boundaries of the soul. An inner feeling of discontentment regarding the "ways of the world" is experienced, but the world is moving on, and you are a part of its movement. You cannot simply jump off the social train. You are caught up in issues or ideas that you helped create. Still, you are uncomfortable. It is easy to get caught up in energies that take you outside, or beyond, the realm of your "Sun," outside the realm of consciousness, beyond intended purpose, away from your own truth.

Mercury continues to slow until it stops at its retrograde station. This represents a time in the cycle when all ambitious, forward movement must stop in order to evaluate where it is leading. In some way, you have become trapped in society's movements and have lost your Self in the process. Mercury's retrograde station requires you to focus. Stop all progressive movement to ponder over where you have been and what it has led to. Begin to disassociate yourself from mass-consciousness to find your inner light, your inner truth. Back up to find what you have lost, or left behind, in your search for social integration. Ask yourself: what parts of me have I sacrificed to ambition, or to attain acceptance of others?

When seen in transit, the Epimethean retrograde Mercury marks a time when systems begin to break down. People begin to realize how and where they have gone too far, or, in their quest for greater accomplishment, have overlooked important messages or exceeded positive boundaries. Ralph Nadar's life exemplifies the Epimethean retrograde Mercury. He has dedicated his life to evaluate consumer products and to alert society to products that do not meet consumer criteria. Mercury retrograde in the Epimetheus stage marks a time when people must back up, complete, or correct inconsistencies between what the mind (Mercury) has accumulated and what the Self (Sun) truly wants.

If you were born during this stage of Mercury's retrogradation, your life symbolizes society's tendency to exceed limits. You must learn to internalize, to evaluate, to analyze (Virgo) each stage of your intellectual growth. Are you truly attuned to society's ideas? Do you know when to walk away (retrograde) from systems or circumstances that have exceeded appropriate limits? The unconscious sends signals to initiate this reevaluation. But, because all retrograde planets are processed through the unconscious before finding outward expression, these signals can easily be misunderstood.

For example, *timing* is an important issue for all retrograde planets, especially Mercury. In the Prometheus retrograde stage, Mercury often initiates prematurely. In the Epimetheus retrograde stage, Mercury evaluates facts, and may lose its pace with the rest of the world in its process of analysis. This keeps retrograde Mercury out of step from the mainstream and often creates stress when communicating or attempting to acquire sufficient information to allow the mind to be filled and fulfilled.

Any retrograde Mercury, whether Promethean or Epimethean, shows potential frustration in communication. If pressured to communicate spontaneously, you can become tongue-tied, confused, or respond inappropriately in some way. If challenged to use the same logic others use to form opinions and make decisions, you draw inaccurate conclusions. When retrograde, the Mercury mental function is dominant. Due to the power of its influence, you have *issues* around learning and communicating. You take these things more seriously than most. This very preoccupation with the intellect causes potential problems.

If you have natal Mercury retrograde you probably feel comfortable when Mercury is retrograde by transit. At these times, the world is forced to function on your wave length. Still, a problem exists. You are "in synch" with the mainstream during these times, but society, as a whole, has a tendency to make premature decisions or commitments that cannot be met. You can easily make the same mistakes.

When Mercury forms its inferior Solar conjunction, another new phase begins. Mercury has gone full circle in its orbit around the Sun. Before this new cycle can get under way, detachment from an old way of thinking must occur. Detachment begins in the Epimetheus retrograde phase and continues throughout the entire retrograde stage.

Understanding this cyclic unfoldment of Mercury can also be useful when considering how Mercury operates in transit. For example, the pre-retrograde Stage of Mercury's transits warn of the potential to over-extend. By observing Mercury's transit in relation to its Solar cycle, more sense can be made of its retrograde periods.

The following people were born with Mercury retrograde:

William Lilly	Alfred Adler	Earl Stanly Gardner
Paul McCartney	Howard Hughes	Ralph Nadar
John Huston	Nostradames	Mozart

The following people were born with Mercury direct at its greatest elongation:

Socrates	Madam Curie	Orville Wright
Dane Rudhyar	George Washington	William Shakespeare
Isaac Newton	Joan of Arc	Washington Irving
Michalangelo	Alan Arkin	Marc Edmond Jones

MERCURY'S RETROGRADE TRANSIT: Most of us, in our early astrological learning, are indoctrinated about the perils of Mercury's retrograde transits. Don't start new projects. Don't buy anything new. Don't plan elective surgery. Don't have dental work done. Don't make a residential move. Don't make commitments or sign any contracts. Mercury, when retrograde, tends to turn life upside down. Communications break down. Plans fall apart. Progress seems to come to an abrupt standstill. If it's true that nothing in astrology is negative in, and of, itself, how is it that Mercury's retrograde condition can be relied upon to create confusion and cause delays?

By understanding the Stages of Mercury's Solar cycle, as outlined in an earlier chapter, its retrograde periods become less intimidating. When Mercury retrogrades in transit, it advises people to back up and catch up with unfinished business. Realize, prior to the time Mercury actually turns retrograde, it moves into its retrograde zone. During its direct transit into this zone, people, in general, tend to get ahead of themselves. They often over commit. They are often so busy keeping up with life's pressures and society's expectations that important issues or information are overlooked. Once Mercury turns retrograde, they must retrace their steps to complete those things that have been overlooked or tabled due to excessive mental pressures.

Mercury, remember, represents the part of you that links together all other functions of personality. It represents the "phone wires" that keep you on-line with the rest of the world. When these wires get crossed, communications break down. The mind, in its attempt to acquire and distribute information to other parts of personality, begins to "short circuit." Some backtracking must be done to find where the "short" occurred, where the missing link exists that is causing incongruity.

Due to social pressures, you may feel compelled to continue in your progressive attempts to keep up with the world around you. Yet, when making agreements with a world that has also exceeded its limits, the contracts fail to materialize or they are lacking in some way.

Mercury retrograde advises you to slow down and digest what you have already ingested. Back up and complete, or review, what you have already initiated rather than taking on more than you can realistically assimilate. You can be sure that those things you put aside in the recent past, because you didn't have time to deal with them, will resurface and force you to confront the results. For example, if you heard your car making a funny noise, but, due to external time pressures, chose not to have it checked, you can expect further difficulty when Mercury turns retrograde. If you over-committed yourself prior to Mercury's retrograde transit, it will become an obvious problem once retrogradation occurs.

The message of retrograde Mercury is: use this time to catch up; use this time to take care of unfinished business. Rather than jumping into something new while Mercury is retrograde, reevaluate what already exists and make reparations where necessary. For example, if you are an author, use this time to edit what you have already created. If you are a teacher, use this time to review materials you have previously introduced. If you are a salesperson, use this time to re-contact previous customers and work out any problems that may interfere with future business deals. If you are searching for truth, look backward to previous experiences. Answers to your questions have been available to you in the past, but you failed to recognize them because you were too busy. The keynote of Mercury retrograde is repetition.

American society has always had difficulty coping with Mercury when retrograde. America's culture is based on progress. Carelessness in production often occurs during Mercury's retrogradation. Little time is permitted to go backward, to review existing materials or products, to find small errors that could create major problems if not discovered retroactively. An overload occurs that interferes with smooth operations in the future. Once these problems surface, rather than backing up to correct them, society simply replaces them, or attempts to cover them up, with something new. Problems stack up. Important information is lost to the past. Mistakes are repeated.

Mercury's rulership of Virgo is particularly evident when retrograde. Mercury's role, in relationship to Virgo, is to assist in digesting information and experience, while Gemini, its primary ruler, thirsts for new data. Mercury, when retrograde, wants you to take time out from your hectic schedule to evaluate the importance of the various fragments of data you have accumulated. If you don't welcome these reflective, digestive, corrective moments, you become saturated with so much information that you can no longer function productively.

Our clocks are designed to continually move forward. Yet, the planets, in their relation to Earth, do not always agree with this constant. Astrology advises us that sometimes it is wise to regress, to re-think, to re-evaluate, to re-align ourselves with our planetary energies in order to re-veal that which has value. Any retrograde planet deals with this concept of realignment and revelation. The only time retrograde Mercury works against us is when we choose to work against, or ignore, its message.

If, for example, you choose to purchase a new car when Mercury is retrograde, rather than using this time to evaluate whether you need a new car, what kind of car would suit you best, the economics of buying a new car, etc., you are choosing to work against the flow of nature. Not only is your timing off due to excessive stress in life, but the entire world is in transition. This factor must be considered when making decisions while Mercury is retrograde.

If Mercury is retrograde in your natal chart, you probably feel good when it retrogrades in transit. Society suddenly begins to operate on your wave-length. While you find these periods comfortable, it is important that you don't interpret this comfort as a green light to make important decisions. Even though you may function creatively while Mercury is retrograde, the rest of the world is in transition. Agreements, appointments or purchases initiated during these periods are still subject to revision. The basic premise of Mercury retrograde in transit applies regardless of its cyclic stage at the time of your birth.

An entire book could be written about experiences encountered by people when Mercury was retrograde. Mistakes are made. Misunderstandings occur. Appliances break down, and on and on it goes. If Mercury were a living entity, s/he would probably be sitting in a corner laughing at the comedy of errors committed by we Earthlings ... all because we fail to heed the loud, persistent messages Mercury has so consistently provided. "How many times" Mercury might say, "must you be told to stop, to rest your mind, to reflect and catch up?"

For three weeks at a time, once every four months, Mercury is retrograde. A mere nine weeks of every year we are asked to slow down and clean up our desks, clean out our closets, dust our minds so that they can function with greater efficiency. Many inconveniences and many frustrations could be avoided by using Mercury's retrograde periods to catch up with yourself. Many times, people don't connect the confusion and stress of Mercury retrograde to the realities experienced in life. They fail to see the effect of the cause. Every time Mercury retrogrades, they continue to forge ahead, making plans for the future, rather than completing projects of the past.

Eventually they find they have overextended themselves. Projects do not reach a positive completion. Life becomes a carnival ride that never stops.

The house through which Mercury retrogrades by transit describes an area of life requiring review. Here, you are challenged to evaluate what you have been doing and where you want to go in the future. You are challenged to take care of unfinished business, to review the past, to clean out the cobwebs in that room of your life. It is likely that you have overextended yourself in matters defined by this house.

To use Mercury's retrograde periods effectively, use the first half of its retrograde period, before the Solar conjunction, to complete unfinished business, clear the slate, "clean house" at some level. This is a time to "edit" your life and your activities. Go back over the "manuscript" of your life and eliminate or enhance the experiences you have acquired. Fine tune your life. Then, during the second half of its retrograde stage (after the Solar conjunction), plan for future action. Once Mercury has turned direct, you will be ready to move ahead and act on your plans. By heeding the messages provided by Mercury throughout each Stage of its Solar cycle, a well-organized, well-synchronized, clear mental process is assured.

Delays are not a disadvantage when they occur while Mercury is retrograde. Often, the Universe provides signals, in the form of delays, that make you re-assess what is taking place around you. When you force things to happen while Mercury is retrograde, you are forced to later retrace your steps to make corrections for omissions or defects in the original plan or project. Action taken while Mercury is retrograde is frequently premature. Important information is missing or misunderstood. You can avoid experiencing overload here if you use this time to reorganize.

Another interesting phenomenon occurs when examining Mercury's entire retrograde patterns over a period of years. Because Mercury retrogrades once every four months, it will spend several of its sequential retrograde transits in signs of the same Element. For example, notice in the Table of Mercury in the Appendix, that in December 1989 throughout 1990, Mercury retrograded in Earth signs. In early 1991 it made its transition from Earth into Fire. By November of 1991, it was solidly in the Fire Element and retrogrades in the Fire signs until November 1992. In February 1993, it retrogrades in Water signs. All of its retrograde periods occur in Water until October, 1994.

By noting the Element influenced by Mercury's retrograde cycles throughout any giving year, you are cued to what basic personal processes need attention.

For example, Mercury retrograde in **Water signs** suggests a need to reevaluate all matters that influence your emotional makeup. Matters of security, intimacy, and the past, will be a focus for review throughout the course of the time Mercury retrogrades in signs of the Water Element. Use these times to work at cleaning out your emotional storehouse.

In **Earth Signs**, Mercury retrograde challenges you to reorganize your practical life. Reevaluate what has value, from a material and psychological perspective. Clean up your financial records. Bring all practical matters up to par.

When Mercury retrogrades in **Air Signs**, you are challenged to reevaluate relationships. How do you communicate with others? How do you relate? What aspects of your intellect need reorganized?

In **Fire Signs**, Mercury retrograde advises you to examine how you go about realizing your goals. Creative energy must be redirected. What has provided enthusiasm and vision in the past may not have meaning in the future.

It is important to remember that Mercury, when retrograde, requires you to get some mental distance between yourself and the world around you. This distance breeds objectivity that helps you to clarify and prioritize. The entire retrograde phenomenon is one of reorientation. Stand back and review what you have already learned in order to get a clear picture of where the future is leading.

VENUS

Venus represents the capacity to appreciate all that life offers. It shows what you want for yourself, what gives you personal enjoyment, and what you want from social interaction. Venus is your personal "magnet." It enables you to attract experiences that cultivate self worth and promote creative relationships. Venus is love. Your level of self love qualifies what and whom you attract. It also plays a part in determining whether you accept or reject what comes to you.

Venus' simple but profound promise is: If you don't want it, you won't keep it. Whatever you choose to accept and keep in your life serves some value to you or you would not accept it. A well-developed Venus provides an ability to know what's good for you and what will bring happiness. On the other hand, conflicts involving what, or whom, you attract are always in some way connected to this powerfully magnetic planet. If you use its attracting energy to draw unhealthy experiences, or self-degrading relationships, your self worth obviously needs attention. However Venus functions, positively or negatively, its basic principle of attraction always operates. You attract substances and people because you want something from them. If they serve no purpose in life, your "magnet" would not draw or hold them to you.

Venus provides the capacity to attract what gives you personal pleasure. This self-loving Venus is represented by Venus and its rulership of Taurus. The ability to *weigh* the value of experience through objective evaluation comes from its rulership of Libra, the scales. Venus is a planet of comparison. It represents the part of you that knows what you want. Then it to weighs the value of what filling desires might "cost."

Venus represents all that is feminine. In the natal chart, it describes how (sign) and where (house) your feminine urges are developed and expressed. Venus, in a female's chart, defines how she feels about her femininity, her sexuality as a woman. In a man's chart, Venus describes the type of women he attracts. In today's less sexually-discriminating society, men are becoming more attuned to their own feminine natures. They no longer must act out their femininity through a female partner.

Like Mercury, Venus orbits inside the Earth's pathway around the Sun. This is a personal planet. In itself, it is unfettered by social or collective concerns. Planets outside the Earth's orbit are always shaped by worldly affairs because they cannot function without social exposure. The energies of Venus belong solely to you. Yet, unlike Mercury, Venus is not neutral. Venus wants what gives pleasure. It represents the part of you that wants to possess, to love, to be surrounded in beauty and comfort. Based on the house, sign, aspect, and stage of Venus' Solar cycle at the moment of birth, each individual has a different perspective of what creates comfort, what constitutes beauty, what possessions are desirable, and what love truly means.

A natal retrograde Venus has traditionally been blamed for limiting one's ability to attract valuable substances and supportive partners. It is said to be an inhibitive factor, causing low self esteem and separations in relationships. When viewing retrograde Venus in context with its Solar cycle, this myth is dissolved. Like all planets when retrograde, Venus retrograde functions powerfully in life. The attraction force it represents is dynamic. The urge to acquire valuable experiences is probably stronger in those having Venus retrograde than those having Venus direct. Remember, Venus is at its closest point to Earth when retrograde. Its urges are powerful, sometimes overwhelming, when hovering so close to our planet.

Like Mercury, Venus is never far from the Sun in the natal chart. However, while Mercury retrogrades with great frequency, Venus retrogrades only once throughout its 584 day synodic cycle. Only Mars retrogrades less frequently. Because Venus is retrograde for only about 6 weeks of its total cycle, it is the least seen retrograde planet in natal charts.

Venus, like Mercury, is either a morning or an evening star. It either rises before or after the Sun, and is never more than 48 degrees ahead or behind it. Therefore, its potential Solar aspects are minimal. The Stage at which Venus was operative in its Solar cycle at the time of birth adds significant information regarding how it functions in your life.

Like the Prometheus Mercury mind, Venus, when rising before the Sun, functions spontaneously and with enthusiasm regarding the possibilities of the future. Rudhyar calls Venus, when rising before the Sun, Venus Lucifer ... bearer of the light. This is the maiden Venus, who looks forward with a certain naivety, based on lack of experience, to what the future offers. There is an innocence to Venus Lucifer, a vulnerability combined with a blind faith about the future. Venus, when rising before the Sun, learns after the fact, and therefore can be easily disillusioned when she realizes her naivety and confronts her vulnerability. Frequent disappointments in love can leave Venus Lucifer *appearing* emotionally cold.

The inferior Solar conjunction marks the birth of a new Venus/Sun cycle. Venus switches places with the Sun to become an evening star. Like a New Moon personality, little consciousness is available in the earlier phase of Venus Lucifer. If you were born during this half of the Venus cycle, you go after what you want without always considering the consequences. You are simply, but profoundly, following your heart's desire.

At its inferior Solar conjunction, Venus is retrograde. It is closest to Earth than at any other time in its cycle. If you were born during this Stage, you are challenged to develop values around personal experiences instead of accepting socially-defined beliefs regarding what has value. To do this, you must to turn your back (R) on accepted social values to discover your own truth and define what gives your life meaning.

You were born shortly after society had overextended safe, or constructive, boundaries regarding ownership and relating. You must examine your personal values and compare them to what is considered "normal" in the world around you. What society considers important in relationships, acquisition, all issues of personal survival, may not compute with your inner reality.

The inferior Solar conjunction occurs half way through the retrograde stage. A new cycle is being born, and awareness that old values have become antiquated has taken place. Full awareness of what the future holds is not yet present. If you were born at such a time, you know that you don't belong in the value structures set by society. Yet, what you want is not clear. Minimal objectivity regarding what gives pleasure is available. You must naively move into the world to discover what you want. Only as a result of trial and error do you find your place, define what you want, and discover what makes you feel good about who you are and what you represent. For this reason, retrograde Venus suggests insecurities regarding the capacity to get what you want. Few social precedents have been set that support your inner yearnings.

It is not unusual for people with Venus retrograde to turn their backs on "normal" relationships. They often choose to follow an aesthetic life, or pursue an alternative life style. Venus Lucifer, the bearer of light, moves you into the darkness with only your own "Solar power" to light the way. All you know for sure, regarding what you want, is that you don't want what satisfies the norm. You want something more than what others accept without question. You find that the world does not offer you what others take for granted.

There is an "adolescent" quality to Venus when it rises before the Sun. There is an eagerness regarding what lies ahead, and a discontentment with society's existing values. When retrograde, your visions are not clear. Still, you must move toward them, and away from the precedents set by society, to find your own worth and beauty.

Retrograde Venus describes an emotional life geared toward the future but trapped in the past. You are challenged to turn away from natural instincts or values that influence or sway others. In the process, self denial becomes a potential problem for retrograde Venus. There is a tendency to turn away from the pleasures life offers. You want more from life than what the world currently offers. This can lead to a highly spiritual orientation toward life, or you could become pessimistic or self sacrificing. You are always comparing your life to others. Through comparison, you realize that you don't fit in with the mainstream. Your values, your feminine urges, work counter to the norm.

Women having Venus retrograde often question their femininity. They may turn their backs on their desire to be appreciated and feel attractive. Society's views of what is attractive and desirable somehow differ from yours. A man having Venus retrograde might turn his back on his feminine qualities as well, inhibiting his capacity to attract satisfactory relationships. Rejection or denial is not foreign to the retrograde Venus personality.

You need to learn to please yourself rather than seeking approval from others. What brings you happiness is not in synch with the norm. The more you conform to social standards, the more disappointment you experience.

You were born to "walk to the beat of a different drummer." Trust your own senses to determine what is beautiful in your world. Pursuing tradition leads to disillusionment.

While we are all influenced by social pressures, it is not unusual for those having Venus retrograde to, at first, engulf themselves in traditional values in an attempt to "fit in." Doing so only magnifies the fact that the values of your society won't work for you. It is easy to succumb to social pressures. Eventually, however, you will come face-to-face with what you want, what gives your life value and meaning. An inner voice tells you that the path society is taking is not the way for you.

It is difficult to live *in* a world and yet feel *apart* from it. It requires true commitment to what you know to be truth. Social pressures, especially peer pressures of youth, are difficult to ignore. You sense that the world has either overstepped important boundaries in its attempt to get what it collectively wants, or old values are not consistent with the future's requirements. You may feel you are working against all odds. At the same time, you inwardly hear a calling that beseeches you to walk into the unknown.

Because Venus is hovering close to the Earth at the time of the inferior Solar conjunction, relationships are strongly emphasized. The desire for a partner is powerful. The Venus function can become obsessive. Yet your capacity to accept love is questionable in the early part of life. When you learn to approve of yourself, and find value in your personal views, you no longer attract others who try to mold you into a value-structure that is inappropriate for you. Until you come to terms with your unique perspective of life's beauty, you may attract people who are non-supportive.

When Venus becomes stationary in preparation to turn direct, a certain doggedness is shown in one's determination to get what one wants from life. The conflicts of retrogradation are lifted and opportunities open the door to further exploration. The maiden's veil is lifted and she faces the future with new hope. From this point until the superior Solar conjunction occurs, the true qualities of Venus Lucifer are evident.

As Venus begins to accelerate in speed, it soon moves out of the retrograde zone to reach its maximum speed near the direct Solar conjunction. Enthusiasm is met with social acceptance, rather than the rejection evident during retrogradation. If you were born at this Stage of the Venus cycle, society's values are in harmony with what you want from life. And, you move into life to get what you want with zest and anticipation. Unfettered by the past, you are free to experiment and discover. You define your worth around what is possible rather than what is already affirmed. The past, and what you have accumulated from it, is of little importance. Your sense of worth is defined by what you are striving to experience rather than what you have thus far accomplished or acquired.

At the superior Solar conjunction, another major transition occurs. Venus again switches places with the Sun to rise after it from this point on in its cycle. Like the Epimetheus Mercury, Venus takes on a more conservative role when rising after the Sun. Rudhyar calls Venus, when rising after the Sun, Venus Hesperus, meaning "western." Venus is Hesperus when its longitude is greater than that of the Sun.

At its superior Solar conjunction, Venus and Earth are in opposition. The Sun is between Venus and our planet. This is the "quasi" full phase of the Venus/Sun cycle. Objectivity is required. While Venus Lucifer's feelings are not conditioned by social values, the opposite is true of Venus Hesperus. If you were born when Venus rose after the Sun, your feelings and values are steeped in tradition. You know what you want, while Venus Lucifer knows she wants something, but is unable to define it. There is less innocence to Venus Hesperus. At one level, it is more reliable when rising after the Sun. At another, it can be more cunning.

Once the superior Solar conjunction occurs, and Venus becomes Hesperus, it begins to decelerate in speed. The Venus function becomes more deliberate, premeditated, and objective. The desire to get what you want requires you to integrate with the mainstream, to "socialize" your values.

You know what you want for yourself, and in relationships, because there is historical or past evidence that proves what you want exists or is possible to attain. Relationship choices are based on social norms. Personal tastes, in so far as possessions are concerned, are grounded in tradition or existing social values. Like the Epimethean Mercury mind, Venus Hesperus *uses society* to acquire substance. It uses magnetism to get what it wants from the world. If you have Venus Hesperus, you need to belong. You need acceptance for the role you play and the value you give and receive via relationships. For this reason, your values are more conservative than those of Venus Lucifer. Your attitudes regarding relationships are based on the protocols of society. You want to attract substances and people that confirm your social belonging.

Because Venus Hesperus demonstrates greater maturity or control than Venus Lucifer, passion accompanies this position. From a positive level, this promotes success. Negatively, due to lack of spontaneity, passion can become destructive and result in fear or excessive possessiveness.

As Venus moves into the retrograde zone, prior to actual retrogradation, the next crisis of unfoldment occurs. Once having jumped on the social bandwagon and reaped the benefits of working with the system to get what you want, it is important to assess when that social wagon has taken you farther than your personal values want you to go. When does the urge to acquire valuable substances and relationships cease being an asset? When Venus enters the retrograde zone, before reaching its retrograde station, the world, as a whole, tends to exceed important limits that it will later need to confront.

If you were born during this stage of the Venus cycle, it is important to you to fit in. Yet, you must be aware that fitting in can lead to ill-timed "investments." This stage brings to mind the age-old advise: Just because everyone else wants it doesn't mean its good for you.

Collectively, Venus Hesperus, direct but in the retrograde zone, suggests a time of overextension. Everyone seems to want a slice of the "pie in the sky" only to later find the "pie" has already been eaten. There is a tendency to hold on long after the value of the product or relationship to which you are clinging has served its purpose. Cyclically, purchases, commitments, or other Venus-ruled activities initiated during this Stage are often inappropriate or ill-timed. You may not want what you thought you wanted once Venus has moved on to its next Solar cycle. From a natal perspective, the same concept applies. Venus Hesperus in the retrograde zone suggests a tendency to hold on too long, or acquire too much too late, only to be disillusioned after the commitment has been made.

Soon after moving into the retrograde zone, Venus comes to a complete stop. Venus again is forced to examine life from a personal rather than social perspective. Excessive desire for accumulation and self serving involvements must now be confronted. When Venus Hesperus reaches the retrograde station, it marks a time when society must come to terms with its quest for pleasure and comfort. Have desires extended moral limits? Has expenditure exceeded the "budget?" If you were born during this stage of Venus' Solar cycle, you are constantly challenged to focus on where you stand with regard to society's existing values. As with Mercury, when stationary, you have an ability to evaluate life with profundity. The "frozen" status of Venus provides a clear perspective regarding what is possible and what must change in order to leave one cycle and begin a new one while maintaining integrity. You could use this insight for positive or negative purposes. From a positive level, you are acutely aware of your own value and how it compares with social standards. Negatively, your sense of worth (good or bad) could be used to manipulate others.

As Venus begins to retrograde, social errors in judgement must be confronted and rectified. Society must now come to terms with how and where it has exceeded limits in its desire to get what it wants. People must confront their own greed, not only for material comforts, but their desires to find pleasure through relationships.

If you were born during this stage of Venus' retrogradation, your life exemplifies the need for frequent "reality" checks regarding what provides pleasure and what truly has value. You will live out the consequences of excess. It is essential to evaluate what is truly valuable and compare that to society's programs. Venus Hesperus, when retrograde, must return to the "source" to meet the Sun at the inferior conjunction. Likewise, you must walk away from pressures to conform to an overly-permissive or greed-ridden society to get a clear picture of what is important, what truly brings happiness, what you want as apart from what you were taught was important. Like retrograde Venus Lucifer, you do not fit in the mainstream. You must be totally objective when making value judgments. To do so, you must put "distance" between yourself and the world around you. By walking away from the mainstream, you get a broader picture of the value of your life, the relationships you attract, the value of ownership, the value of pleasure, and the value of love. Your resulting evaluation will be different from the majority because it is based on a totally objective perspective. Your role, like the new person on the block, is to see the reality of the neighborhood with greater clarity and objectivity than those who have been long-term residents. Your concept of personal worth comes from introspection. What you ultimately find important may be contradictory to what others deem valuable. You could feel isolated because of the contrasts you see. From a spiritual perspective, you are a "witness," while Venus Lucifer is a "seeker."

Venus retrograde, whether rising before or after the Sun, suggests some problems regarding relationships. There is a tendency to discover, after the fact, that the relationships you have chosen do not support your inner values. This often occurs because peoples' natural tendency is to succumb to social pressures regarding the importance of relationships, marriage, contracts, etc. Later, you find that what you were taught is not in harmony with your inner yearnings.

At the inferior Solar conjunction, Venus begins a new cycle. Still retrograde, Venus switches places with the Sun to become, again, Venus Lucifer ... the seeker, the child maiden in search of a future.

The following list of recognizable personalities were born with Venus retrograde:

VENUS LUCIFER	**VENUS HESPERUS**

Alfred Adler	Socrates
John Steinbeck	Anne Besant
Alan Leo	Adolf Hitler
Michelangelo	Winston Churchill
Otto Preminger	Norman Rockwell
C.C. Zain	Elizabeth Barret Browning

TRANSIT OF VENUS RETROGRADE: It is important to understand the cyclic pattern of Venus to fully comprehend the full import of its retrograde transits. Its retrograde periods are equal in potency to those of Mercury's. These two planets, because they reside inside the Earth's Solar orbit, represent dynamic aspects of personal development. Venus touches you at core levels. It describes what you want from life, what gives you pleasure. It describes the kinds of people with whom you want to share life experiences, not only because they offer you comfort and pleasure, but because they complement your life.

Venus is retrograde less time than any other planet in the Solar system. While Mars retrogrades less frequently, Venus is more rarely retrograde. In a 584 day period, Venus is retrograde less than 6 weeks.

Realize that just prior to the time Venus turns retrograde, it has theoretically gone "out of bounds." As it transits the degree at which it will later make its direct station, it begins to function beyond your ability to consciously direct its energy. Once it makes its retrograde station, you are challenged to cease moving forward in your desire to acquire more for yourself. Stop to assess whether or not what you want is in harmony with what you need to enhance your life. As you grow, your values change. Venus retrograde provides time to assess what you have accumulated and determine if those things still hold meaning for you. Are you attracting substances, or people, based on values that do not reflect the needs of the future? Are you caught up in society's concepts of what has value to the degree you have lost touch with your own value, your own desires? Do you know what you want? How have your values changed over the last 1 1/2 years? When Venus retrogrades, it presents opportunity to reevaluate where you are in life, and how your values are reflected through your relationships and acquisitions.

There is often a sense of desperation that surfaces when Venus is retrograde. You know things are changing. You sense that certain aspects of your relationships are subject to revision. Fear of making adjustments sometimes compels people to make new commitments rather than reviewing the content and value of the relationships currently operative in life.

While Mercury is impersonal, Venus is totally focussed on self-gratification. When retrograde, you are encouraged to examine what truly provides personal gratification versus what society has defined as valuable or desirable. Have you become so caught up in your effort to attract what the majority defines as attractive that you have lost touch with what you really want?

You may feel that your mate is moving away from you, or you may be the one who is growing in a different direction. Do you stop to evaluate the transition occurring? Or, does your fear of adjustment lead you to act on premature decisions? It is not unusual for people to marry when Venus is retrograde, only to find out later that they no longer want what their partner provides. Important details are not considered prior to making Venus retrograde commitments.

On the other hand, relationships are often severed when Venus retrogrades, only to later find that the separation was premature or inappropriate. Venus retrograde wants you to back up and examine the quality of the relationships in your life. It is not a time to make external changes, but a time to evaluate how and where changes are in order. Only after Venus has turned direct have you completed the process of reevaluation. Any overt or final action taken while Venus is retrograde is premature.

I have no reservations when I see Venus about to retrograde in advising clients to postpone making long-term commitments in relationships until after it has turned direct. Use its retrograde transit to objectively reassess relationships. Make sure that they are what you really want. Often, throughout the course of Venus' retrogradation, issues come up that must be addressed. When Venus retrogrades, it brings home (conjunction to Earth) all those things you have wanted in the past. The question you must ask is: does what you once wanted still have credibility? Is it enough? New values emerge out of these reflective questions. New desires prompt you to reevaluate past criteria. As Venus turns direct, new values can be implemented.

This is not to say that relationships always break down when Venus is retrograde. It is, however, a time of reassessment. Adjustments must be made regarding what you perceive brings value to your life. This is a time to deal with issues from the past that have not yet been completed or resolved. Expectations regarding all things, or people, you value must be examined. Take care of an unfinished past before attempting to create a new future.

Rather than accepting everything that comes to you, stop and ask yourself: is this what I really want? Examine closely what you have acquired or attracted to yourself. Does it still hold value for you? It is not unusual to attract people from your past while Venus is retrograde as a means of comparing the quality of your life now in relation to your earlier sense of self worth. This is particularly the case when Venus retrogrades in Houses of Relationship (3, 7, 11).

Because Venus is close to Earth when retrograde, you must examine the very basis of your power to attract. This includes not only your capacity to attract people, but your ability to accumulate assets that provide comfort and personal pleasure. All these matters must now be scrutinized. How have your values changed? What kinds of adjustments must be made to realign your outer life with your newly emerging values? This is a time to psychologically strip away the adornments society calls attractive, and look inside to find your true beauty. Apart from social conventions, what do you want? What do you find valuable? Take time out from social pressures to reestablish a relationship with yourself.

In some way, society, as a whole, has overstepped positive boundaries in its quest to sustain itself and find pleasure. You need to stand back and look to see where you may have gone beyond what's right for you. Has society's greed gone too far? If so, consequences of indulgence become evident when Venus turns retrograde. If you have "bitten off more than you can chew," in an attempt to feed your "appetite," you will come face-to-face with the results of excess when Venus retrogrades by transit.

It is easy to get caught up in habits of acquisition to the degree you are no longer conscious of the value those acquisitions provide. Your "magnet" can function indiscriminately. When Venus turns retrograde, you must examine this process. Begin to weed out those things in your life that no longer represent what you want, that no longer reflect your worth. Your values have changed since the last time Venus was retrograde. Now is the time to adjust to those changes so that your life can continue to evolve. Stand back and take a close look at your life. Do your relationships reflect your current level of self worth? Are your possessions a reflection of your values? Review and assess. When Venus turns direct, you will have your answers. While retrograde, you are in the *process* of analysis, comparison, and transition. Any action taken while Venus is retrograde is premature.

The house through which Venus retrogrades by transit points to the area of life where this transition occurs. It describes where you are challenged to examine whether or not the experiences being encountered are valuable with regard to what you want in the future. What once provided pleasure or personal gratification may no longer be adequate. You are challenged to use this time to stand back and view, from a larger perspective, the activities defined by this house. Are you gauging your values around what society defines as desirable and, in the process, ignoring your personal needs. Have you over-extended safe boundaries here? Have you accumulated so much in this area of life that you can no longer find value in your acquisitions? Are you attracting people through these experiences that fill your personal needs and complement your life? Or, have you attracted companions that fill a space in your life but leave your heart empty?

It is interesting to note that Venus, like Mercury, follows a pattern in its retrograde motion through the signs. Venus retrogrades sequentially through signs that are quincunx. The quincunx is an aspect of adjustment, an aspect indicating a time when you must alter the course you have chosen to walk in order to meet new experiences that could not be foreseen. It is easy to get caught up in habits of interacting and attracting. When Venus retrogrades, you are challenged to examine these habits and make adjustments if deemed to be operating counter to your personal growth needs.

INTRODUCTION TO TRANS-EARTH PLANETS

Any natal planet in opposition to the Sun is retrograde; a fact seldom mentioned in books designed around aspect interpretation. Any planet opposing the Sun is at its closest point to, or conjunct, Earth; another fact often overlooked in aspect evaluation. The approximate midpoint of all planetary retrogradation (except for Mercury and Venus) occurs at its Solar opposition. This phenomenon suggests a need to reevaluate the significance of the opposition aspect from its traditional interpretation.

The Sun is the source of all life on our planet. Astrologically, it represents the core of your being, the center of consciousness, the life force. Any planet opposite the Sun represents a part of personality that must be confronted and realigned with the Solar energy. It represents a part of personality that separated (opposition) from its source (Sun). This part of you must stop attempting to move ahead on society's momentum, and back up to find new meaning, to reunite with its true essence.

Retrograde planets represent personality functions that do not find comfort in conformity. The very nature of the opposition aspect that occurs midway through the retrograde phase, suggests a need to observe. Back up from the mainstream to compare and evaluate your needs in contrast to the norm. The "mirror" provided by the opposition gives you a clear picture of who you are.

All natal retrograde planets are not in opposition to the Sun. The opposition is experienced near the midpoint of the retrograde stage. This midpoint must be considered to understand the full significance of the retrograde condition. The opposition introduces the Full Phase of a planet's cycle. Cyclically, it represents a time when you must cease functioning solely on instinct. You must begin operating with full consciousness, full awareness of the results of action and how your actions ultimately affect the lives of others. The opposition requires you to think before you act. When involving the Sun, it describes a need to be aware of how your urge to integrate with society supports or detracts from your life purpose. You must consider not only how your life influences the lives of others, but how society has influenced you, both positively and negatively. Oppositions require full objectivity when making choices or initiating action.

It is important to keep these principles in mind as you consider the retrogradation of Mars through Pluto.

MARS

Mars acts on what Venus wants. It is the go-between of the inner and outer life. While Mercury sends messages to the various functions of personality, Mars initiates action based on Mercury's information.

Mars offers courage to meet the world on your own terms. It motivates you to get what you want from life. By using its energy to initiate action, you begin the process of socialization. While Venus represents passive magnetism, Mars is active aggression. Your Venus urges rely on the incentive of Mars to get what you want. These planets share a special relationship. They represent polarizing forces of personality.

Mars is the first planet outside Earth's orbit. It unlocks the door to the outer world and takes you to the world of society. Mars represents pure masculine energy. It represents the part of you that is provocative, aggressive, and often combative in your quest to prove yourself capable of independent action. Mars provides the drive to fight for what you want, to assertively and courageously meet new experiences. In a man's chart, Mars shows how he presents his masculinity. At one time, Mars, in a woman's chart, described what she needed from a male counterpart to survive. In today's world, Mars identifies her own masculine urges. Without the energy of Mars, you would be unable to function as an independent being.

Mars' cycle begins at its Solar conjunction. It is direct and at its farthest point from Earth. Objectivity is minimal while instinct is powerful during the New Phase of the Sun/Mars cycle. Like Prometheus Mercury or Venus Lucifer, Mars functions spontaneously, if not recklessly, when conjunct the Sun. This is particularly true when Mars is within the combust zone. Little awareness is evident during the birth of any New Phase experience.

Geocentric Mars orbits Earth once every two years, while the Sun circles the ecliptic once every year. It is important to realize that when Mars and the Sun conjunct, the Sun has moved to meet Mars. The opposite is true with Mercury and Venus. The Sun comes to Mars to get courage. It relies on Mars to increase its level of consciousness by creating new experiences. Your Sun needs Mars to stimulate new activity that leads to growth. Mars motivates you to move into the world outside personality, outside your safe cocoon. As the actions that Mars stimulates are new to the Sun, Mars must offer courage to the life force. The Sun reimburses Mars by giving direction to the masculine drive. Before Mars can function with full power in your life, it must get approval from your Venus. Abstractly, Mercury informs Venus of what Mars is able to do. Venus either accepts or rejects based on what she wants or what she is capable of receiving. If accepted, Mars pierces the Solar consciousness and plants new seeds.

Once energized by the Mars function, the Sun moves away from the conjunction point. Objectivity increases and greater awareness regarding *how* aggressive instincts are functioning begin to emerge.

If you were born during the first half of the Mars cycle, Mars operates with confidence. You use its energy to pave the way into the future. There is little concern for getting results. The purpose of Mars, in the early stages, is to create and activate. Mars moves into the world to acquire experiences to bring home once it returns to align with Earth at the time of its next Solar opposition.

You eagerly move into the world to create new experiences. You are courageous and act largely on instinct. Not always aware of what the future holds, you move toward it with confidence, brevity, and sometimes with careless abandon. You are provocative, restless, and eager to put things in motion. You are a "soldier," willing to fight the battle even though you don't always know the strategies of war. The phase and aspect between Mars and the Sun give further information regarding how your aggressive instincts function, i.e. with stress (square) or with grace (trine).

When Mars, due to the Sun's movement, moves into the retrograde zone, the assertive, combative, "me first" energies begin to exceed constructive limits. From a cyclic perspective, this marks a time when people often go too far in their quest to get what they want. If you were born during this stage of Mars' transit, you could easily overexert yourself. You have a tendency to push too far, go too fast, get carried away with your own desires. Eventually you find yourself isolated in territory that is foreign to you. Only after the fact do you realize you have gone beyond the limits consciousness can assimilate. This realization challenges you to reconsider the value of your actions and adjust when deemed necessary.

At a cyclic level, Mars has entered territory it must later assess. Mars will later retrograde over this same point, requiring revisions based on the objectivity provided by the Sun's coming opposition. If born during this pre-retrograde phase of Mars' cycle, life will challenge you to learn to control the masculine, assertive urges that potentially lead to conflict.

When Mars is in the first half of its Solar cycle, action is initiated before consciousness. You learn to direct your masculine urges after you have experienced the consequences of aggression. When direct, but in the retrograde zone, important lessons must be learned about the use of personal power.

As with all planets at their retrograde stations, Mars takes on a dogged persistence to use its power. This can result in an individual who is obstinate and unbending in his/her desire to maintain control. When Mars begins its retrogradation, desires are internalized and, because of its approach to Earth, Mars becomes a powerful energy with which to reckon. This turning point begins a period of realignment regarding the aggressive nature. If you have Mars retrograde, you don't feel you fit in the world around you. You must define ways to get what you want that are counter to the norm. At one level, you realize how and where you easily exceed limits. You learn as you retreat to heal your resulting wounds. At another level, you realize that your energy can be used more efficiently if you retreat to construct strategies.

"Normal" or socially-defined means of exerting yourself, living out your masculine urges, do not work for you. You must turn your back on passion, as defined and demonstrated by society, to find a new source of vitality. Your desires are not in rhythm with society's. Normal methods of fulfilling desires don't work for you. You must go through Scorpio's "death" to be born in Aries, to find your own truth.

Issues of anger are also evident when Mars is retrograde. You don't know how to direct anger in a way others accept or condone. You might hold on to your anger, only to watch it surface at inappropriate times. You may lack spontaneity, or, a clear perspective of the purpose of anger. Any pent-up aggression must eventually find release. Mars retrograde needs a focus for its energy. Sometimes, projects that require intense involvement help you focus your passion. On the other hand, excessive involvement in outside-the-self activities can magnify your tendency to ignore your own physical urges and needs.

The past (personal, cultural, social or collective) has had a strong influence on how you assimilate your masculine, assertive, sexual energies.

You need to confront the past to define a future. In some way, your life exemplifies society's mis-use of Martian energy.

Freud's chart offers a classic example of Mars retrograde. His retrograde Mars is a singleton planet. His entire life was built on Mars themes. His fascination with sexuality and the past could be called obsessive. Yet, his unique perspective, based on his internal exploration, is also called genius. Freud spent his life coming to terms with his sexuality. His perception of man's aggressive "animal" instincts was certainly unique in his era. He turned his back on society's previous definition of instinct and brought in a new understanding of masculine energy. He challenged society to become conscious of the importance of acknowledging, expressing, and using Mars' power.

A lot can be learned about retrograde planets by studying the lives of people who made an important contribution (positive or negative) to society's understanding of itself. You may not be aware of the social statement your retrograde planets make, especially if born in the first half of the retrograde stage. But rest assured, a statement is evident via your behaviors and beliefs.

Mars retrograde is associated with sexual repression, uncontrollable or inhibited anger, and suppression of survival instincts. It has been associated with weakness, submission and violence. These are symptoms, not the cause behind the retrograde dilemma.

When pressured by social influences to act in a certain way, to define desires in terms others' understand, to act spontaneously, you fail to meet the requirements of retrograde Mars. These pressures, usually induced by social exposure, can lead to any number of symptoms. The root cause for suppression, or excessive show of anger, is pressure to conform. You don't feel comfortable reacting to external stimuli in the same way others find natural. You need time to review what is taking place within and without.

Mars is in its retrograde zone for approximately 6 months of its 26 month cycle. Each retrograde cycle lasts 9 to 10 weeks. It is in its retrograde zone 1/4th of its complete cycle, during which time energy is transmuted and redirected. If Mars never retrograded, society would never stop long enough to examine what motivates it. There would be no morality to man. The retrograde Mars individual must examine the purpose of his/her desires. This awareness can come out of the results of violence inflicted on, or caused by, the individual him/herself. Or, it can come as a result of stepping off the social trolley to question the value of reaching its destination.

Greater awareness of the differences between your desires and the "norm" is evident at the Solar opposition. At this time, Earth is between Sun and

Mars. The inner self (Sun) pulls you in one direction while desire, stimulated by external circumstances, pulls you in the opposite. While the stress level is high at the opposition point you *see*, through objective experience, the conflict. Prior to the opposition, no "mirror" is available.

If you were born when Mars was opposite the Sun, your Mars is retrograde. Much like the Epimethean Mercury, or Venus Hesperus, you were born when society was challenged to be attentive to the results of action. At the Solar opposition, this awareness comes out of stress. You are aware of the conflicts in your own nature, ie: the desire to prove yourself in worldly terms versus the urge for personal fulfillment and commitment to your inner sense of purpose. For every action you initiate, you will attract strong reactions from the world. You will come face-to-face with your own desires and realize how they contrast with the norm. This can lead to enlightenment (Full Phase), or, when ignored, conflict and fragmentation. Because Mars is retrograde, you must come to terms with your desires. Your instincts are leading you in a unique direction. Moving with the mainstream of society leads you away from your own center. Pursuing desires defined by the outer world leads you away from your own power. You need to define unique methods of getting what you want to satisfy your desires. This requires forethought. As the Sun and Mars separate, greater objectivity is developed. You learn methods to get what you want.

If you were born when Mars was in the second half of its retrogradation, your methods of getting what you want are more sophisticated than people born in the first half of the retrograde cycle. While you stand apart from the mainstream, you are aware of the differences. You know how to design modes of action that are appropriate for you. While Mars, in its early phase with the Sun, functions with little objectivity, this is not the case with you. You know what you want, and you know that the only way to get it is by acting against, or turning away from, the norm.

You are aware of what separates you from others. This does not make the retrograde condition of Mars easy. Awareness of your "abnormal" desires can intensify the frustration of retrogradation and create strong feelings of isolation. Aspects to Mars indicate the comfort or stress involved with your particular idiosyncracies. What motivates you, what "turns you on" is based on your internal realities rather than what excites the mainstream of society. You need to define your own truths around issues of sexuality and self assertion.

Any symptoms (described earlier) of Mars retrograde are results of frustration regarding masculine energy. There is a tendency to be overly controlling in an attempt to get what you want. Because your desires do not conform to the norm, you could attempt to control the world around you to gain acceptance in it, or power over it. On the other hand, it is not unusual for people having Mars retrograde to sublimate sexual energy and direct their desires toward spiritual development or fighting for social or global causes. In the latter case, control is focussed on the self.

If you have Mars retrograde, and are unable to get what you want, maybe it's because you pattern your desires around what others want. Are you attempting to use aggressive techniques that are not in harmony with your "source?" If so, you will feel as if you are fighting against all odds. As you attempt to initiate new activity, you are rejected because your desire is not sincere. It is not congruent with what you internally crave.

Mars, when moving counter to the normal planetary tide, has difficulty finding external avenues through which to live out Venus's values. Mars retrograde shows highly developed regenerative energy at one level, and self destructive energy at another. Retrograde Mars challenges you to free yourself from the compulsive desires and instincts that are typical in society.

When Mars reaches its direct station, re-integration with society takes place. As with all stationary direct planets, there is a dynamic urge to join the world and benefit through interaction. You know who you are. You know what you want. And you are prepared to move into the world to get it. A compulsive quality is evident at the time of Mars' direct station. This is because of the freedom you feel from its pre-birth retrogradation. Like a wild lyon released from entrapment, you rush to meet your "pride," to reintegrate with your group.

Once Mars turns direct, it follows the Sun over the horizon. When rising before Mars, the Sun lightens its path. It enables you to know where you are going and to see the potential outcomes of activity you initiate. Unlike Mars in the first half of its Solar cycle, you need to know why you are asked, or compelled, to think before initiating action. You need to see a potential result. While Mars, when rising before the Sun, is likened to a soldier who goes out to fight a war and often knows not why, you are the general. You need to have the strategies that can lead you to where you want to go. You need to be in control, not always of others, but over your own desires. You recognize how society fits into your strategies for self discovery. Therefore, you need to be aware of how your actions and desires are received by the world around you. You go out to get what you want based on social protocol or what history has already proven works. Your actions are more deliberate, more controlled.

During the time Mars is retrograde, it is trying to "catch up" with itself. This is a time when Mars is busy recycling past experiences and integrating the results into new activities. Once free from the retrograde zone, there is no further need to examine old patterns. You are free to initiate activity without tripping over old construction.

Mars represents the first step man takes into the world of society. If you were born after Mars had left its retrograde zone, and before its Solar conjunction, you must take your first steps into new experiences aware of where you are and whom you will meet. You act after consciousness rather than before. Because of the social experiences you encounter, you grow. Your desires expand. Cyclically, you are being led toward a new Solar conjunction where a new phase of action is initiated.

A unique relationship is found between Venus and Mars in the natal chart. These two planets surround the Earth ... Venus lying inside the Earths orbit and Mars orbiting just outside its path. Venus describes what you want. Mars goes into the world to get it. At times, Mars acts counter to Venus' values. The desire energy of Mars can oppose, or differ from, your inner values. Mars may be unable to provide Venus with what she wants due to inappropriate techniques of aggression, either because of suppressed energy or excessive combativeness. The Solar cycles of these planets show how they operate together. Regardless of whether aspects exist between Venus and Mars, conflicts can be experienced. For example, during the second half of Mars' cycle, Mars, through the function of Mercury, tells Venus: "This is what I can get for you. And, this is how I can get it." Venus accepts or rejects according to her values. Challenging aspects between Mars and Venus suggest disagreements between these two functions of personality. Conflicts and complements can also be seen by comparing the cyclic position of Venus to that of Mars.

It is interesting to consider planets as separate parts of personality communicating with each other. Doing so gives you a different perspective of the workings of your own psyche. The following is what you might hear between Mars and Venus, based on the stages of their individual Solar Cycles. This dialogue demonstrates the potential compatibility, or stress, associated with their partnership.

Venus Rising Before the Sun: Mars Rising Before the Sun:

Venus: "I want it now! Go for it!"

Mars: "I'm out of here!"

Venus Rising Before the Sun: Mars Rising After the Sun:

Venus: " This is what I want. I don't know why, but I really want it and I want it now! Will you get it for me? Please? Hurry!"

Mars: "Keep your pants on. What's your hurry? I need to design a strategy to get the job done. I can handle it, but don't pressure me! I need to find what avenues are open before I can get what you want."

Venus Rising After the Sun: Mars Rising After the Sun:

Venus: "After giving this some thought, I'd like you to work out a way to get what I want. Be sure you think before you act."

Mars: "Be glad to. I'll work out a plan and get back to you."

Venus Rising After the Sun: Mars Rising Before the Sun:

Venus: "This is what I want so I'll be accepted and acceptable. Don't rush. Be sure you know what you're doing and don't risk my social reputation."

Mars: "Don't worry about all that! I'll just follow my instincts regardless of social protocol."

RETROGRADE MARS IN TRANSIT: When Mars turns retrograde in transit, you come face to face with your own power. As the Earth moves ahead to align with Mars, you must realign your aggressive instincts. You are challenged to evaluate what motivates you to take assertive action. Are your actions supporting growth? Are your actions building consciousness (Sun)? Or, are they prohibiting or even destroying it? Have you become swept up in passion or adrenalin to the degree you are no longer in control of your own power? Have you gone too far in your attempt to get what you want? Are you overwhelmed by social pressures that cause excessive anxiety? Could it be that you are pursuing desires defined by society that are incongruent with your own needs?

If you have overextended yourself, you will reap the results when Mars turns retrograde. Your Mars energy now comes to the forefront to be examined, redirected, integrated, or exorcised. Any pent-up frustrations must now be examined. Face your anger, acknowledge your natural instincts, and take control of them. Rather than acting spontaneously while Mars is retrograde, use this time to develop new strategies for aggression. This process requires objectivity. It requires you to stand back to examine your life and where you are going. Are you piloting your own ship or have outside forces taken control of the helm? What are you doing with your life, and why?

There are distinct similarities in the messages sent by the personal planets, Mercury, Venus, and Mars when retrograde. All point to times when reflection, reevaluation, and redirection of energy is required. Mars, due to its aggressive nature, challenges you to cease forging ahead to create new experiences on instinct only. Take time out to evaluate. Come to terms with your masculine urges, your aggression, your sexuality, your passions. Consider potential outcomes of action and face the results or consequences of all action initiated since Mars' previous Solar conjunction. Make adjustments where needed. You will confront the past when either Mercury, Venus, or Mars turn retrograde. If you have exceeded appropriate limits in your life, or if you have not constructively and consciously met the challenges thus far presented, you will reap the results during this stage of these planets' cycles. On the other hand, if you have met the challenges introduced since the beginning of the Solar cycle, you can now relax and reap the rewards.

Once Mars enters the retrograde zone, you begin functioning beyond your ability to assimilate ... beyond consciousness. As outlined in Chapter XVI, this Stage is especially critical in all planetary cycles. Because Mars' energy is particularly volatile, when it functions beyond the boundaries of consciousness it opens the door to excessive stress and anxiety. Mars retrograde points to a time when you need to slow down, examine how stress is influencing your attitudes and behaviors. How are you handling stress in your life? Look for strategies to relieve stress and establish techniques for managing aggression. Ask yourself: do I really want what I have been aggressively attempting to acquire?

The Mars function is powerful when retrograde. So powerful, in fact, that it requires special attention. You need to use its retrograde periods to regain control over its energy. You need to recognize and take responsibility for past actions. On the other hand, if you have repressed your power, Mars, when retrograde, provides an opportunity to reclaim it and redirect it. This is not a time to give your power to others. It is a time to embrace, and hold dear, your capacity to be independent and to function as a separate, yet complete, individual. By claiming ownership of your ability to function independently you also confront a need to take responsibility for the consequences of your actions. All these issues must be addressed when Mars turns retrograde in transit.

The house through which Mars retrogrades describes the area of life where you may have overextended yourself. Here, you are challenged to back up and take care of unfinished business. You are challenged to become more conscious of how your actions, passions, and personal power influence the degree of success or failure you have recently experienced in this area of your life. Have you been directing your power into activities simply because its "the thing to do?" Or, do you really want what you have been striving to acquire? It is important to use this time to realign your life and to design new modes for getting what you want. Use this time to re-act to what you have thus far experienced or created. Rather than impulsively moving ahead, use this period to catch up with yourself. When Mars turns direct, you will be ready to begin forging new trails. But first use its retrograde periods to make sure the destiny you are moving toward, and the passion or power you are using to propel you, are in harmony with where you truly want to go.

Retrograde Mars demonstrates the intensity of its secondary rulership of Scorpio. You must direct the power of this sign into constructive channels or it will either turn in on itself in destructive ways, or impose itself on others in an attempt to control what it does not rightfully possess. When Mars is retrograde, personal motivation must be carefully scrutinized. This can be a time of life providing opportunity to meet your power and regenerate it, or it can be a time when you are shown how that same power can destroy.

Mars retrograde provides a rare opportunity to redirect assertive power. In order to do so constructively, you must recognize how you have used your power in the past and discern how you want to direct it in the future. This is a time to stand back, take time out and internalize. This is a time for problem solving. Any energies, or desires, that have been misplaced, misused, or abused are intense when Mars is retrograde. This very process of intensification draws your attention. A yellow caution sign replaces the green light.

The point at which Mars opposes the Sun shows when full consciousness is achieved. At this time, you are challenged to take responsibility for directing your power. Use the first half of its retrograde phase to wrap up unfinished business. Confront your past and make adjustments required to continue moving ahead with new goals once Mars turns direct. Use the second half (after the Solar opposition) of the retrograde period to set the stage for new directives. Progressive actions taken while Mars is retrograde is premature. This is a time for internalizing energy rather than provoking external action. Confront and adjust is the keynote of all retrograde planets. It is vitally important to use the retrograde periods of Mars to realign action patterns, examine previous habits established around assertion, and design strategies for moving ahead into new, unexplored territory once Mars turns direct.

JUPITER

Once you expend Mars' energy and go out to meet the world, you are greeted by Jupiter, who opens the door to society. While Mars represents the process of moving toward socialization, Jupiter represents society's welcome mat. It encourages you to integrate with society and offers opportunity to reap benefits from the contacts you make. Jupiter represents the process of social assimilation.

Jupiter is the first of the social planets. Mars represents the vehicle that gets you out the door to meet society. Jupiter's role is one of expansion. It invites you to participate in life, to be a member of society. From a positive level, Jupiter represents acceptance of all that is outside, or foreign from, the self.

Jupiter is optimistic, open minded and philosophical. Negatively, it describes prejudices that stem from lack of social integration, or fear of losing your separateness by merging with the larger community. Jupiter is a planet of extremes. It represents the part of you that wants to experience all of life. While Jupiter provides the power to accumulate wealth, it also rules excess.

It is difficult to separate the role of Jupiter from that of Saturn. These planets represent a powerful social polarity. They must function as partners to guarantee a satisfactory social life. Jupiter urges you to experience the fullness life offers in terms of social opportunity. If Jupiter's appetite is not curbed by Saturn's discipline, excessiveness at all levels occurs. Obesity, greed, fanaticism, or an over-inflated sense of one's importance are characteristics of an undisciplined Jupiter.

Jupiter's role is to expose you to worldly things. Saturn provides discipline to choose wisely from what society offers. Jupiter without Saturn is like an adolescent who, after having experienced freedom of choice, decides s/he wants it all! There is no sense of limitation, only exhilaration and a thirst for more of whatever life presents. While Jupiter promises opportunity for expansion, it must work with Saturn to assure that the opportunities it provides are directed into positive channels. Likewise, Saturn must occasionally loosen its reigns to allow Jupiter freedom to continue moving toward the future. Jupiter welcomes you to the world of tomorrow. It is considered the Great Benefic of the Solar system.

Jupiter offers promises of what could be. It encourages you to reach out toward the future with zest and enthusiasm. It wants you to have everything you need and more. Jupiter exposes you to worldly things. It also expands consciousness, enabling you to understand broad ideas and abstractions that can only be assimilated through social participation. Jupiter teaches you of mankind's inalienable rights. Saturn enforces those rights.

When Jupiter is met by the Sun to begin a new cycle, its natural enthusiasm is abundant. The Sun/Jupiter conjunction occurs when Jupiter is direct and at its farthest distance from Earth. Your urge for more functions spontaneously and enthusiastically. Jupiter's function is infused by Solar power. If you were born between Jupiter's Solar conjunction and the time it entered its retrograde zone, you are eager to prove your social skills. There is little objectivity regarding the potential results of your expansive urges. You discover your destination only after you have ended your journey. As with all planets, that rise before the Sun, the potential results of Jupiter's expansion are not perceived before action is taken. The urge to move forward to expand both understanding and opportunity is not well-defined. There is great charisma evident with Jupiter conjunct Sun. There is an innocence evident in your urge to experience all that life offers. Social instincts are strong and magnetism is dynamic. You want to experience the fullness of what society provides. You are a part of society's progressive trends. While you may not know where society is taking you, you are eager to move with it.

When Jupiter, by direct motion, enters its retrograde zone, its expansive urges begin to exceed positive limits. Society, as a whole, tends to get ahead of itself. If you were born during this stage of Jupiter's cycle, you are caught in social movements that can easily fall apart because of society's tendency to go too far. As Jupiter begins to slow in motion, it introduces a time of life when the urge for expansion must be tamed.

Jupiter retrogrades every 13 months and remains retrograde for 4 months. It is in its retrograde zone for 10 months of its 13 month Solar cycle. When it first enters the retrograde zone, you must begin to integrate its function into consciousness. You begin to slow down. Evaluate how social aspirations, and urges to get more from the outer world, interface with your inner values and sense of purpose. From a cyclic level, excessive activities initiated during the pre-retrograde stage of Jupiter must be confronted at the time of its retrograde station. From a natal perspective, Jupiter in the pre-retrograde zone warns you to cease moving into society solely on instinct. You need to take responsibility for your extravagant urges.

Jupiter retrograde suggests that principles upon which society is based are not always appropriate for you. What society defines as opportunity is not congruent with your inner needs. I have seen little evidence to support a common theory that people having Jupiter retrograde shy away from social activity. Many of these people are gifted with considerable social skills.

What is consistent with Jupiter retrograde is an urge to back away from society's philosophical belief systems. If you have Jupiter retrograde, you must define your own philosophies, your own morality, your own perspective on religion and cultural values. You must define a process of socialization that is uniquely your own. The lives' of Shirley MacLaine, Nostradamis, Mark Twain and Karl Marx are examples of how retrograde Jupiter operates.

Usual means by which society seeks truth, wisdom and social integration do not work for you. You need to go inside, rather than looking outside, for moral support and guidelines for expansion. You need to focus on inner expansion in order to maintain a progressive social role. This can produce acute objectivity regarding social affairs. You understand the expansive mechanisms of society because you can separate yourself from the larger arena. You must separate yourself from society's urge toward excess to discover what you can contribute to broaden society's consciousness.

Jupiter retrograde does not create the same kind of personal dilemmas, or complexes, that are evident when personal planets are retrograde. Jupiter represents a part of you that may influence personality, but is not a part of it. It is a social planet, defining the need to learn existing social principles in order to integrate with society and expand your influence. It describes what society offers you. It describes the benefits that come from socialization. It describes the wealth (material, intellectual and spiritual) that comes from taking advantage of worldly offerings. When Jupiter is retrograde, you cannot accept all that society offers. Normal social vehicles used to attain knowledge and social expansion do not transport you to where you need to go. This does not mean you are unable to attract opportunity to advance in social terms. It suggests a need to define, in your own terms, what wealth and opportunity represent. Each step you take in the outer world must be balanced with an inner step toward personal enlightenment.

Jupiter was close to Earth when you were born, bringing its blessings to you. Its power is so great, when retrograde, that you must psychologically prepare yourself for receiving its blessings. Each opportunity met in the outer world must be internalized and digested before further external opportunity can occur at a positive level. You must be aware of the personal ramifications of all society's offerings. Just because something is available, doesn't mean its good for you.

Jupiter retrograde cultivates wisdom. Its co-rulership of Pisces functions strongly when in the retrograde stage. Jupiter retrograde challenges you to challenge society's accepted beliefs and behaviors. Look beyond society to find your own truth. All that Jupiter offers is taken inside and recycled.

At the point of Jupiter's Solar opposition, it is closer to Earth than at any other time in its cycle. The opposition represents the climatic point of its entire retrograde cycle. Unless conscious (opposition) of the complexities of Jupiter in your life, you will feel out of step with society's values. Lack of conformity to established religions, for example, can result in intense faith, a profound personal belief system that carries you through life. It can also result in a sense of religious depravation, or isolation, if you fail to find peace with your own God because you are expending all of your energy trying to conform.

A dis-integrated retrograde Jupiter promotes prejudice. If you are not centered, you will be unable to merge with society. On the other hand, retrograde Jupiter can provide universal understanding because it enables you to detach from society's existing level of consciousness.

You must prepare yourself for outer expansion before you can accept opportunity from the outside world. Inner expansion must precede elevation of social influence. You are searching for wisdom. The world, as you know it, cannot provide the knowledge you seek. You are searching for opportunity and influence. But, you must first expand within.

Jupiter, when retrograde after its Solar conjunction, functions with greater consciousness. You know that your philosophical ideas are inconsistent with the mainstream of society. The Sun preceded Jupiter over the horizon on the date of your birth to light your way into the world of society. This gives you a keen understanding of what is possible to attain in worldly terms. You realize how your expansive urges operate, even though they contrast with the norm. You see the possibilities of society's future. While the social mainstream may not be ready to change its perspective, you see where current social patterns are leading. You could be ahead of your time, able to prophesy where society is heading from both a positive and negative level.

Once Jupiter turns direct, there is no longer a feeling of isolation or contradiction between your visions and the expectations of society. Until the next Solar conjunction, Jupiter functions objectively to move you ahead with the mainstream, to reap the rewards of social integration. Because Jupiter is in the last half of its Solar cycle, there is maturity evident in your urge to expand and integrate with society. You move toward society having something of value to contribute. Your objectivity regarding the expansive qualities of Jupiter, combined with your understanding of where society is headed, gives you the capacity to integrate with it without losing yourself to it.

More information on the significance of Jupiter through Pluto, in transit, is provided at the end of this chapter.

SATURN

Rudhyar called Saturn the "ring pass not." Saturn defines limits. It describes the parameters of activity society has defined as safe. It represents rules, regulations, social responsibilities and obligations that must be met in order to guarantee acceptance by society and to establish your territory within its structures. While Jupiter represents expansion, Saturn draws limits that keep you from overextending energy or reaching for unattainable goals.

Saturn is likened to a teacher who outlines lessons that must be learned. In itself, Saturn represents the part of you that wants to belong in a social sense, and wants you to be safe while functioning as a social being. It creates obstructions or restrictions when it senses you have come close to extending the boundaries it deems safe for you to live within. Saturn will not allow you to progress through the various stages of life until it has determined you are ready to learn the next lesson. It knows that you cannot jump from grade six to twelve without completing the lessons of each stage, thereby making each transition in sequential steps.

Saturn is a social planet. It describes the rules that you must follow to reach your ultimate life goals in worldly terms. Its house describes where social responsibilities will be met. Its sign describes how you approach these life lessons. Before you can free yourself from social limitations, you must first learn all there is to know about the system of which you are a part, or feel you are trapped within. Saturn requires work, effort, and self discipline. It encourages you to be responsible (able to respond) to social requirements. It rules your capacity to become an authority, respected by society. Until you have reached this level, it operates through the authoritive figures you meet in life ...your father, the legal system, schools, and all others who have authority over your life and the results of the choices you make.

When Saturn is direct, you are able to integrate with authoritive figures and define your place, or social importance, once early lessons of responsibility have been met. If retrograde, however, you find that society's rules are not congruent with your individualistic needs. Role models provided by society may lead you away from your place in the puzzle of life rather than toward it.

Saturn is always direct when conjunct the Sun. As the Sun moves away from Saturn, and Earth nears it, issues centering around social limitations and protocols must be reevaluated. Once Saturn begins to retrograde back to meet Earth, opportunity to more clearly see and assess the appropriateness of social rules and how they influence the personal life is met.

If you were born with Saturn retrograde, you entered life at a time when society was being challenged to restructure old systems of operations. Reorganization was a requirement of the moment. Your life reflects these social issues. You are acutely aware of the inadequacies of existing systems and structures.

Saturn retrograde challenges you to detach from existing social patterns or expectations in order to objectively evaluate them. Authority figures do not provide appropriate guidelines to help you establish your place in society. Often there is a sense of estrangement from the father, whose role is to provide structures for social integration and a sense of social belonging. Guidelines you need in preparation for finding your social place are not clearly defined.

Saturn provides the ability to define boundaries to protect your territory. When retrograde, it is difficult to outwardly defend your "place" because your role models were not operating in synch with your reality. It is difficult to know when, or where, you have reached responsible limits because you have not been taught how to recognize limits that appropriately define your life. On one hand, you could accept more responsibility than is rightfully yours. Or, you could shun all social responsibility and design a personal belief that it is okay for you to reject responsibility and social rules because of your lack of a positive role model. It is important to realize, when Saturn is retrograde in the natal chart, that the authoritive role models available in your early life cannot provide the direction you need to find success in worldly terms.

Because of this, you could easily let others take advantage of you. Or, at the other extreme, you might be overly defensive in protecting your territory due to inner insecurity. Saturn's role is to teach you about limits ... teach you how to say: I'll go this far and no farther. When Saturn is retrograde, your boundaries are not clearly defined. Others may not recognize when they have pushed you to your limits because your limits are not congruent with the norm. You may fluctuate when defining or defending boundaries, never knowing for sure where you should set limits and when it is appropriate to let down your guard.

In some way, you will be challenged to walk away (retrograde) from normal or usual ambitions to establish your social place. This by no means implies that you will not reach success in social terms. It suggests, however, that success, for you, comes out of non-conformity to the structures or protocols defined by the authoritive figures in your personal life or prevalent social attitudes. You must rebel against the limits society normally sets on its participants in order to find your place within it. You must evaluate your separateness from the mainstream before finding where you fit in it. This is particularly evident when Saturn and the Sun are in opposition, but applies to Saturn throughout its entire retrograde stage. You must play a part in reorganizing existing social rules and attitudes.

It is interesting to note that Saturn is free from its retrograde zone for only about three weeks of its entire solar cycle. It is retrograde for about 4 1/2 months of its 12 1/2 month solar cycle. From a collective perspective, this demonstrates the slow, but persistent and steady, growth patterns of society.

As retrograde Saturn approaches the opposition to the Sun, greater awareness is developed regarding the difference between personal purpose (Sun) and social expectations or tutoring (Saturn). What you need to accomplish to find personal satisfaction in life (Sun), seems counter to what the world has attempted to lead you toward (Saturn). You must realize the importance of functioning in a manner that is acceptable to society without ignoring your own truth.

If you were born between the time Saturn was direct and conjunct the Sun and the time it entered its retrograde zone, you are strongly influenced by society's rules. You have been powerfully influenced by Saturn's messages regarding responsibility. You are conscientious of social protocols. Strong authority figures have influenced your life. In youth, your consciousness may have been obscured because of the strong Saturn disciplines to which you were exposed. While Saturn's function is infused by the Solar rays, the Solar energies are often dimmed by the strong Saturnian forces that shape your life. You are instinctively living out Saturn's principles of discipline and self protection. When Saturn is direct, and the Sun is moving toward its opposition, there is little objectivity regarding Saturn's influence on consciousness. There is little awareness of where Saturn's disciplines are leading you. While there is a driving urge to find your place in society, there is little objectivity regarding where you belong. In some way, Saturn forces, whether positive or negative, are leading you to where you belong in the social structure. You realize this, however, only after you have established your territory and found your niche.

Saturn, when direct, implies that you are instinctively moving with the flow of society's mainstream. Once Saturn has entered its retrograde zone, however, existing social attitudes must be examined more objectively. The closer Earth moves to conjoin Saturn, and the Sun nears Saturn's opposition, the stronger Saturn's forces operate until it becomes important to seriously examine society's systems and structures to find how they shape your life. The capacity to understand social influences becomes stronger as Saturn turns retrograde and moves to its Solar opposition. This objectivity can only be developed by detaching yourself from the system ... distance enables you to see social patterns unfold. If you try to conform and merge with existing social structures, you are unable to clearly see the whole system. You must stand back to get a total picture of what the system represents. A piece of a jigsaw puzzle cannot see the picture of the whole puzzle as long as it remains only a piece. Only by separating yourself from the pieces of society can you objectively evaluate its credibility or value.

Retrograde Saturn, like all retrograde planets, functions differently before its Solar opposition than when after. If born with Saturn retrograde, but prior to its Solar opposition, you see significant differences between your personal perspective of success and society's concepts of success. But, you may not have a clear picture of how these differences shape your life or where you are going because of them.

Saturn, in the second half of its retrograde stage, provides greater objectivity. The crisis involved in defining your needs as separate from conditioned beliefs is less stressful because greater consciousness is evident. Your challenge is to develop confidence in what you have to offer society apart from what it already has, and move into the world to contribute to it by offering new systems for growth.

More information on the significance of Saturn's retrograde transit is provided later in this chapter.

THE COLLECTIVE PLANETS

The outer planets, Uranus, Neptune and Pluto, deal with energies that extend beyond personality or socially conditioned personality projections. These planets represent collective energies that have global influences. They are non-personal planets, ruling forces at work in life that extend beyond personality or culture. Uranus, Neptune, and Pluto urge you to look at your life in reference to some larger, evolutionary pattern. They challenge you to view life from a larger than ego perspective. They encourage you to examine and define how you make a difference in the world and how, or if, you are contributing to social and global evolution and survival.

It is interesting to note that Neptune and Pluto are always in their retrograde zones. Uranus, the bridge between the conscious and unconscious, is free of the retrograde zone for less than one day each year. These planets, in transit, always repeat an aspect to a natal planet at least three times ... once during their first direct transit over a specific degree, once by retrograde motion and again in the direct transit as they move into a new Solar cycle.

Because collective planets function outside ego, the differences between their direct and retrograde stages are subtle. Some astrologers argue that the functions of collective planets can become conscious functions of personality. Certainly, those who are more "evolved," or function at a high level, have attuned themselves to the principles they represent. However, once Uranus, for example, has awakened you to a new way of life, or you become a "reborn" individual as a result of Pluto's regenerative powers, these new aspects of self become part of consciousness, no longer under the rule of the outer planets. Once Uranus has broken barriers, it has done its job. Once you have integrated these new experiences into your life pattern, they are henceforth ruled by planets inside the orb of Saturn.

Uranus rules change. Once change has occurred, the issues it has brought to your conscious attention are no longer a Uranus factor. Uranus moves on to create further reform. In other words, the outer planets deal with the unconscious. They rule forces at work in life that are outside personal control. Control only enters the experiences these planets rule in regard to how you respond.

Collective planets describe global issues that extend beyond one's particular society ... issues that influence not just an individual, or a society, but the entire Earth, and possibility the solar system. Collective planets show how conditions on our planet are changing. You, as a part of the larger structure, must adapt to these collective changes. The outer planets remind us that we are all a part of the larger picture. We all play some part, no matter how great or small, in its evolution or destruction. Uranus, Neptune and Pluto rule energies that awaken you to that reality. They often indicate, particularly by transit, where and when conditions outside personal control, shape your life. While you may be unable to control these forces, you can direct them, use them, and learn from them. By welcoming these transforming experiences, you evolve. But once you have personalized the experiences they bring, once you have been changed by the events or illuminations, once you have integrated the new experiences they provide, those very experiences are no longer ruled by the collective planets. They have entered into the ring of Saturn. The outer planets enter your life to give you a new experience, a new perspective. Then they move on to explore new territory. Their intrinsic functions are always outside consciousness.

When collective planets are retrograde, they are closer to our planet than when direct. Individuals and societies meet opportunities to examine issues that influence all life on our planet. Everyone is challenged to be more objective about life issues that extend beyond ego and personal control. From a cyclic level, outer planets, when retrograde, suggest times of global transition. In the natal chart, these planets encourage you to stand back and examine what larger-than-life issues must be addressed. The point of the Solar opposition is the apex of the retrograde stage. Even if a retrograde collective planet in your chart is not in opposition to the Sun, the degree at which the opposition occurs is important to consider. It points to the main collective crisis needing to be examined. It is this crisis that you live out in your personal life.

URANUS

The retrograde pattern of Uranus is interesting to observe. The point at which it turns retrograde in one Solar cycle is the same point at which it will turn direct in its next cycle. For this reason, Uranus always aspects each planet, within a one degree orb, three times. Natal planets at the degree at which its stations occur are particularly emphasized.

Uranus retrograde challenges you to stand back and examine your urge to reform. Are you rebelling because it's the thing to do? Or, are you really aware of the need for change? Do you invite chaos into your life for the sake of excitement only? Or is there a valid reason for the changes you attract or create? Before rebelling against the status quo, be sure you understand the full import of the status. Before tearing down structures in life, be sure you understand the full significance of these structures. The only way to do so is to enter the structure, or system, you want to change. Doing so gives you more information about what actually needs reformed.

You will attract unstable, unexpected, or chaotic conditions in the area of life described by the house of Uranus, whether it is retrograde or direct. If retrograde, because Uranus is near to our planet, you must be prepared to take personal responsibility for the changes you create, or those imposed on you by outside forces. As with all retrograde planets, you are challenged to deal with Uranus' energy in a way that is unique to the norm. You are challenged to stand back and observe before taking action. Use this powerful planet objectively.

While you may not be able to control what Uranus brings to your life, you must become conscious of how you direct its energy. When the world around you is in the throws of change, rebelling against outdated or misused systems and rules, you are challenged to observe in order to get a clear picture of where the rebellion is leading. Unlike direct Uranus, which encourages instinctive reaction that requires risk, you must have a vision of a potential outcome of the changes occurring around you and within you.

Realize that the urge to create change is strengthened when Uranus is retrograde. The urge to reform is strong. This can manifest in positive reformation or in eccentric behavior that separates you from the masses and its perspective of what needs changed. John F. Kennedy had Uranus stationary retrograde. Hitler also had Uranus retrograde. Through their lives we see the extremes of Uranus at work. Kennedy directed his Uranian energies to promote equal rights and create reform. Hitler's ego interfered with the energy trying to function through it. Uranus still functioned, and powerfully so. His life played a significant role in collective chaos. Both Hitler and Kennedy were strong social reformers. Both allowed collective influences to shape and guide their lives. Hitler demonstrated the negativity in the collective while Kennedy lived out the role of the humanitarian.

Of those well-known in the astrological arena, Evangeline Adams had Uranus retrograde. She changed the laws in New York City by going to court to fight for astrology to be legalized. This is classic example of working within the system to change or reform it, rather than operating outside its laws. Rudhyar also had Uranus retrograde. He gave credibility to astrology because of his academic accomplishments.

This is not to say that Uranus direct is not a powerful force in life. Direct Uranus infers that as the collective changes, you move with it. A powerfully aspected direct Uranus can operate as potently as when retrograde. However, it functions differently. Uranus, when direct, seldom needs to become a part of what it wants to change. As instinct is strong, objective evaluation of the need to reform is less needed. Circumstances met in life "lead" you toward finding your individuality. Things happen in your world and you react to them. You don't need to examine, you simply react. You live out the pure Uranus concepts.

As mentioned earlier, the function of Uranus is not a conscious one. The differences between direct and retrograde Uranus do not show in personality. However, upon examining how you respond to crises, or how you react to what comes to you with lightening force (inspiration or accident), its direct or retrograde condition is evident.

NEPTUNE

Neptune's function is also intensified when found retrograde in the natal chart. It requires objectivity regarding all issues of faith. Rather than moving ahead into the unknown on blind faith, Neptune retrograde challenges you to question, to attempt to "unveil the mysteries of life" by examining them and testing their authenticity.

Neptune, when retrograde, is no less illusive than when direct. Its energy is no less dissolving. In fact, due to its nearness to our planet, Neptune's energy is magnified when retrograde. Because of the intensification of the Neptune function, there is a need to understand how its energies not only influence your personal life, but how it inspires, or confuses, the masses.

The unconscious is stimulated by retrograde Neptune. Dream activity is often intensified. Messages are trying to get through from the unconscious to help you dissolve boundaries that inhibit inspiration and faith. Rather than repressing Neptune's function, the retrograde condition enhances it. Everything that Neptune represents becomes an "issue" in your life. All things that cannot be proven real, all that has no form, structure, or physical value, are ruled by Neptune. Commonly accepted attitudes about faith must be explored. What society simply accepts as truth, or fears because of lack of understanding, are things you examine and question. You find truth, faith, and acceptance using methods that are alternative to the norm.

The lives of Carl Jung, Martin Luther King, Marc Edmond Jones and Aleister Crowley all exemplify the truest essence of Neptune retrograde. All were compelled to pursue dream-work at some level ... Jung studied and wrote about dreams, Jones designed the Sabian Symbols as tools to explore the unconscious. Martin Luther King's life revolved around his dream for a better life. Aleister Crowley designed a Tarot Deck saturated with symbolism. These people all left society with powerful Neptunian messages. All had Neptune retrograde.

Others, in their search of Neptune, found its truths through drugs, phobic behaviors or escapism. The point to be stressed with Neptune retrograde is that it functions powerfully in life. Those born with Neptune retrograde are compelled to address Neptunian issues. Its nearness to our planet, when retrograde, calls your attention to its message. How you choose to listen to, and interpret, its symbolic messages is an individual choice.

Neptune can bring true spirituality and an understanding of your "connectedness" with the universe. It reminds you that all rivers flow into the same oceans. Fear of losing yourself to the collective leads to phobias, neurosis, or escapism. On the other hand, giving yourself to the collective, and losing yourself in the process, is another one of Neptune's traps.

Neptune is illusive. Neptune is confusing. Neptune rules both faith and fear, dreams and illusions, acceptance and escapism. If you have Neptune retrograde, these issues are important for you to examine. You must view them in your own terms. What is blindly accepted by the norm must be questioned and addressed from your own unique perspective.

When dreams are realized, they no longer exist. Dreams (Neptune) have become reality (Saturn). When fears are faced, there is no more fear. Neptune rules what has no substance. Once Neptune's visions take form, they are no longer Neptunian. New dreams, new visions, new fears, new ego-dissolving conditions begin to present themselves. When retrograde, this process must be examined. The fears, fantasies, inspiration, or faith, stimulated by Neptune in the natal chart, evolve, just as all aspects of life either evolve or self destruct. If your Neptune is retrograde, you are challenged to analyze your fears, examine your faith, evaluate your visions. Find meaning in life by seeking your spiritual source.

PLUTO

Because of Pluto's eccentric orbit, it can spend as few as 11 years, or as many as 30 years, in a sign. The rate of its motion corresponds to the rate of evolution or growth taking place on the planet. For example, Pluto was discovered in 1930, during the time of the Great Depression. At the time of its discovery, Pluto was beginning to move closer to Neptune. Since that time, it has entered Neptune's orbit. It is now in the sign of Scorpio, where it completes its total transit through Scorpio in only 11 years.

It is interesting to equate the rate of Pluto's motion to the rate of social change. For example, as Pluto increases in speed, the rate at which significant global events unfold also accelerates. People living on Earth at this time in history are experiencing three times the rate of change than those living in the 1800's. In the span of one life-time, the world has gone from the horse and buggy to manned space exploration.

We have reached a point in our evolutionary growth where the entire planet must comprehend how global influences affect not only mankind as a whole, but each individual on the planet. As the world closed in on World War II, people were forced to recognize Pluto's message.

We must all recognize how small and delicate our planet is. We must all recognize our individual roles in humanity's larger purpose. The process of global evolution and change, due to technology developed in the second half of the 20th Century, has intensified. People must now recognize, not only the responsibilities they have to sustain their individual lives, but with the state of the world. Global survival has reached a critical state ... a state that requires the attention of all.

Could it be possible that each of us, individually, represent one cell in the body of humanity? If so, Pluto describes the importance of your place in the larger picture. Are you contributing to global survival and evolution? Or is your "cell" contributing to its disease and ultimate decay? How does your life reflect the conditions of our planet? How have you been influenced by your generation and its purpose (sign)? Where (house) are you living out that purpose? What parts of humanity are you purging and helping to regenerate, to give new power?

Because it takes Pluto longer to orbit the Sun than any other planet, the changes it provokes take time. Pluto represents challenges met, not by one individual, but by a generation of people born not only to evolve individually, but collectively. Pluto represents the ultimate power, the "God-power," the power to create, to destroy, to evolve or to perish. You will live out its purpose regardless of your level of consciousness. You may be a living example of society's sins, or you might be an example of its future potential.

Because Pluto is now well within Neptune's orbit, its role is becoming more a part of society's consciousness. People are now aware of the need for conservation, recycling, environmental control, etc. They are becoming aware of the vulnerability and fragility of the planet. People are now questioning their roles in the larger picture. They ask: how does my life make a difference? While people have always lived out the purpose of their time, the changing roles of their generations, they must now do so with greater awareness.

The sign Pluto occupied at the time of your birth describes the need for change met by your generation as a whole. If Pluto is in an early degree, you were born at the beginning of some major global shifts in consciousness. If born with Pluto in a later degree, you were born well into the period of social transition. These global issues involved:

Pluto in Gemini: introduction of mass communication that changed the world.

Pluto in Cancer: major changes in the family structure.

Pluto in Leo: liberation in self expression.

Pluto in Virgo: technological developments that change the course of history.

Pluto in Libra: changing attitudes about equal rights, women's liberation and major changes in social attitudes about marriage and relationships.

Pluto in Scorpio: major issues regarding the use of sexual power, nuclear power, waste disposal, recycling, man's potential to destroy.

The house Pluto occupies describes the area of life where these collective changes influence your personal experiences. Here, you will live out the prophesies of your generation. This house shows where, positively or negatively, you will play a part (big or small) in shaping humanity's future.

You are living out the problems, the challenges, and the promises of the future. You may feel you are a "vehicle" used to activate or mobilize some greater-than-personal purpose. Regardless of whether your Pluto is direct or retrograde, it will function through your life.

Pluto is retrograde for five months of its Solar cycle. It is always in the retrograde zone. The differences between its retrograde and direct conditions are very subtle. Because it is retrograde almost half of the time, its direct or retrograde condition has no bearing on personality, nor does it influence your ability to function at a social level.

Pluto's role is to create global regeneration or evolution. When retrograde, the need for social reform, demonstrated by your generation as a whole, may be incongruent with the larger role you need to play in life's drama. You must observe the path that the world is taking. In the process, you see global change more objectively than those having Pluto direct. You must realize that change cannot occur unless each individual recognizes the importance of his/her own actions. You are challenged to make personal changes that promote global survival. While those having Pluto direct live out Pluto's regenerative powers in what they do, you must demonstrate Pluto's message in who you are. You must experience personal rebirth before finding opportunity to play a part in global regeneration.

RETROGRADE TRANSITS OF TRANS-PERSONAL PLANETS

Because Jupiter and Saturn are social planets, their transiting retrograde stages do not have the same degree of personal impact as those of Mercury, Venus and Mars. The transits of Uranus, Neptune and Pluto are even more obscure in their personal significance. Collective planets are retrograde almost half of the time. Their retrograde periods mark times of social and collective transition. This is not to say that the retrograde periods of these planets have no personal meaning. They don't, however, make the obvious impact on everyday activities as do Mercury, Venus and Mars.

Jupiter turns retrograde when society's urge for expansion has exceeded positive limits. In some way, society, as a whole, has gotten ahead of itself in its urge to expand. From a personal perspective, Jupiter's retrograde transits are best spent using its expansive energy for internal growth. Its retrogradation marks times during the year when you need to become more aware of the personal ramifications that result from the opportunities society offers. This is a time to expand consciousness in preparation for social expansion once it turns direct. Those who never heed the retrograde messages of Jupiter frequently find themselves psychologically unprepared to fully use and appreciate opportunities available within the social spectrum. Rather than moving with a society that has over extended itself, stop to look where it is headed and how its tendency toward excess could cause eventual problems.

The basic implication of the retrograde phenomenon applies to all planets ... personal, social or collective. Jupiter retrograde marks a time of inner growth. It is of vital importance to expand your security boundaries while Jupiter is retrograde in order to greet, and fully use, the opportunities for external expansion this planet offers when direct.

As an example, consider the lives of people who, for one reason or another, meet experiences that rapidly take them from "rags to riches." If these people are not emotionally or psychologically prepared to make this leap, crisis is experienced. If they do not expand their inner sense of worth, they cannot effectively deal with financial windfalls. All new, potentially expansive opportunities, be they material, emotional or mental, must be internalized and evaluated with reference to their personal import. The results of opportunities must be assimilated for creative growth to be realized. Retrograde periods mark times when you are encouraged to take responsibility and "own" what society has offered. If you evaluate the offerings provided by Jupiter, and find them to be incongruent with your personal values, the retrograde periods challenge you to walk away from society's promises and find your own truth.

Saturn's retrograde periods challenge you to stop and reevaluate the structures and rules that have defined the parameters of your life up to this point. Awareness is the keynote. This is a time to restructure and rebuild. For those functioning in the world of business or politics, this marks an excellent time for reformulating the systems you have used up to this point and reevaluate the protocols you have previously used to make business decisions. If some rebuilding is not done during the retrograde periods of Saturn, the competition will soon surpass these individuals in their quests for success.

At a personal level, this is a time to evaluate where you fit in, and where you don't, in reference to the rules that influence your life. Are you allowing society's boundaries to limit your personal power?

At another level, you need to ask yourself: are you using your power in a way that is acceptable within the rules defined by your world? While Saturn is retrograde in transit, you are challenged to be more socially aware. At the time of the Saturn/Sun opposition, occurring approximately mid way through its retrograde phase, awareness reaches its peak. The houses in which this opposition occurs provide further definition to the retrograde challenge.

The collective planets, Uranus, Neptune and Pluto are even more obscure from a personal perspective. Their retrograde periods mark times when you are challenged to stop and look at where the world, as a whole, is headed. Look beyond what is happening only in your society, to consider the evolution and changes occurring at a global level. Then ask yourself where and how you fit into these changes. Pay particular attention to global issues and realize that, if only in an obscure way, you are plugged into the larger cycles of mankind. How is the shift in global consciousness shaping your life? What are you doing to contribute to global issues?

Obviously, many people never make a conscious connection between world change and personal transformation. The world, as a whole, changes slowly but continually. If you don't adjust and contribute to global change, you cannot survive. In most cases, however, these changes occur so gradually that they are not a part of our daily thoughts.

As an example of how collective planets operate when direct and retrograde, consider the events of in September, 1989. Saturn, a social planet, and Uranus and Neptune, collective planets, all turned direct in the sign of Capricorn. This marked a time of massive and active change (direct) that would shake (Uranus) and dissolve (Neptune) the very foundations of governmental structures (Saturn). The focus of planetary energy was on outer, overt, direct social reform. Massive political unrest and revolution was experienced in the eastern block countries.

By the spring of 1990, these planets turned retrograde, marking a time when the forward thrust toward reformation was forced to slow down so that the societies influenced by the changes could adjust. The historical events occurring from the fall of 1989 to the spring of 1990 were marked by the rare conjunction of these three powerful planets in a sign ruling government and structure (Capricorn). Uranus and Neptune, representing the collective, merged with the preexisting structures defined by Saturn. These structures were forced to change. The results of these changes became a part of the collective consciousness during their retrograde transits.

The outer planets are not personal. Yet, each individual is in some way affected by the changes they provoke. The retrograde periods of the outer planets will not create any evident changes in your personal life unless they make their stations on powerful degrees in your chart. They are, however, always interesting to observe from a societal point of view, and equally interesting when comparing these global changes to the personal events occurring in your life.

For a more thorough evaluation of these planets, when retrograde, I refer you to the sections describing their natal import.

PROGRESSIONS

It is interesting to watch planets move from one Stage into another by secondary progressions. Secondary progressions move planets ahead in the chart based on the theory that each day after birth equals one day of life.

While transits indicate life changes promoted by outside circumstances, secondary progressions describe an internal growth process. They indicate, by their progression through degrees, signs, and houses, a maturing process that enables you to become more than what your birth chart promises.

For example, you may have been born having no planets occupying Mutable signs. This indicates a potential difficulty in adapting to change. By progression, as planets move into the Mutable signs, you learn, through experience, to adapt and adjust. While the natal chart sets the tone for life, secondary progressions add new dimensions to life. Secondary progressions describe internal unfoldment.

Transits, on the other hand, indicate external conditions that constantly challenge you to grow. Transits tend to be more forceful in their influence because they describe issues that are often outside personal control. They are stimulants, offered by the outside world, that encourage personal change.

Social and collective planets (Jupiter through Pluto) progress very slowly. They seldom make major aspects to natal planets, or move from one Stage of their Solar cycle into another. The personal planets (Moon through Mars), however, progress significantly and are always worth watching.

If you were born with Mercury retrograde, it will turn direct, by progression, sometime before your mid 20's. Venus and Mars may take longer to change direction by progression. The years when planets make their stations (either from direct to retrograde, or retrograde to direct) often mark important times of change in an individual's life. Likewise, when planets change from one Stage of their Solar cycle to another, they begin to take on the qualities characterized by the progressed Stage.

While in most cases, when dealing with progressions, we watch progressed planets aspect natal planets, it is also important to consider them as a progressed-to-progressed phenomenon. The changes in expression of these planetary energies are often subtle. However, they always produce interesting shifts in an individual's perspective of, or means of acting out, the planetary energy. For example, you may have been born with a planet direct and free from its retrograde zone. By secondary progression, it might move into the retrograde zone, marking a time when it is easy to over-project the energy of the planet. Likewise, a planet may change from retrograde to direct, indicating a time in your life when you begin to experience less need for introspection.

Important events frequently correspond to years when planets change direction by progression. The years when this occurs should be noted, and the occurrences of those years evaluated with reference to the issues brought to play by the activated planet. As with transits, orbs for progressions must be kept very narrow. A one degree orb is generally recommended.

IN CONCLUSION

While there are similarities in the outer manifestation of intercepted signs and retrograde planets, they occur due to very different astrological phenomenons. The location, or environment, of the birth place has little affect on the retrograde condition. Rather than finding an environment that does not adequately support individual development, retrogradation infers just the opposite. When planets are retrograde, you are challenged to objectively evaluate your individual needs apart from environmental or social trends and tendencies. Often it becomes necessary to "turn your back" on social customs in order to find yourself. In either case, individuality becomes an issue.

When you look away from the mainstream, you find sources of inspiration, and define concepts for living, that are uniquely your own. Both intercepted and retrograde planets encourage originality and individuality, but both do so in completely different ways and for different purposes.

Intercepted signs can be defined as personal needs that society does not readily recognize. *Interceptions work from the inside out.* Retrograde planets describe functions of personality that work counter to the norm or mainstream of society. Rather than being an environmental factor, retrograde planets describe the need for introspection. *Retrograde planets take the outside in.*

It is important that you do not fall into the trap of considering retrogrades or interceptions as weaknesses or handicaps in the chart. These conditions can result in creative genius once they are understood and integrated. Without them, society as a whole might never evolve, new concepts for living might never be defined. If everyone fit the status quo, life would remain static ... no new discoveries would be made. Appreciate your interceptions and/or retrograde planets. While they may be frustrating and, at times, debilitating, they are also your mark of individuality and describe your potential to create.

RETROGRADE PLANETS

APPENDIX

The following Tables track Mercury through Saturn through their retrograde zones from 1920 through 1999. Tables are based on GMT and are accurate to within one degree. Allow a one day orb on either side of their retrograde and direct stations.

MERCURY

Enter Retrograde Zone...	02/25/20 at 21 Pisces	06/26/20 at 29 Cancer	10/13/20 at 16 Scorpio
STATIONARY RETROGRADE...	03/10/20 at 04 **ARIES**	07/13/20 at 10 **LEO**	11/05/20 at 02 **SAGITTARIUS**
Solar Conjunction.......	03/20/20 at 29 Pisces	07/27/20 at 03 Leo	11/16/20 at 23 Scorpio
STATIONARY DIRECT.......	04/02/20 at 21 Pisces	08/06/20 at 29 Cancer	11/25/20 at 16 Scorpio
Leave Retrograde Zone...	04/21/20 at 04 Aries	08/20/20 at 10 Leo	12/12/20 at 02 Sagittarius
Enter Retrograde Zone...	02/07/21 at 03 Pisces	06/08/21 at 11 Cancer	09/29/21 at 00 Scorpio
STATIONARY RETROGRADE...	02/21/21 at 17 **PISCES**	06/21/21 at 20 **CANCER**	10/20/21 at 16 **SCORPIO**
Solar Conjunction.......	03/03/21 at 12 Pisces	07/08/21 at 15 Cancer	10/31/21 at 07 Scorpio
STATIONARY DIRECT.......	03/16/21 at 03 Pisces	07/19/21 at 11 Cancer	11/09/21 at 00 Scorpio
Leave Retrograde Zone...	04/04/21 at 17 Pisces	08/02/21 at 20 Cancer	11/25/21 at 16 Scorpio
Enter Retrograde Zone...	01/21/22 at 16 Aquarius	05/21/22 at 22 Gemini	09/12/22 at 14 Libra
STATIONARY RETROGRADE...	02/05/22 at 01 **PISCES**	06/05/22 at 00 **CANCER**	10/03/22 at 00 **SCORPIO**
Solar Conjunction.......	02/14/22 at 24 Aquarius	06/18/22 at 26 Gemini	10/15/22 at 21 Libra
STATIONARY DIRECT.......	02/27/22 at 16 Aquarius	06/29/22 at 22 Gemini	10/24/22 at 14 Libra
Leave Retrograde Zone...	03/19/22 at 01 Pisces	07/14/22 at 00 Cancer	11/09/22 at 00 Scorpio
Enter Retrograde Zone...	01/04/23 at 29 Capricorn	05/03/23 at 02 Gemini	08/26/23 at 28 Virgo
STATIONARY RETROGRADE...	01/20/23 at 14 **AQUARIUS**	05/17/23 at 10 **GEMINI**	09/16/23 at 13 **LIBRA**
Solar Conjunction.......	01/29/23 at 08 Aquarius	05/27/23 at 06 Gemini	09/29/23 at 05 Libra
STATIONARY DIRECT.......	02/10/23 at 29 Capricorn	06/10/23 at 02 Gemini	10/08/23 at 28 Virgo
Leave Retrograde Zone...	03/01/23 at 14 Aquarius	06/25/23 at 10 Gemini	10/22/23 at 13 Libra
Enter Retrograde Zone...	12/18/23 at 12 Capricorn	04/13/24 at 12 Taurus	08/08/24 at 12 Virgo
STATIONARY RETROGRADE...	01/04/24 at 28 **CAPRICORN**	04/27/24 at 21 **TAURUS**	08/29/24 at 26 **VIRGO**
Solar Conjunction.......	01/13/24 at 21 Capricorn	05/08/24 at 17 Taurus	09/11/24 at 18 Virgo
STATIONARY DIRECT.......	01/24/24 at 12 Capricorn	05/21/24 at 12 Taurus	09/20/24 at 12 Virgo
Leave Retrograde Zone...	02/12/24 at 28 Capricorn	06/06/24 at 21 Taurus	10/04/24 at 26 Virgo
Enter Retrograde Zone...	11/30/24 at 26 Sagittarius	03/25/25 at 22 Aries	07/23/25 at 26 Leo
STATIONARY RETROGRADE...	12/18/24 at 13 **CAPRICORN**	04/08/25 at 02 **TAURUS**	08/11/25 at 09 **VIRGO**
Solar Conjunction.......	12.27/24 at 05 Capricorn	04/18/25 at 28 Aries	08/25/25 at 01 Virgo
STATIONARY DIRECT.......	01/06/25 at 26 Sagittarius	05/02/25 at 22 Aries	09/04/25 at 26 Leo
Leave Retrograde Zone...	01/26/25 at 13 Capricorn	05/19/25 at 02 Taurus	09/18/25 at 09 Virgo
Enter Retrograde Zone...	11/13/25 at 10 Sagittarius	03/07/26 at 02 Aries	07/06/26 at 09 Leo
STATIONARY RETROGRADE...	12/02/25 at 27 **SAGITTARIUS**	03/21/26 at 14 **ARIES**	07/24/26 at 21 **LEO**
Solar Conjunction.......	12/11/25 at 19 Sagittarius	03/31/26 at 09 Aries	08/07/26 at 14 Leo
STATIONARY DIRECT.......	12/21/25 at 10 Sagittarius	04/13/26 at 02 Aries	08/17/26 at 09 Leo
Leave Retrograde Zone...	01/09/26 at 27 Sagittarius	05/02/26 at 14 Aries	08/31/26 at 21 Leo
Enter Retrograde Zone...	10/27/26 at 25 Scorpio	02/17/27 at 13 Pisces	06/18/27 at 21 Cancer
STATIONARY RETROGRADE...	11/15/26 at 11 **SAGITTARIUS**	03/04/27 at 27 **PISCES**	07/06/27 at 02 **LEO**
Solar Conjunction.......	11/25/26 at 03 Sagittarius	03/13/27 at 22 Pisces	07/19/27 at 26 Cancer
STATIONARY DIRECT.......	12/05/26 at 25 Scorpio	03/27/27 at 13 Pisces	07/30/27 at 21 Cancer
Leave Retrograde Zone...	12/23/26 at 11 Sagittarius	04/15/27 at 27 Pisces	08/13/27 at 02 Leo

MERCURY

Enter Retrograde Zone...	10/10/27 at 09 Scorpio	01/31/28 at 26 Aquarius	05/31/28 at 03 Cancer
STATIONARY RETROGRADE...	**10/30/27 at 25 SCORPIO**	02/15/28 at 10 **PISCES**	06/16/28 at 12 **CANCER**
Solar Conjunction.......	11/10/27 at 16 Scorpio	02/24/28 at 04 Pisces	06/29/28 at 07 Cancer
STATIONARY DIRECT.......	11/19/27 at 09 Scorpio	03/08/28 at 26 Aquarius	07/10/28 at 03 Cancer
Leave Retrograde Zone...	12/06/27 at 25 Scorpio	03/28/28 at 10 Pisces	07/25/28 at 12 Cancer
Enter Retrograde Zone...	09/12/28 at 23 Libra	01/13/29 at 08 Aquarius	05/13/29 at 13 Gemini
STATIONARY RETROGRADE...	10/12/28 at 09 **SCORPIO**	01/29/29 at 24 **AQUARIUS**	05/28/29 at 22 **GEMINI**
Solar Conjunction.......	10/24/28 at 00 Scorpio	02/07/29 at 17 Aquarius	06/09/29 at 18 Gemini
STATIONARY DIRECT.......	11/02/28 at 23 Libra	02/19/29 at 08 Aquarius	06/21/29 at 13 Gemini
Leave Retrograde Zone...	11/18/28 at 09 Scorpio	03/11/29 at 24 Aquarius	07/06/29 at 22 Gemini
Enter Retrograde Zone...	09/05 29 at 08 Libra	12/27/29 at 22 Capricorn	04/24/30 at 23 Taurus
STATIONARY RETROGRADE...	09/25/29 at 23 **LIBRA**	01/13/30 at 08 **AQUARIUS**	05/08/30 at 02 **GEMINI**
Solar Conjunction.......	10/08/29 at 14 Libra	01/22/30 at 01 Aquarius	05/20/30 at 28 Taurus
STATIONARY DIRECT.......	10/17/29 at 08 Libra	02/02/30 at 22 Capricorn	06/02/30 at 23 Taurus
Leave Retrograde Zone...	11/01/29 at 23 Libra	02/22/30 at 08 Aquarius	06/17/30 at 02 Gemini
Enter Retrograde Zone...	08/18/30 at 22 Virgo	12/11/30 at 06 Capricorn	04/05/31 at 03 Taurus
STATIONARY RETROGRADE...	09/08/30 at 06 **LIBRA**	12/27/30 at 22 **CAPRICORN**	04/19/31 at 13 **TAURUS**
Solar Conjunction.......	09/21/30 at 28 Virgo	01/06/31 at 14 Capricorn	04/30/31 at 09 Taurus
STATIONARY DIRECT.......	09/30/30 at 22 Virgo	01/17/31 at 06 Capricorn	05/13/31 at 03 Taurus
Leave Retrograde Zone...	10/15/30 at 06 Libra	02/05/31 at 22 Capricorn	05/30/31 at 13 Taurus
Enter Retrograde Zone...	08/02/31 at 05 Virgo	11/24/31 at 20 Sagittarius	03/17/32 at 13 Aries
STATIONARY RETROGRADE...	08/22/31 at 19 **VIRGO**	12/11/31 at 06 **CAPRICORN**	03/31/32 at 25 **ARIES**
Solar Conjunction.......	09/04/31 at 11 Virgo	12/21/31 at 28 Sagittarius	04/10/32 at 20 Aries
STATIONARY DIRECT.......	09/14/31 at 05 Virgo	12/31/31 at 20 Sagittarius	04/24/32 at 13 Aries
Leave Retrograde Zone...	09/28/31 at 19 Virgo	01/19/32 at 06 Capricorn	05/12/32 at 25 Aries
Enter Retrograde Zone...	07/15/32 at 19 Leo	11/06/32 at 04 Sagittarius	02/27/33 at 24 Pisces
STATIONARY RETROGRADE...	08/03/32 at 01 **VIRGO**	11/24/32 at 20 **SAGITTARIUS**	03/13/33 at 07 **ARIES**
Solar Conjunction.......	08/17/32 at 24 Leo	12/04/32 at 12 Sagittarius	03/23/33 at 02 Aries
STATIONARY DIRECT.......	08/27/32 at 19 Leo	12/14/32 at 04 Sagittarius	04/05/33 at 24 Pisces
Leave Retrograde Zone...	09/10/32 at 01 Virgo	01/01/33 at 20 Sagittarius	04/24/33 at 07 Aries
Enter Retrograde Zone...	06/29/33 at 02 Leo	10/01/33 at 18 Scorpio	02/10/34 at 06 Pisces
STATIONARY RETROGRADE...	07/16/33 at 13 **LEO**	11/08/33 at 04 **SAGITTARIUS**	02/24/34 at 20 **PISCES**
Solar Conjunction.......	07/30/33 at 06 Leo	11/18/33 at 26 Scorpio	03/06/34 at 14 Pisces
STATIONARY DIRECT.......	08/09/33 at 02 Leo	11/28/33 at 18 Scorpio	03/19/34 at 06 Pisces
Leave Retrograde Zone...	08/23/33 at 13 Leo	12/15/33 at 04 Sagittarius	04/07/34 at 20 Pisces
Enter Retrograde Zone...	06/11/34 at 14 Cancer	10/02/34 at 02 Scorpio	01/23/35 at 18 Aquarius
STATIONARY RETROGRADE...	06/28/34 at 23 **CANCER**	10/22/34 at 18 **SCORPIO**	02/08/35 at 03 **PISCES**
Solar Conjunction.......	07/11/34 at 18 Cancer	11/03/34 at 10 Scorpio	02/17/35 at 27 Aquarius
STATIONARY DIRECT.......	07/22/34 at 14 Cancer	11/12/34 at 02 Scorpio	03/02/35 at 18 Aquarius
Leave Retrograde Zone...	08/05/34 at 23 Cancer	11/28/34 at 18 Scorpio	03/21/35 at 03 Pisces

MERCURY

Enter Retrograde Zone...	05/24/35 at 25 Gemini	09/15/35 at 17 Libra	01/06/36 at 01 Aquarius
STATIONARY RETROGRADE...	06/08/35 at 04 **CANCER**	10/06/35 at 02 **SCORPIO**	01/23/36 at 17 **AQUARIUS**
Solar Conjunction.......	06/21/35 at 29 Gemini	10/18/35 at 23 Libra	01/03/36 at 10 Aquarius
STATIONARY RETROGRADE...	07/03/35 at 25 Gemini	10/27/35 at 17 Libra	02/13/36 at 01 Aquarius
Leave Retrograde Zone...	07/18/35 at 04 Cancer	11/11/35 at 02 Scorpio	03/04/36 at 17 Aquarius
Enter Retrograde Zone...	05/05/36 at 05 Gemini	08/28/36 at 01 Libra	12/20/36 at 15 Capricorn
STATIONARY RETROGRADE...	05/19/36 at 14 **GEMINI**	09/18/36 at 16 **LIBRA**	01/05/37 at 01 **AQUARIUS**
Solar Conjunction.......	05/31/36 at 09 Gemini	10/01/36 at 07 Libra	01/14/37 at 24 Capricorn
STATIONARY DIRECT.......	06/12/36 at 05 Gemini	10/10/36 at 01 Libra	02/15/37 at 15 Capricorn
Leave Retrograde Zone...	06/28/36 at 14 Gemini	10/24/36 at 16 Libra	02/15/37 at 01 Aquarius
Enter Retrograde Zone...	04/16/37 at 15 Taurus	08/11/37 at 15 Virgo	12/03/37 at 29 Sagittarius
STATIONARY RETROGRADE...	04/30/37 at 24 **TAURUS**	09/02/37 at 29 **VIRGO**	12/20/37 at 15 **CAPRICORN**
Solar Conjunction.......	05/11/37 at 20 Taurus	09/14/37 at 21 Virgo	12/30/37 at 08 Capricorn
STATIONARY DIRECT.......	05/24/37 at 15 Taurus	09/23/37 at 15 Virgo	01/09/38 at 29 Sagittarius
Leave Retrograde Zone...	06/09/37 at 24 Taurus	10/07/37 at 29 Virgo	01/29/38 at 15 Capricorn
Enter Retrograde Zone...	03/28/38 at 25 Aries	07/25/38 at 28 Leo	11/16/38 at 13 Sagittarius
STATIONARY RETROGRADE...	04/11/38 at 05 **TAURUS**	08/14/38 at 12 **VIRGO**	12/04/38 at 29 **SAGITTARIUS**
Solar Conjunction.......	04/21/38 at 01 Taurus	08/28/38 at 04 Virgo	12/14/38 at 21 Sagittarius
STATIONARY DIRECT.......	05/05/38 at 25 Aries	09/06/38 at 28 Leo	12/24/38 at 13 Sagittarius
Leave Retrograde Zone...	05/22/38 at 05 Taurus	09/21/38 at 12 Virgo	01/12/39 at 29 Sagittarius
Enter Retrograde Zone...	03/10/39 at 05 Aries	07/09/39 at 12 Leo	10/30/39 at 27 Scorpio
STATIONARY RETROGRADE...	03/24/39 at 17 **ARIES**	07/27/39 at 24 **LEO**	11/18/39 at 13 **SAGITTARIUS**
Solar Conjunction.......	04/03/39 at 12 Aries	08/10/39 at 17 Leo	11/28/39 at 05 Sagittarius
STATIONARY DIRECT.......	04/16/39 at 05 Aries	08/20/39 at 12 Leo	12/08/39 at 27 Scorpio
Leave Retrograde Zone...	05/05/39 at 17 Aries	09/03/39 at 24 Leo	12/25/39 at 13 Sagittarius
Enter Retrograde Zone...	02/20/40 at 16 Pisces	06/21/40 at 24 Cancer	10/12/40 at 12 Scorpio
STATIONARY RETROGRADE...	03/06/40 at 00 **ARIES**	07/08/40 at 05 **LEO**	11/02/40 at 27 Scorpio
Solar Conjunction.......	03/15/40 at 24 Pisces	07/22240 at 29 Cancer	11/11/40 at 19 Scorpio
STATIONARY DIRECT.......	03/29/40 at 16 Pisces	08/02/40 at 24 Cancer	11/21/40 at 12 Scorpio
Leave Retrograde Zone...	04/17/40 at 00 Aries	08/15/40 at 05 Leo	12/07/40 at 27 Scorpio
Enter Retrograde Zone...	02/02/41 at 28 Aquarius	06/03/41 at 06 Cancer	09/25/41 at 26 Libra
STATIONARY RETROGRADE...	02/17/41 at 13 **PISCES**	06/19/41 at 15 **CANCER**	10/15/41 at 12 **SCORPIO**
Solar Conjunction.......	02/26/41 at 07 Pisces	07/02/41 at 10 Cancer	10/27/41 at 03 Scorpio
STATIONARY DIRECT.......	03/11/41 at 28 Aquarius	07/14/41 at 06 Cancer	11/05/41 at 26 Libra
Leave Retrograde Zone...	03/31/41 at 13 Pisces	07/28/41 at 15 Cancer	11/21/41 at 12 Scorpio
Enter Retrograde Zone...	01/16/42 at 11 Aquarius	05/17/42 at 17 Gemini	09/08/42 at 10 Libra
STATIONARY RETROGRADE...	02/02/42 at 26 **AQUARIUS**	05/31/42 at 25 **GEMINI**	09/28/42 at 25 **LIBRA**
Solar Conjunction.......	02/09/42 at 20 Aquarius	06/12/42 at 21 Gemini	10/11/42 at 17 Libra
STATIONARY DIRECT.......	02/22/42 at 11 Aquarius	06/24/42 at 17 Gemini	10/20/42 at 10 Libra
Leave Retrograde Zone...	03/14/42 at 26 Aquarius	07/09/42 at 25 Gemini	11/03/42 at 25 Libra

MERCURY

Enter Retrograde Zone...	12/30/42 at 24 Aquarius	04/28/43 at 27 Taurus	08/22/43 at 24 Virgo
STATIONARY RETROGRADE...	01/15/43 at 10 **AQUARIUS**	05/12/43 at 05 **GEMINI**	09/11/43 at 09 Libra
Solar Conjunction.......	01/24/43 at 03 Aquarius	05/23/43 at 01 Gemini	09/24/43 at 00 Libra
STATIONARY DIRECT.......	02/05/43 at 24 Aquarius	06/05/43 at 27 Taurus	10/03/43 at 24 Virgo
Leave Retrograde Zone...	02/25/43 at 10 Aquarius	06/20/43 at 05 Gemini	10/18/43 at 09 Libra
Enter Retrograde Zone...	12/13/43 at 08 Capricorn	04/07/44 at 06 Taurus	08/04/44 at 08 Virgo
STATIONARY RETROGRADE...	12/30/43 at 24 **CAPRICORN**	04/22/44 at 16 **TAURUS**	08/24/44 at 22 **VIRGO**
Solar Conjunction.......	01/08/44 at 17 Capricorn	05/02/44 at 12 Taurus	09/06/44 at 14 Virgo
STATIONARY DIRECT.......	01/19/44 at 08 Capricorn	05/15/44 at 06 Taurus	09/16/44 at 08 Virgo
Leave Retrograde Zone...	02/08/44 at 24 Capricorn	06/01/44 at 16 Taurus	09/30/44 at 22 Virgo
Enter Retrograde Zone...	11/25/44 at 22 Sagittarius	03/20/45 at 16 Aries	07/18/45 at 21 Leo
STATIONARY RETROGRADE...	12/13/44 at 08 **CAPRICORN**	04/03/45 at 27 **ARIES**	08/06/45 at 04 **VIRGO**
Solar Conjunction.......	12/23/44 at 01 Capricorn	04/13/45 at 23 Aries	08/20/45 at 27 Leo
STATIONARY DIRECT.......	01/02/45 at 22 Sagittarius	04/27/45 at 16 Aries	08/30/45 at 21 Leo
Leave Retrograde Zone...	01/21/45 at 08 Capricorn	05/14/45 at 27 Aries	09/13/45 at 04 Virgo
Enter Retrograde Zone...	11/08/45 at 06 Sagittarius	03/03/46 at 29 Pisces	07/01/46 at 04 Leo
STATIONARY RETROGRADE...	11/27/45 at 23 **SAGITTARIUS**	03/16/46 at 10 **ARIES**	07/19/46 at 16 **LEO**
Solar Conjunction.......	12/07/45 at 15 Sagittarius	03/26/46 at 05 Aries	08/02/46 at 09 Leo
STATIONARY DIRECT.......	12/17/45 at 06 Sagittarius	04/03/46 at 29 Pisces	08/12/46 at 04 Leo
Leave Retrograde Zone...	01/04/46 at 23 Sagittarius	04/27/46 at 10 Aries	08/26/46 at 16 Leo
Enter Retrograde Zone...	10/24/46 at 21 Scorpio	02/13/47 at 09 Pisces	06/14/47 at 17 Cancer
STATIONARY RETROGRADE...	11/11/46 at 07 **SAGITTARIUS**	02/27/47 at 23 **PISCES**	07/02/47 at 27 **CANCER**
Solar Conjunction.......	11/21/46 at 28 Scorpio	03/08/47 at 17 Pisces	07/14/47 at 21 Cancer
STATIONARY DIRECT.......	12.02/46 at 21 Scorpio	03/22/47 at 09 Pisces	07/25/47 at 17 Cancer
Leave Retrograde Zone...	12/18/46 at 07 Sagittarius	04/11/47 at 23 Pisces	07/25/47 at 27 Cancer
Enter Retrograde Zone...	10/05/47 at 05 Scorpio	01/27/48 at 21 Aquarius	05/26/48 at 28 Gemini
STATIONARY RETROGRADE...	10/25/47 at 21 **SCORPIO**	02/11/48 at 06 **PISCES**	06/11/48 at 07 **CANCER**
Solar Conjunction.......	11/05/47 at 12 Scorpio	02/20/48 at 00 Pisces	06/24/48 at 02 Cancer
STATIONARY DIRECT.......	11/15/47 at 05 Scorpio	03/04/48 at 21 Aquarius	07/05/48 at 28 Gemini
Leave Retrograde Zone...	12.01/47 at 21 Scorpio	03/23/48 at 06 Pisces	07/20/48 at 07 Cancer
Enter Retrograde Zone...	09/17/48 at 19 Libra	01/09/49 at 04 Aquarius	05/08/49 at 08 Gemini
STATIONARY RETROGRADE...	10/08/48 at 05 **SCORPIO**	01/24/49 at 20 **AQUARIUS**	05/23/49 at 17 **GEMINI**
Solar Conjunction.......	10/20/48 at 26 Libra	02/02/49 at 13 Aquarius	06/03/49 at 13 Gemini
STATIONARY DIRECT.......	10/28/48 at 19 Libra	02/14/49 at 04 Aquarius	06/16/49 at 08 Gemini
Leave Retrograde Zone...	11/13/48 at 05 Scorpio	03/07/49 at 20 Aquarius	07/01/49 at 17 Gemini
Enter Retrograde Zone...	08/31/49 at 03 Libra	12/23/49 at 18 Capricorn	04/19/50 at 18 Taurus
STATIONARY RETROGRADE...	09/21/49 at 19 **LIBRA**	01/08/50 at 04 **AQUARIUS**	05/03/50 at 27 **TAURUS**
Solar Conjunction.......	10/03/49 at 10 Libra	01/17/50 at 27 Capricorn	05/14/50 at 23 Taurus
STATIONARY DIRECT.......	10/12/49 at 03 Libra	01/29/50 at 18 Capricorn	05/27/50 at 18 Taurus
Leave Retrograde Zone...	10/28/49 at 19 Libra	02/18/50 at 04 Aquarius	06/12/50 at 27 Taurus

MERCURY

Enter Retrograde Zone...	08/14/50 at 17 Virgo	12/05/50 at 01 Capricorn	03/31/51 at 28 Aries
STATIONARY RETROGRADE...	09/04/50 at 02 **LIBRA**	12/23/50 at 18 **CAPRICORN**	04/14/51 at 08 **TAURUS**
Solar Conjunction.......	09/17/50 at 23 Virgo	01/01/51 at 10 Capricorn	04/25/51 at 04 Taurus
STATIONARY DIRECT.......	09/26/50 at 17 Virgo	01/12/51 at 01 Capricorn	05/08/51 at 28 Aries
Leave Retrograde Zone...	10/11/50 at 02 Libra	02/01/51 at 18 Capricorn	05/25/51 at 08 Taurus
Enter Retrograde Zone...	07/28/51 at 01 Virgo	11/19/51 at 16 Sagittarius	03/12/52 at 08 Aries
STATIONARY RETROGRADE...	08/17/51 at 15 **VIRGO**	12/07/51 at 02 **CAPRICORN**	03/26/52 at 20 **ARIES**
Solar Conjunction.......	08/31/51 at 07 Virgo	12/17/51 at 24 Sagittarius	04/05/52 at 15 Aries
STATIONARY DIRECT.......	09/09/51 at 01 Virgo	12/27/51 at 16 Sagittarius	04/19/52 at 08 Aries
Leave Retrograde Zone...	09/24/51 at 15 Virgo	01/15/52 at 02 Capricorn	05/07/52 at 20 Aries
Enter Retrograde Zone...	07/10/52 at 14 Leo	11/01/52 at 00 Sagittarius	02/22/53 at 19 Pisces
STATIONARY RETROGRADE...	07/29/52 at 27 **LEO**	11/20/52 at 16 **SAGITTARIUS**	03/09/53 at 02 **ARIES**
Solar Conjunction.......	08/12/52 at 19 Leo	11/30/52 at 08 Sagittarius	03/18/53 at 27 Pisces
STATIONARY DIRECT.......	08/22/52 at 14 Leo	12/10/52 at 00 Sagittarius	04/02/53 at 19 Pisces
Leave Retrograde Zone...	09/05/52 at 27 Leo	12/27/52 at 16 Sagittarius	04/19/53 at 02 Aries
Enter Retrograde Zone...	06/24/53 at 27 Cancer	10/15/53 at 14 Scorpio	02/05/54 at 01 Pisces
STATIONARY RETROGRADE...	07/11/53 at 08 **LEO**	11/03/53 at 00 **SAGITTARIUS**	02/20/54 at 16 **PISCES**
Solar Conjunction.......	07/25/53 at 02 Leo	11/14/53 at 22 Scorpio	03/01/54 at 10 Pisces
STATIONARY DIRECT.......	08/04/53 at 27 Cancer	11/23/53 at 14 Scorpio	03/14/54 at 01 Pisces
Leave Retrograde Zone...	08/18/53 at 08 Leo	12/10/53 at 00 Sagittarius	04/03/54 at 16 Pisces
Enter Retrograde Zone...	06/06/54 at 09 Cancer	09/27/54 at 28 Libra	01/19/55 at 14 Aquarius
STATIONARY RETROGRADE...	06/23/54 at 18 **CANCER**	10/18/54 at 14 **SCORPIO**	02/03/55 at 29 **AQUARIUS**
Solar Conjunction.......	07/06/54 at 13 Cancer	10/29/54 at 05 Scorpio	02/12/55 at 23 Aquarius
STATIONARY DIRECT.......	07/17/54 at 09 Cancer	11/07/54 at 28 Libra	02/25/55 at 14 Aquarius
Leave Retrograde Zone...	07/31/54 at 18 Cancer	11/23/54 at 14 Scorpio	03/17/55 at 29 Aquarius
Enter Retrograde Zone...	05/20/55 at 20 Gemini	09/11/55 at 13 Libra	01/02/56 at 27 Capricorn
STATIONARY RETROGRADE...	06/03/55 at 28 **GEMINI**	10/02/55 at 28 **LIBRA**	01/18/56 at 13 **AQUARIUS**
Solar Conjunction.......	06/16/55 at 24 Gemini	10/13/55 at 19 Libra	01/27/56 at 06 Aquarius
STATIONARY DIRECT.......	06/27/55 at 20 Gemini	10/22/55 at 13 Libra	02/08/56 at 27 Capricorn
Leave Retrograde Zone...	07/12/55 at 28 Gemini	11/07/55 at 28 Libra	02/28/56 at 13 Aquarius
Enter Retrograde Zone...	04/30/56 at 00 Gemini	08/24/56 at 27 Virgo	12/15/56 at 11 Capricorn
STATIONARY RETROGRADE...	05/13/56 at 08 **GEMINI**	09/13/56 at 12 **LIBRA**	01/02/57 at 27 **CAPRICORN**
Solar Conjunction.......	05/25/56 at 04 Gemini	09/26/56 at 03 Libra	01/10/57 at 20 Capricorn
STATIONARY DIRECT.......	06/07/56 at 00 Gemini	10/05/56 at 27 Virgo	01/21/57 at 11 Capricorn
Leave Retrograde Zone...	06/22/56 at 08 Gemini	10/20/56 at 12 Libra	02/10/57 at 27 Capricorn
Enter Retrograde Zone...	04/10/57 at 09 Taurus	08/07/57 at 11 Virgo	11/28/57 at 25 Sagittarius
STATIONARY RETROGRADE...	04/25/57 at 19 **TAURUS**	08/27/57 at 25 **VIRGO**	12/16/57 at 11 **CAPRICORN**
Solar Conjunction.......	05/06/57 at 15 Taurus	09/09/57 at 16 Virgo	12/25/57 at 03 Capricorn
STATIONARY DIRECT.......	05/19/57 at 09 Taurus	09/19/57 at 11 Virgo	01/05/58 at 25 Sagittarius
Leave Retrograde Zone...	06/04/58 at 19 Taurus	10/03/57 at 25 Virgo	01/24/58 at 11 Capricorn

MERCURY

Enter Retrograde Zone...	03/23/58 at 19 Aries	07/21/58 at 24 Leo	11/11/58 at 09 Sagittarius
STATIONARY RETROGRADE...	**04/06/58 at 00 TAURUS**	08/09/58 at 07 **VIRGO**	11/30/58 at 25 **SAGITTARIUS**
Solar Conjunction.......	04/16/58 at 26 Aries	08/23/58 at 00 Virgo	12/10/58 at 17 Sagittarius
STATIONARY DIRECT.......	04/30/58 at 19 Aries	09/02/58 at 24 Leo	12/20/58 at 09 Sagittarius
Leave Retrograde Zone...	05/17/58 at 00 Taurus	09/16/58 at 07 Virgo	01/07/59 at 25 Sagittarius
Enter Retrograde Zone...	03/05/59 at 00 Aries	07/04/59 at 07 Leo	10/25/59 at 23 Scorpio
STATIONARY RETROGRADE...	03/19/59 at 13 **ARIES**	07/22/59 at 19 **LEO**	11/14/59 at 09 **SAGITTARIUS**
Solar Conjunction.......	03/29/59 at 08 Aries	08/05/59 at 12 Leo	11/24/59 at 01 Sagittarius
STATIONARY DIRECT.......	04/12/59 at 00 Aries	08/15/59 at 07 Leo	12/03/59 at 23 Scorpio
Leave Retrograde Zone...	05/01/59 at 13 Aries	08/29/59 at 19 Leo	12/21/59 at 09 Sagittarius
Enter Retrograde Zone...	02/16/60 at 12 Pisces	06/16/60 at 19 Cancer	10/08/60 at 08 Scorpio
STATIONARY RETROGRADE...	03/02/60 at 25 **PISCES**	07/03/60 at 00 **LEO**	10/27/60 at 24 **SCORPIO**
Solar Conjunction.......	03/10/60 at 20 Pisces	07/17/60 at 24 Cancer	11/07/60 at 15 Scorpio
STATIONARY DIRECT.......	03/12/60 at 12 Pisces	07/27/60 at 19 Cancer	11/16/60 at 08 Scorpio
Leave Retrograde Zone...	04/12/60 at 25 Pisces	08/10/60 at 00 Leo	12/03/60 at 24 Scorpio
Enter Retrograde Zone...	01/29/61 at 24 Aquarius	05/30/61 at 01 Cancer	09/20/61 at 22 Libra
STATIONARY RETROGRADE...	02/12/61 at 09 **PISCES**	06/14/61 at 10 **CANCER**	10/10/61 at 08 **SCORPIO**
Solar Conjunction.......	02/21/61 at 03 Pisces	06/27/61 at 05 Cancer	10/22/61 at 29 Libra
STATIONARY DIRECT.......	03/06/61 at 24 Aquarius	07/08/61 at 01 Cancer	10/31/61 at 22 Libra
Leave Retrograde Zone...	03/27/61 at 09 Pisces	07/23/61 at 10 Cancer	11/16/61 at 08 Scorpio
Enter Retrograde Zone...	01/12/62 at 07 Aquarius	05/11/62 at 11 Gemini	09/03/62 at 06 Libra
STATIONARY RETROGRADE...	01/27/62 at 22 **AQUARIUS**	05/26/62 at 20 **GEMINI**	09/24/62 at 21 **LIBRA**
Solar Conjunction.......	02/05/62 at 16 Aquarius	06/07/62 at 16 Gemini	10/06/62 at 12 Libra
STATIONARY DIRECT.......	02/17/62 at 07 Aquarius	06/19/62 at 11 Gemini	10/16/62 at 06 Libra
Leave Retrograde Zone...	03/09/62 at 22 Aquarius	07/04/62 at 20 Gemini	10/30/62 at 21 Libra
Enter Retrograde Zone...	12/25/62 at 20 Capricorn	04/22/63 at 21 Taurus	08/17/63 at 20 Virgo
STATIONARY RETROGRADE...	01/11/63 at 06 **AQUARIUS**	05/06/63 at 00 **GEMINI**	09/06/63 at 05 **LIBRA**
Solar Conjunction.......	01/20/63 at 29 Capricorn	05/18/63 at 26 Taurus	09/20/63 at 26 Virgo
STATIONARY DIRECT.......	02/02/63 at 20 Capricorn	05/30/63 at 21 Taurus	09/29/63 at 20 Virgo
Leave Retrograde Zone...	02/20/63 at 06 Aquarius	06/15/63 at 00 Gemini	10/14/63 at 05 Libra
Enter Retrograde Zone...	12/09/63 at 04 Capricorn	04/02/64 at 01 Taurus	07/30/64 at 04 Virgo
STATIONARY RETROGRADE...	12/26/63 at 20 **CAPRICORN**	04/16/64 at 11 **TAURUS**	08/19/64 at 17 **VIRGO**
Solar Conjunction.......	01/04/64 at 13 Capricorn	04/27/64 at 07 Taurus	09/02/64 at 09 Virgo
STATIONARY DIRECT.......	01/15/64 at 04 Capricorn	05/10/64 at 01 Taurus	09/11/64 at 04 Virgo
Leave Retrograde Zone...	02/03/64 at 20 Capricorn	05/27/64 at 11 Taurus	09/25/64 at 17 Virgo
Enter Retrograde Zone...	11/21/64 at 18 Sagittarius	03/15/65 at 11 Aries	07/13/65 at 17 Leo
STATIONARY RETROGRADE...	12/09/64 at 04 **CAPRICORN**	03/29/65 at 23 **ARIES**	08/02/65 at 00 **VIRGO**
Solar Opposition........	12/18/64 at 27 Sagittarius	04/08/65 at 18 Aries	08/15/65 at 22 Leo
STATIONARY DIRECT.......	12/29/64 at 18 Sagittarius	04/22/65 at 11 Aries	08/25/65 at 17 Leo
Leave Retrograde Zone...	01/16/65 at 04 Capricorn	05/10/65 at 23 Aries	09/09/65 at 00 Virgo

MERCURY

Enter Retrograde Zone...	11/04/65 at 02 Sagittarius	02/25/66 at 22 Pisces	06/27/66 at 00 Leo
STATIONARY RETROGRADE...	11/23/65 at 19 **SAGITTARIUS**	03/12/66 at 05 **ARIES**	07/14/66 at 11 **LEO**
Solar Conjunction.......	12/03/65 at 10 Sagittarius	03/21/66 at 00 Aries	07/28/66 at 05 Leo
STATIONARY DIRECT.......	12/12/65 at 02 Sagittarius	04/04/66 at 22 Pisces	08/07/66 at 00 Leo
Leave Retrograde Zone...	12/31/65 at 19 Sagittarius	04/22/66 at 05 Aries	08/21/66 at 11 Leo
Enter Retrograde Zone...	10/18/66 at 17 Scorpio	02/08/67 at 04 Pisces	06/08/67 at 12 Cancer
STATIONARY RETROGRADE...	11/06/66 at 03 **SAGITTARIUS**	02/23/67 at 18 **PISCES**	06/26/67 at 21 **CANCER**
Solar Conjunction.......	11/17/66 at 24 Scorpio	03/04/67 at 13 Pisces	07/09/67 at 16 Cancer
STATIONARY DIRECT.......	11/26/66 at 17 Scorpio	03/17/67 at 04 Pisces	07/20/67 at 12 Cancer
Leave Retrograde Zone...	12/14/66 at 03 Sagittarius	04/06/67 at 18 Pisces	08/03/67 at 21 Cancer
Enter Retrograde Zone...	10/01/67 at 01 Scorpio	01/22/68 at 17 Aquarius	05/22/68 at 23 Gemini
STATIONARY RETROGRADE...	10/21/67 at 17 **SCORPIO**	02/06/68 at 02 **PISCES**	06/06/68 at 02 **CANCER**
Solar Conjunction.......	11/01/67 at 08 Scorpio	02/15/68 at 26 Aquarius	06/18/68 at 27 Gemini
STATIONARY DIRECT.......	11/10/67 at 01 Scorpio	02/28/68 at 17 Aquarius	06/30/68 at 23 Gemini
Leave Retrograde Zone...	11/27/67 at 17 Scorpio	03/19/68 at 02 Pisces	07/15/68 at 02 Cancer
Enter Retrograde Zone...	09/12/68 at 15 Libra	01/04/69 at 00 Aquarius	05/03/69 at 03 Gemini
STATIONARY RETROGRADE...	10/03/68 at 01 **SCORPIO**	01/20/69 at 16 **AQUARIUS**	05/17/69 at 12 **GEMINI**
Solar Conjunction.......	10/15/68 at 22 Libra	01/29/69 at 09 Aquarius	05/29/69 at 07 Gemini
STATIONARY DIRECT.......	10/24/68 at 15 Libra	02/10/69 at 00 Aquarius	06/10/69 at 03 Gemini
Leave Retrograde Zone...	11/09/68 at 01 Scorpio	03/02/69 at 16 Aquarius	06/26/69 at 12 Gemini
Enter Retrograde Zone...	08/26/69 at 29 Virgo	12/18/69 at 13 Capricorn	04/14/70 at 13 Taurus
STATIONARY RETROGRADE...	09/16/69 at 14 **LIBRA**	01/06/70 at 29 **CAPRICORN**	04/28/70 at 22 **TAURUS**
Solar Conjunction.......	09/29/69 at 06 Libra	01/13/70 at 22 Capricorn	05/09/70 at 18 Taurus
STATIONARY DIRECT.......	10/08/69 at 29 Virgo	01/24/70 at 13 Capricorn	05/22/70 at 13 Taurus
Leave Retrograde Zone...	10/23/69 at 14 Libra	02/13/70 at 29 Capricorn	06/07/70 at 22 Taurus
Enter Retrograde Zone...	08/09/70 at 13 Virgo	12/01/70 at 27 Sagittarius	03/27/71 at 23 Aries
STATIONARY RETROGRADE...	08/30/70 at 28 **VIRGO**	12/19/70 at 14 **CAPRICORN**	04/09/71 at 03 **TAURUS**
Solar Conjunction.......	09/12/70 at 19 Virgo	12/28/70 at 06 Capricorn	04/19/71 at 29 Aries
STATIONARY DIRECT.......	09/22/70 at 13 Virgo	01/08/71 at 27 Sagittarius	05/03/71 at 23 Aries
Leave Retrograde Zone...	10/06/70 at 28 Virgo	01/27/71 at 14 Capricorn	05/20/71 at 03 Taurus
Enter Retrograde Zone...	07/24/71 at 27 Leo	11/14/71 at 11 Sagittarius	03/06/72 at 03 Aries
STATIONARY RETROGRADE...	08/12/71 at 10 **VIRGO**	12/03/71 at 28 **SAGITTARIUS**	03/21/72 at 15 **ARIES**
Solar Conjunction.......	08/26/71 at 02 Virgo	12/12/71 at 20 Sagittarius	03/31/72 at 10 Aries
STATIONARY DIRECT.......	09/05/71 at 27 Leo	12/22/71 at 11 Sagittarius	04/14/72 at 03 Aries
Leave Retrograde Zone...	09/19/71 at 10 Virgo	01/10/72 at 28 Sagittarius	05/02/72 at 15 Aries
Enter Retrograde Zone...	07/06/72 at 10 Leo	10/27/72 at 26 Scorpio	02/18/73 at 15 Pisces
STATIONARY RETROGRADE...	07/24/72 at 28 **LEO**	11/15/72 at 12 **SAGITTARIUS**	03/04/73 at 28 **PISCES**
Solar Conjunction.......	08/07/72 at 15 Leo	11/26/72 at 04 Sagittarius	03/13/73 at 23 Pisces
STATIONARY DIRECT.......	08/17/72 at 10 Leo	12/05/72 at 26 Scorpio	03/27/73 at 15 Pisces
Leave Retrograde Zone...	08/31/72 at 22 Leo	12/23/72 at 12 Sagittarius	04/15/73 at 28 Pisces

MERCURY

Enter Retrograde Zone...06/19/73 at 22 Cancer   10/10/73 at 10 Scorpio   02/01/74 at 27 Aquarius
STATIONARY RETROGRADE...07/06/73 at 03 **LEO**   10/30/73 at 26 **SCORPIO**   02/15/74 at 11 **PISCES**
Solar Conjunction.......07/20/73 at 27 Cancer   11/10/73 at 17 Scorpio   02/24/74 at 05 Pisces
STATIONARY DIRECT.......07/30/73 at 22 Cancer   11/19/73 at 10 Scorpio   03/09/74 at 27 Aquarius
Leave Retrograde Zone...08/13/73 at 03 Leo   12/06/73 at 26 Scorpio   03/29/74 at 11 Pisces

Enter Retrograde Zone...06/01/74 at 04 Cancer   09/23/74 at 24 Libra   01/14/75 at 09 Aquarius
STATIONARY RETROGRADE...06/17/74 at 13 **CANCER**   10/13/74 at 10 **SCORPIO**   01/30/75 at 25 **AQUARIUS**
Solar Conjunction.......06/30/74 at 08 Cancer   10/25/74 at 01 Scorpio   02/08/75 at 19 Aquarius
STATIONARY DIRECT.......07/12/74 at 04 Cancer   11/03/74 at 24 Libra   02/20/75 at 09 Aquarius
Leave Retrograde Zone...07/26/74 at 13 Cancer   11/19/74 at 10 Scorpio   03/12/75 at 25 Aquarius

Enter Retrograde Zone...04/27/75 at 15 Gemini   09/06/75 at 09 Libra   12/29/75 at 23 Capricorn
STATIONARY RETROGRADE...05/29/75 at 23 **GEMINI**   09/26/75 at 24 **LIBRA**   01/14/76 at 09 **AQUARIUS**
Solar Conjunction.......06/10/75 at 19 Gemini   10/09/75 at 15 Libra   01/23/76 at 02 Aquarius
STATIONARY DIRECT.......06/22/75 at 15 Gemini   10/18/75 at 09 Libra   02/03/76 at 23 Capricorn
Leave Retrograde Zone...07/07/75 at 23 Gemini   11/02/75 at 24 Libra   02/24/76 at 09 Aquarius

Enter Retrograde Zone...04/24/76 at 24 Taurus   08/19/76 at 23 Virgo   12/11/76 at 07 Capricorn
STATIONARY RETROGRADE...05/09/76 at 03 **GEMINI**   09/08/76 at 07 **LIBRA**   12/28/76 at 23 **CAPRICORN**
Solar Conjunction.......05/20/76 at 29 Taurus   09/22/76 at 29 Virgo   01/06/77 at 15 Capricorn
STATIONARY DIRECT.......06/02/76 at 24 Taurus   10/02/76 at 23 Virgo   01/17/77 at 07 Capricorn
Leave Retrograde Zone...06/17/76 at 03 Gemini   10/15/76 at 07 Libra   02/06/77 at 23 Capricorn

Enter Retrograde Zone...04/05/77 at 04 Taurus   08/02/77 at 06 Virgo   11/24/77 at 21 Sagittarius
STATIONARY RETROGRADE...04/20/77 at 14 **TAURUS**   08/22/77 at 20 **VIRGO**   12/12/77 at 07 **CAPRICORN**
Solar Conjunction.......04/30/77 at 10 Taurus   09/05/77 at 12 Virgo   12/21/77 at 29 Sagittarius
STATIONARY DIRECT.......05/13/77 at 04 Taurus   09/14/77 at 06 Virgo   12/31/77 at 21 Sagittarius
Leave Retrograde Zone...05/30/77 at 14 Taurus   09/28/77 at 20 Virgo   01/19/78 at 07 Capricorn

Enter Retrograde Zone...03/18/78 at 14 Aries   07/17/78 at 20 Leo   11/07/78 at 05 Sagittarius
STATIONARY RETROGRADE...04/02/78 at 26 **ARIES**   08/04/78 at 03 **VIRGO**   11/25/78 at 21 **SAGITTARIUS**
Solar Conjunction.......04/11/78 at 21 Aries   08/18/78 at 25 Leo   12/05/78 at 13 Sagittarius
STATIONARY DIRECT.......04/25/78 at 14 Aries   08/28/78 at 20 Leo   12/15/78 at 05 Sagittarius
Leave Retrograde Zone...05/13/78 at 26 Aries   09/11/78 at 03 Virgo   01/02/79 at 21 Sagittarius

Enter Retrograde Zone...02/28/79 at 25 Pisces   06/30/79 at 03 Leo   10/21/79 at 19 Scorpio
STATIONARY RETROGRADE...03/15/79 at 08 **ARIES**   07/17/79 at 14 **LEO**   11/09/79 at 05 **SAGITTARIUS**
Solar Conjunction.......03/24/79 at 03 Aries   07/31/79 at 07 Leo   11/20/79 at 27 Scorpio
STATIONARY DIRECT.......04/07/79 at 25 Pisces   08/11/79 at 03 Leo   11/29/79 at 19 Scorpio
Leave Retrograde Zone...04/26/79 at 08 Aries   08/24/79 at 14 Leo   12/16/79 at 05 Sagittarius

Enter Retrograde Zone...02/11/80 at 07 Pisces   06/12/80 at 15 Cancer   10/02/80 at 03 Scorpio
STATIONARY RETROGRADE...02/26/80 at 21 **PISCES**   06/28/80 at 25 **CANCER**   10/23/80 at 19 **SCORPIO**
Solar Conjunction.......03/06/80 at 15 Pisces   07/11/80 at 19 Cancer   11/03/80 at 11 Scorpio
STATIONARY DIRECT.......03/19/80 at 07 Pisces   07/22/80 at 15 Cancer   11/12/80 at 03 Scorpio
Leave Retrograde Zone...04/08/80 at 21 Pisces   08/06/80 at 25 Cancer   11/28/80 at 19 Scorpio

MERCURY

Enter Retrograde Zone...	01/24/81 at 19 Aquarius	05/25/81 at 26 Gemini	09/16/81 at 18 Libra
STATIONARY RETROGRADE...	02/08/81 at 04 **PISCES**	06/09/81 at 05 **CANCER**	10/06/81 at 03 **SCORPIO**
Solar Conjunction.......	02/17/81 at 28 Aquarius	06/22/81 at 00 Cancer	10/18/81 at 24 Libra
STATIONARY DIRECT.......	03/02/81 at 02 Aquarius	07/03/81 at 26 Gemini	10/27/81 at 18 Libra
Leave Retrograde Zone...	03/21/81 at 04 Pisces	07/18/81 at 05 Cancer	11/11/81 at 03 Scorpio
Enter Retrograde Zone...	01/07/82 at 02 Aquarius	05/05/82 at 06 Gemini	08/30/82 at 02 Libra
STATIONARY RETROGRADE...	01/23/82 at 18 **AQUARIUS**	05/21/82 at 15 **GEMINI**	09/19/82 at 17 **LIBRA**
Solar Conjunction.......	02/01/82 at 11 Aquarius	06/01/82 at 11 Gemini	10/02/82 at 08 Libra
STATIONARY DIRECT.......	02/13/82 at 02 Aquarius	06/13/82 at 06 Gemini	10/11/82 at 02 Libra
Leave Retrograde Zone...	03/05/82 at 18 Aquarius	06/29/82 at 15 Gemini	10/26/82 at 17 Libra
Enter Retrograde Zone...	12/21/82 at 16 Capricorn	04/17/83 at 16 Taurus	08/13/83 at 16 Virgo
STATIONARY RETROGRADE...	01/07/83 at 02 **AQUARIUS**	05/02/83 at 25 **TAURUS**	09/02/83 at 00 **LIBRA**
Solar Conjunction.......	01/16/83 at 25 Capricorn	05/12/83 at 21 Taurus	09/15/83 at 22 Virgo
STATIONARY DIRECT.......	01/27/83 at 16 Capricorn	05/25/83 at 16 Taurus	09/24/83 at 16 Virgo
Leave Retrograde Zone...	02/15/83 at 02 Aquarius	06/10/83 at 25 Taurus	10/09/83 at 00 Libra
Enter Retrograde Zone...	12/04/83 at 00 Capricorn	03/29/84 at 26 Aries	07/26/84 at 00 Virgo
STATIONARY RETROGRADE...	12/22/83 at 16 **CAPRICORN**	04/11/84 at 06 **TAURUS**	08/14/84 at 13 **VIRGO**
Solar Conjunction.......	12/31/83 at 09 Capricorn	04/22/84 at 02 Taurus	08/28/84 at 05 Virgo
STATIONARY DIRECT.......	01/11/83 at 00 Capricorn	05/05/84 at 26 Aries	09/07/84 at 00 Virgo
Leave Retrograde Zone...	01/30/83 at 16 Capricorn	05/22/84 at 06 Taurus	09/21/84 at 13 Virgo
Enter Retrograde Zone...	11/16/84 at 14 Sagittarius	03/10/85 at 06 Aries	07/09/85 at 13 Leo
STATIONARY RETROGRADE...	12/04/84 at 00 **CAPRICORN**	03/24/85 at 18 **ARIES**	07/28/85 at 25 **LEO**
Solar Conjunction.......	12/14/84 at 22 Sagittarius	04/03/85 at 13 Aries	08/10/85 at 18 Leo
STATIONARY DIRECT.......	12/24/84 at 14 Sagittarius	04/17/85 at 06 Aries	08/20/85 at 13 Leo
Leave Retrograde Zone...	01/12/85 at 00 Capricorn	05/05/85 at 18 Aries	09/03/85 at 25 Leo
Enter Retrograde Zone...	10/30/85 at 28 Scorpio	02/20/86 at 17 Pisces	06/22/86 at 25 Cancer
STATIONARY RETROGRADE...	11/18/85 at 15 **SAGITTARIUS**	03/07/86 at 01 **ARIES**	07/09/86 at 06 **LEO**
Solar Conjunction.......	11/28/85 at 06 Sagittarius	03/16/86 at 25 Pisces	07/23/86 at 00 Leo
STATIONARY DIRECT.......	12/08/85 at 28 Scorpio	03/30/86 at 17 Pisces	08/03/86 at 25 Cancer
Leave Retrograde Zone...	12/26/85 at 15 Sagittarius	04/18/86 at 01 Aries	08/17/86 at 06 Leo
Enter Retrograde Zone...	10/13/86 at 13 Scorpio	02/03/87 at 29 Aquarius	06/05/87 at 07 Cancer
STATIONARY RETROGRADE...	11/02/86 at 29 **SCORPIO**	02/18/87 at 14 **PISCES**	06/21/87 at 16 **CANCER**
Solar Conjunction.......	11/13/86 at 20 Scorpio	02/27/87 at 08 Pisces	07/04/87 at 11 Cancer
STATIONARY DIRECT.......	11/22/86 at 13 Scorpio	03/13/87 at 29 Aquarius	07/15/87 at 07 Cancer
Leave Retrograde Zone...	12/09/86 at 29 Scorpio	04/01/87 at 14 Pisces	07/29/87 at 16 Cancer
Enter Retrograde Zone...	09/26/87 at 27 Libra	01/17/88 at 12 Aquarius	05/17/88 at 18 Gemini
STATIONARY RETROGRADE...	10/16/87 at 13 **SCORPIO**	02/02/88 at 28 **AQUARIUS**	05/31/88 at 26 **GEMINI**
Solar Conjunction.......	10/28/87 at 04 Scorpio	02/11/88 at 21 Aquarius	06/13/88 at 22 Gemini
STATIONARY DIRECT.......	11/06/87 at 27 Libra	02/23/88 at 12 Aquarius	06/24/88 at 18 Gemini
Leave Retrograde Zone...	11/21/87 at 13 Scorpio	03/15/88 at 28 Aquarius	07/09/88 at 26 Gemini

MERCURY

Enter Retrograde Zone...	09/08/88 at 11 Libra	12/31/88 at 26 Capricorn	04/28/89 at 28 Taurus
STATIONARY RETROGRADE...	09/28/88 at 27 **LIBRA**	01/16/89 at 11 **AQUARIUS**	05/12/89 at 06 **GEMINI**
Solar Conjunction.......	10/11/88 at 18 Libra	01/25/89 at 05 Aquarius	05/23/89 at 02 Gemini
STATIONARY DIRECT.......	10/20/88 at 11 Libra	02/05/89 at 26 Capricorn	06/05/89 at 28 Taurus
Leave Retrograde Zone...	11/21/88 at 27 Libra	02/25/89 at 11 Aquarius	06/20/89 at 06 Gemini
Enter Retrograde Zone...	08/22/89 at 25 Virgo		
STATIONARY RETROGRADE...	09/11/89 at 10 **LIBRA**		
Solar Conjunction.......	09/24/89 at 01 Libra		
STATIONARY DIRECT.......	10/03/89 at 25 Virgo		
Leave Retrograde Zone...	10/18/89 at 10 Libra		
Enter Retrograde Zone...	12/13/89 at 09 Capricorn	04/08/90 at 07 Taurus	08/05/90 at 09 Virgo
STATIONARY RETROGRADE...	12/30/89 at 25 **CAPRICORN**	04/23/90 at 17 **TAURUS**	08/25/90 at 23 **VIRGO**
Solar Conjunction.......	01/09/90 at 18 Capricorn	05/03/90 at 13 Taurus	09/08/90 at 15 Virgo
STATIONARY DIRECT.......	01/20/90 at 09 Capricorn	05/17/90 at 07 Taurus	09/17/90 at 09 Virgo
Leave Retrograde Zone...	02/08/90 at 25 Capricorn	06/02/90 at 17 Taurus	10/01/90 at 23 Virgo
Enter Retrograde Zone...	11/26/90 at 23 Sagittarius	03/21/91 at 17 Aries	07/20/91 at 23 Leo
STATIONARY RETROGRADE...	12/14/90 at 09 **CAPRICORN**	04/04/91 at 29 **ARIES**	08/07/91 at 05 **VIRGO**
Solar Conjunction.......	12/24/90 at 02 Capricorn	04/14/91 at 24 Aries	08/21/91 at 28 Leo
STATIONARY DIRECT.......	01/03/91 at 23 Sagittarius	04/28/91 at 17 Aries	08/31/91 at 23 Leo
Leave Retrograde Zone...	01/22/91 at 09 Capricorn	05/16/91 at 29 Aries	09/14/91 at 05 Virgo
Enter Retrograde Zone...	11/09/91 at 07 Sagittarius	03/02/92 at 26 Pisces	07/01/92 at 05 Leo
STATIONARY RETROGRADE...	11/28/91 at 24 **SAGITTARIUS**	03/17/92 at 16 **ARIES**	07/20/92 at 17 **LEO**
Solar Conjunction.......	12/08/91 at 16 Sagittarius	03/26/92 at 06 Aries	08/02/92 at 10 Leo
STATIONARY DIRECT.......	12/18/91 at 07 Sagittarius	04/09/92 at 28 Pisces	08/13/92 at 05 Leo
Leave Retrograde Zone...	01/05/92 at 24 Sagittarius	04/28/92 at 11 Aries	08/27/92 at 17 Leo
Enter Retrograde Zone...	10/23/92 at 22 Scorpio	02/13/93 at 10 Pisces	06/15/93 at 18 Cancer
STATIONARY RETROGRADE...	11/11/92 at 08 **SAGITTARIUS**	02/27/93 at 24 **PISCES**	07/02/93 at 28 **CANCER**
Solar Conjunction.......	11/21/92 at 29 Scorpio	03/09/93 at 18 Pisces	07/15/93 at 22 Cancer
STATIONARY DIRECT.......	12/02/92 at 22 Scorpio	03/22/93 at 10 Pisces	07/25/93 at 18 Cancer
Leave Retrograde Zone...	12/18/92 at 08 Sagittarius	04/11/93 at 24 Pisces	08/09/93 at 28 Cancer
Enter Retrograde Zone...	10/05/93 at 06 Scorpio	01/27/94 at 22 Aquarius	05/28/94 at 29 Gemini
STATIONARY RETROGRADE...	10/25/93 at 22 **SCORPIO**	02/11/94 at 07 **PISCES**	06/12/94 at 08 **CANCER**
Solar Conjunction.......	11/06/93 at 13 Scorpio	02/20/94 at 01 Pisces	06/25/94 at 03 Cancer
STATIONARY DIRECT.......	11/15/93 at 06 Scorpio	03/05/94 at 22 Aquarius	07/06/94 at 29 Gemini
Leave Retrograde Zone...	12/01/03 at 22 Scorpio	03/25/94 at 07 Pisces	07/21/94 at 08 Cancer
Enter Retrograde Zone...	09/18/94 at 20 Libra	01/10/95 at 05 Aquarius	05/09/95 at 09 Gemini
STATIONARY RETROGRADE...	10/09/94 at 06 **SCORPIO**	01/26/95 at 21 **AQUARIUS**	05/24/95 at 18 **GEMINI**
Solar Conjunction.......	10/21/94 at 27 Libra	02/03/95 at 14 Aquarius	06/05/95 at 14 Gemini
STATIONARY DIRECT.......	10/30/94 at 20 Libra	02/16/95 at 05 Aquarius	06/17/95 at 09 Gemini
Leave Retrograde Zone...	11/14/94 at 06 Scorpio	03/08/95 at 21 Aquarius	07/02/95 at 18 Gemini

MERCURY

Enter Retrograde Zone...	09/02/95 at 05 Libra	12/24/95 at 19 Capricorn	04/19/96 at 19 Taurus
STATIONARY RETROGRADE...	09/22/95 at 20 **LIBRA**	01/09/96 at 05 **AQUARIUS**	05/03/96 at 28 **TAURUS**
Solar Conjunction.......	10/05/95 at 11 Libra	01/18/96 at 28 Capricorn	05/15/96 at 24 Taurus
STATIONARY DIRECT.......	10/14/95 at 05 Libra	01/30/96 at 19 Capricorn	05/27/96 at 19 Taurus
Leave Retrograde Zone...	10/29/95 at 20 Libra	02/19/96 at 05 Aquarius	06/12/96 at 28 Taurus
Enter Retrograde Zone...	08/15/96 at 19 Virgo	12/06/96 at 02 Capricorn	04/01/97 at 29 Aries
STATIONARY RETROGRADE...	09/04/96 at 03 **LIBRA**	12/23/96 at 19 **CAPRICORN**	04/15/97 at 09 **TAURUS**
Solar Conjunction.......	09/17/96 at 24 Virgo	01/02/97 at 11 Capricorn	04/25/97 at 05 Taurus
STATIONARY DIRECT.......	09/26/96 at 19 Virgo	01/12/97 at 02 Capricorn	05/08/97 at 29 Aries
Leave Retrograde Zone...	10/11/96 at 03 Libra	02/01/97 at 19 Capricorn	05/25/97 at 09 Taurus
Enter Retrograde Zone...	07/28/97 at 02 Virgo	11/19/97 at 17 Sagittarius	03/13/98 at 09 Aries
STATIONARY RETROGRADE...	08/17/97 at 16 **VIRGO**	12/07/97 at 03 **CAPRICORN**	03/27/98 at 21 **ARIES**
Solar Conjunction.......	08/31/97 at 08 Virgo	12/17/97 at 25 Sagittarius	04/06/98 at 16 Aries
STATIONARY DIRECT.......	09/10/97 at 02 Virgo	12/27/97 at 17 Sagittarius	04/20/98 at 09 Aries
Leave Retrograde Zone...	09/24/97 at 16 Virgo	01/15/98 at 03 Capricorn	05/09/98 at 21 Aries
Enter Retrograde Zone...	07/11/98 at 15 Leo	11/02/98 at 01 Sagittarius	02/23/99 at 20 Pisces
STATIONARY RETROGRADE...	07/31/98 at 28 **LEO**	11/21/98 at 17 **SAGITTARIUS**	03/10/99 at 28 **PISCES**
Solar Conjunction.......	08/13/98 at 20 Leo	12/01/98 at 09 Sagittarius	03/19/99 at 28 Pisces
STATIONARY DIRECT.......	08/23/98 at 15 Leo	12/11/98 at 01 Sagittarius	04/02/99 at 20 Pisces
Leave Retrograde Zone...	09/06/98 at 28 Leo	12.29/98 at 17 Sagittarius	04/21/99 at 04 Aries
Enter Retrograde Zone...	06/25/99 at 28 Cancer	10/16/99 at 15 Scorpio	
STATIONARY RETROGRADE...	07/12/99 at 09 **LEO**	11/05/99 at 01 **SAGITTARIUS**	
Solar Conjunction.......	07/26/99 at 03 Leo	11/15/99 at 23 Scorpio	
STATIONARY DIRECT.......	08/06/99 at 28 Cancer	11/25/99 at 15 Scorpio	
Leave Retrograde Zone...	08/20/99 at 09 Leo	12/12/99 at 01 Sagittarius	

VENUS

Enter Retrograde Zone...02/27/21 at 23 Aries	10/03/22 at 24 Scorpio	05/07/24 at 01 Cancer
STATIONARY RETROGRADE...04/01/21 at 10 **TAURUS**	11/04/22 at 09 **SAGITTARIUS**	06/10/24 at 17 **CANCER**
Solar Conjunction.......04/22/21 at 02 Taurus	11/25/22 at 02 Sagittarius	07/01 24 at 09 Cancer
STATIONARY DIRECT.......05/14/21 at 23 Aries	12/15/22 at 24 Scorpio	07/23/24 at 01 Cancer
Leave Retrograde Zone...06/05/21 at 10 Taurus	01/15/23 at 09 Sagittarius	08/25/24 at 17 Cancer
Enter Retrograde Zone...12/17/25 at 10 Aquarius	07/17/27 at 08 Virgo	02/24/29 at 21 Aries
STATIONARY RETROGRADE...01/17/26 at 26 **AQUARIUS**	08/20/27 at 24 **VIRGO**	03/30/29 at 08 **TAURUS**
Solar Conjunction.......02/07/26 at 18 Aquarius	09/10/27 at 17 Virgo	04/20/29 at 29 Aries
STATIONARY DIRECT.......02/28/26 at 10 Aquarius	10/02/27 at 08 Virgo	05/11/29 at 21 Aries
Leave Retrograde Zone...04/01/26 at 26 Aquarius	11/03/27 at 24 Virgo	06/14/29 at 08 Taurus
Enter Retrograde Zone...10/01/30 at 22 Scorpio	05/04/32 at 28 Gemini	12/14/33 at 07 Aquarius
STATIONARY RETROGRADE...11/02/30 at 07 **SAGITTARIUS**	06/07 32 at 15 **CANCER**	01/15/34 at 23 **AQUARIUS**
Solar Conjunction.......11/22/30 at 29 Scorpio	06/29/32 at 07 Cancer	02/05/34 at 15 Aquarius
STATIONARY DIRECT.......12/13/30 at 22 Scorpio	07/20/32 at 28 Gemini	02/25/34 at 07 Aquarius
Leave Retrograde Zone...01/13/31 at 07 Sagittarius	08/23/32 at 15 Cancer	03/29/34 at 23 Aquarius
Enter Retrograde Zone...07/15/35 at 06 Virgo	02/22/37 at 19 Aries	09/28/38 at 19 Scorpio
STATIONARY RETROGRADE...08/18/35 at 22 **VIRGO**	03/27/37 at 05 **TAURUS**	10/30/38 at 04 **SAGITTARIUS**
Solar Conjunction.......09/08/35 at 14 Virgo	04/18/37 at 27 Aries	11/20/38 at 27 Scorpio
STATIONARY DIRECT.......09/29/35 at 06 Virgo	05/09/37 at 19 Aries	12/10/38 at 19 Scorpio
Leave Retrograde Zone...11/01/35 at 22 Virgo	06/11/37 at 05 Taurus	01/10/39 at 04 Sagittarius
Enter Retrograde Zone...05/02/40 at 26 Gemini	12/12/41 at 05 Aquarius	07/13/43 at 04 Virgo
STATIONARY RETROGRADE...06/05/40 at 13 **CANCER**	01/13/42 at 21 **AQUARIUS**	08/15/43 at 20 **VIRGO**
Solar Conjunction.......06/26/40 at 05 Cancer	02/02/42 at 13 Aquarius	09/05/43 at 12 Virgo
STATIONARY DIRECT.......07/18/40 at 26 Gemini	02/23/42 at 05 Aquarius	09/27/43 at 04 Virgo
Leave Retrograde Zone...08/21/40 at 13 Cancer	03/27/42 at 21 Aquarius	10/30/43 at 20 Virgo
Enter Retrograde Zone...02/20/45 at 17 Aries	09/26/46 at 17 Scorpio	04/30/48 at 24 Gemini
STATIONARY RETROGRADE...03/25/45 at 03 **TAURUS**	10/28/46 at 02 **SAGITTARIUS**	06/03/48 at 11 **CANCER**
Solar Conjunction.......04/15/45 at 25 Aries	11/17/46 at 24 Scorpio	06/24/48 at 02 Cancer
STATIONARY DIRECT.......05/06/45 at 17 Aries	12/08/46 at 17 Scorpio	07/16/48 at 24 Gemini
Leave Retrograde Zone...06/08/45 at 03 Taurus	01/08/47 at 02 Sagittarius	08/19/48 at 11 Cancer
Enter Retrograde Zone...12/10/49 at 03 Aquarius	07/11/51 at 02 Virgo	02/17/53 at 14 Aries
STATIONARY RETROGRADE...01/10/50 at 18 **AQUARIUS**	08/13/51 at 18 **VIRGO**	03/23/53 at 01 **TAURUS**
Solar Conjunction.......01/31/50 at 10 Aquarius	09/03/51 at 10 Virgo	04/13/53 at 23 Aries
STATIONARY DIRECT.......02/20/50 at 03 Aquarius	09/25/51 at 02 Virgo	05/04/53 at 14 Aries
Leave Retrograde Zone...03/24/50 at 18 Gemini	10/28/51 at 18 Virgo	06/07 53 at 01 Taurus
Enter Retrograde Zone...09/23/54 at 14 Scorpio	04/28/56 at 22 Gemini	12/07/57 at 00 Aquarius
STATIONARY RETROGRADE...10/25/54 at 00 **SAGITTARIUS**	05/31/56 at 09 **CANCER**	01/08/58 at 16 **AQUARIUS**
Solar Conjunction.......11/15/54 at 22 Scorpio	06/22/56 at 00 Cancer	01/28/58 at 08 Aquarius
STATIONARY DIRECT.......12/05/54 at 14 Scorpio	07/13/56 at 22 Gemini	02/18/58 at 00 Aquarius
Leave Retrograde Zone...01/06/55 at 00 Sagittarius	08/17/56 at 09 Cancer	03/22/58 at 16 Aquarius

VENUS

Enter Retrograde Zone...	07/08/59 at 29 Leo	02/15/61 at 12 Aries	09/21/62 at 12 Scorpio
STATIONARY RETROGRADE...	08/10/59 at 16 **VIRGO**	03/20/61 at 29 **ARIES**	10/23/62 at 27 **SCORPIO**
Solar Conjunction.......	09/01/59 at 08 Virgo	04/10/61 at 20 Aries	11/02/62 at 20 Scorpio
STATIONARY DIRECT.......	09/22/59 at 29 Leo	05/02/61 at 12 Aries	12/03/62 at 12 **SCORPIO**
Leave Retrograde Zone...	10/26/59 at 16 Virgo	06/05/61 at 29 Aries	01/03/63 at 27 Scorpio
Enter Retrograde Zone...	04/25/64 at 20 Gemini	12/05/65 at 28 Capicorn	07/05/67 at 27 Leo
STATIONARY RETROGRADE...	05/29/64 at 06 Cancer	01/05/66 at 13 **AQUARIUS**	08/08/67 at 13 **VIRGO**
Solar Conjunction.......	06/19/64 at 28 Gemini	01/26/66 at 05 Aquarius	08/29/67 at 05 Virgo
STATIONARY DIRECT.......	07/11/64 at 20 Gemini	02/15/66 at 28 Capricorn	09/20/67 at 27 Leo
Leave Retrograde Zone...	08/14/64 at 06 Cancer	03/19/66 at 13 Aquarius	10/22/67 at 13 Virgo
Enter Retrograde Zone...	02/13/69 at 10 Aries	09/17/70 at 09 Scorpio	04/23/72 at 18 Gemini
STATIONARY RETROGRADE...	03/18/69 at 26 **ARIES**	10/20/70 at 25 **SCORPIO**	05/27/72 at 04 **CANCER**
Solar Conjunction.......	04/08/69 at 18 Aries	11/10/70 at 17 Scorpio	06/17/72 at 26 Gemini
STATIONARY DIRECT.......	04/29/69 at 10 Aries	11/30/70 at 09 Scorpio	07/09/72 at 18 Gemini
Leave Retrograde Zone...	06/01/69 at 26 Aries	01/01/71 at 25 Scorpio	08/11/72 at 04 Cancer
Enter Retrograde Zone...	12/02/73 at 25 Capricorn	07/03/75 at 25 Leo	02/11/77 at 08 Aries
STATIONARY RETROGRADE...	01/03/74 at 11 **AQUARIUS**	08/06/75 at 11 **VIRGO**	03/16/77 at 24 **ARIES**
Solar Conjunction.......	01/23/74 at 03 Aquarius	08/27/75 at 03 Virgo	04/06/77 at 16 Aries
STATIONARY DIRECT.......	02/13/74 at 25 Capri	09/18/75 at 25 Leo	04/27/77 at 08 Aries
Leave Retrograde Zone...	03/17/74 at 11 Aquarius	10/20/75 at 11 Virgo	05/30/77 at 24 Aries
Enter Retrograde Zone...	09/15/78 at 07 Cancer	04/21/80 at 16 Gemini	11/30/81 at 23 Capricorn
STATIONARY RETROGRADE...	10/18/78 at 22 **SCORPIO**	05/24/80 at 02 **CANCER**	12/31/81 at 08 **AQUARIUS**
Solar Conjunction.......	11/07/78 at 15 Scorpio	06/15/80 at 24 Gemini	01/21/82 at 01 Aquarius
STATIONARY DIRECT.......	11/28/78 at 07 Scorpio	07/06/80 at 16 Gemini	02/10/82 at 23 Capricorn
Leave Retrograde Zone...	12/29/78 at 22 Scorpio	08/09/80 at 02 Cancer	03/14/82 at 08 Aquarius
Enter Retrograde Zone...	07/01/83 at 23 Leo	02/09/85 at 06 Aries	09/12/86 at 04 Scorpio
STATIONARY RETROGRADE...	08/03/83 at 09 **VIRGO**	03/13/85 at 22 **ARIES**	10/15/86 at 20 **SCORPIO**
Solar Conjunction.......	08/25/83 at 01 Virgo	04/03/85 at 14 Aries	11/05/86 at 12 Scorpio
STATIONARY DIRECT.......	09/15/83 at 23 Leo	04/17/85 at 06 Aries	11/26/86 at 04 Scorpio
Leave Retrograde Zone...	10/18/83 at 09 Virgo	05/28/85 at 22 Aries	12/27/86 at 20 Scorpio
Enter Retrograde Zone...	04/18/88 at 13 Gemini	11/27/89 at 20 Capricorn	06/29/91 at 21 Leo
STATIONARY RETROGRADE...	05/22/88 at 00 **CANCER**	12/29/89 at 06 **AQUARIUS**	08/01/91 at 07 **VIRGO**
Solar Conjunction.......	06/12/88 at 22 Gemini	01/18/90 at 28 Capricorn	08/22/91 at 29 Leo
STATIONARY DIRECT.......	07/04/88 at 13 Gemini	02/08/90 at 20 Capricorn	09/12/91 at 21 Leo
Leave Retrograde Zone...	08/07/88 at 00 Cancer	03/12/90 at 06 Aquarius	10/16/91 at 07 Virgo
Enter Retrograde Zone...	02/06/93 at 03 Aries	09/10/94 at 18 Scorpio	04/16/96 at 11 Gemini
STATIONARY RETROGRADE...	03/11/93 at 20 **ARIES**	11/13/94 at 18 **SCORPIO**	05/20/96 at 28 **GEMINI**
Solar Conjunction.......	04/01/93 at 11 Aries	11/02/94 at 10 Scorpio	06/10/96 at 20 Gemini
STATIONARY DIRECT.......	04/22/93 at 03 Aries	11/23/95 at 02 Scorpio	07/02/96 at 11 Gemini
Leave Retrograde Zone...	05/26/93 at 20 Aries	12/25/94 at 18 Scorpio	08/05/96 at 28 Gemini

VENUS

Enter Retrograde Zone...	11/25/97 at 18 Capricorn	06/25/99 at 18 Leo
STATIONARY RETROGRADE...	12/26/97 at 03 **AQUARIUS**	07/30/99 at 05 **VIRGO**
Solar Conjunction.......	01/16/98 at 26 Capricorn	08/20/99 at 27 Leo
STATIONARY DIRECT......	02/05/98 18 Capricorn	09/11/99 at 18 Leo
Leave Retrograde Zone...	03/09/98 at 03 Aquarius	10/14/99 at 05 Virgo

MARS

Enter Retrograde Zone...	01/10/20 at 21 Libra	03/14/22 at 11 Sagittarius	06/12/24 at 25 Aquarius
STATIONARY RETROGRADE...	03/15/20 at 09 **SCORPIO**	05/08/22 at 25 **SAGITTARIUS**	07/24/24 at 05 **PISCES**
Solar Opposition........	04/21/20 at 01 Scorpio	06/10/22 at 18 Sagittarius	08/23/24 at 00 Pisces
STATIONARY DIRECT.......	05/31/20 at 21 Libra	07/17/22 at 11 Sagittarius	09/22/24 at 25 Aquarius
Leave Retrograde Zone...	07/31/20 at 09 Scorpio	09/04/22 at 25 Sagittarius	11/02/24 at 05 Pisces
Enter Retrograde Zone...	08/09/26 at 04 Taurus	09/20/28 at 24 Gemini	10/15/30 at 27 Cancer
STATIONARY RETROGRADE...	09/29/26 at 19 **TAURUS**	11/12/28 at 09 **CANCER**	12/18/30 at 16 **LEO**
Solar Opposition........	11/04/26 at 11 Taurus	12/21/28 at 29 Gemini	01/27/31 at 06 Leo
STATIONARY DIRECT.......	12/07/26 at 04 Taurus	01/27/29 at 24 Gemini	03/27/31 at 27 Cancer
Leave Retrograde Zone...	01/31/27 at 19 Taurus	04/02/29 at 09 Cancer	05/14/31 at 16 Leo
Enter Retrograde Zone...	11/15/32 at 00 Virgo	12/23/34 at 06 Libra	02/13/37 at 19 Scorpio
STATIONARY RETROGRADE...	01/21/33 at 20 **VIRGO**	02/27/35 at 24 **LIBRA**	04/14/37 at 05 **SAGITTARIUS**
Solar Opposition........	03/01/33 at 10 Virgo	04/06/35 at 16 Libra	05/19/37 at 28 Scorpio
STATIONARY DIRECT.......	04/12/33 at 00 Virgo	05/17/35 at 06 Libra	06/27/37 at 19 Scorpio
Leave Retrograde Zone...	06/17/33 at 20 Virgo	07/19/35 at 24 Libra	08/20/37 at 05 Sagittarius
Enter Retrograde Zone...	05/07/39 at 23 Capricorn	07/22/41 at 11 Aries	09/01/43 at 04 Gemini
STATIONARY RETROGRADE...	06/22/39 at 04 **AQUARIUS**	09/06/41 at 23 **ARIES**	10/28/43 at 22 **GEMINI**
Solar Opposition........	07/23/39 at 29 Capricorn	10/10/41 at 16 Aries	12/05/43 at 12 Gemini
STATIONARY DIRECT.......	08/24/39 at 23 Capricorn	11/10/41 at 11 Aries	01/10/44 at 04 Gemini
Leave Retrograde Zone...	10/05/39 at 04 Aquarius	12/29/41 at 23 Aries	03/11/44 at 22 Gemini
Enter Retrograde Zone...	10/02/45 at 14 Cancer	11/03/47 at 18 Leo	12/07/49 at 22 Virgo
STATIONARY RETROGRADE...	12/04/45 at 03 **LEO**	01/08/48 at 07 **VIRGO**	03/12/50 at 11 **LIBRA**
Solar Opposition........	01/14/46 at 23 Cancer	02/17/48 at 27 Leo	03/23/50 at 02 Libra
STATIONARY DIRECT.......	02/21/46 at 14 Cancer	03/29/48 at 18 Leo	05/03/50 at 22 Virgo
Leave Retrograde Zone...	04/29/46 at 03 Leo	06/04/48 at 07 Virgo	07/07/50 at 11 Libra
Enter Retrograde Zone...	01/22/52 at 01 Scorpio	04/01/54 at 25 Sagittarius	06/29/56 at 13 Pisces
STATIONARY RETROGRADE...	03/25/52 at 18 **SCORPIO**	05/23/54 at 08 **CAPRICORN**	08/10/56 at 23 **PISCES**
Solar Opposition........	05/01/52 at 10 Scorpio	06/24/54 at 02 Capricorn	09/10/56 at 18 Pisces
STATIONARY DIRECT.......	06/10/52 at 01 Scorpio	07/29/54 at 25 Sagittarius	10/10/56 at 13 Pisces
Leave Retrograde Zone...	08/06/52 at 18 Scorpio	09/14/54 at 08 Capricorn	11/22/56 at 23 Pisces
Enter Retrograde Zone...	08/18/58 at 16 Taurus	09/20/60 at 29 Gemini	10/22/62 at 05 Leo
STATIONARY RETROGRADE...	10/10/58 at 02 **GEMINI**	11/20/60 at 18 **CANCER**	12/26/62 at 24 **LEO**
Solar Opposition........	11/16/58 at 23 Taurus	12/30/60 at 08 Cancer	02/04/63 at 14 Leo
STATIONARY DIRECT.......	12/20/58 at 16 Taurus	02/06/61 at 29 Gemini	03/16/63 at 05 Leo
Leave Retrograde Zone...	02/15/59 at 02 Gemini	04/12/61 at 18 Cancer	05/15/63 at 24 Leo
Enter Retrograde Zone...	11/23/64 at 08 Virgo	01/02/67 at 14 Libra	02/28/69 at 01 Sagittarius
STATIONARY RETROGRADE...	01/28/65 at 28 **VIRGO**	03/08/67 at 03 **SCORPIO**	04/27/69 at 16 **SAGITTARIUS**
Solar Opposition........	03/09/65 at 18 Virgo	04/15/67 at 24 Libra	05/31/69 at 10 Sagittarius
STATIONARY DIRECT.......	04/19/65 at 08 Virgo	05/26/67 at 14 Libra	07/08/69 at 01 Sagittarius
Leave Retrograde Zone...	06/24/65 at 28 Virgo	07/26/67 at 03 Scorpio	08/28/69 at 16 Sagittarius

MARS

Enter Retrograde Zone...	05/28/71 at 11 Aquarius	08/02/73 at 25 Aries	09/09/75 at 14 Gemini
STATIONARY RETROGRADE...	07/11/71 at 21 **AQUARIUS**	09/19/73 at 09 **TAURUS**	11/06/75 at 02 **CANCER**
Solar Opposition........	08/10/71 at 17 Aquarius	10/25/73 at 01 Taurus	12/15/75 at 23 Gemini
STATIONARY DIRECT.......	09/09/71 at 11 Aquarius	11/26/73 at 25 Aries	01/20/76 at 14 Gemini
Leave Retrograde Zone...	10/20/71 at 21 Aquarius	01/17/74 at 09 Taurus	03/24/76 at 02 Cancer
Enter Retrograde Zone...	10/10/77 at 22 Cancer	11/10/79 at 25 Leo	12/16/81 at 00 Libra
STATIONARY RETROGRADE...	12/12/77 at 11 **LEO**	01/16/80 at 15 **VIRGO**	02/20/82 at 19 **LIBRA**
Solar Opposition........	01/22/78 at 01 Leo	02/25/80 at 05 Virgo	03/31/82 at 10 Libra
STATIONARY DIRECT.......	03/02/78 at 22 Cancer	04/06/80 at 25 Leo	05/11/82 at 00 Libra
Leave Retrograde Zone...	05/08/78 at 11 Leo	06/12/80 at 15 Virgo	07/13/82 at 19 Libra
Enter Retrograde Zone...	02/04/84 at 11 Scorpio	04/21/86 at 11 Capricorn	07/13/88 at 29 Pisces
STATIONARY RETROGRADE...	04/05/84 at 28 **SCORPIO**	06/08/86 at 22 **CAPRICORN**	08/26/88 at 11 **ARIES**
Solar Opposition........	05/11/84 at 20 Scorpio	07/10/86 at 17 Capricorn	09/28/88 at 05 Aries
STATIONARY DIRECT.......	06/19/84 at 11 Scorpio	08/12/86 at 11 Capricorn	10/28/88 at 29 Pisces
Leave Retrograde Zone...	10/02/84 at 28 Scorpio	09/23/86 at 22 Capricorn	12/13/88 at 11 Aries
Enter Retrograde Zone...	08/26/90 at 27 Taurus	09/27/92 at 08 Cancer	10/30/94 at 13 Leo
STATIONARY RETROGRADE...	10/20/90 at 14 **GEMINI**	11/28/92 at 27 **CANCER**	01/02/95 at 02 **VIRGO**
Solar Opposition........	11/27/90 at 05 Gemini	01/07/93 at 17 Cancer	02/12/95 at 22 Leo
STATIONARY DIRECT.......	01/02/91 at 27 Taurus	02/15/93 at 08 Cancer	03/24/95 at 13 Leo
Leave Retrograde Zone...	03/02/91 at 14 Gemini	03/29/93 at 27 Cancer	05/09/95 at 02 Virgo
Enter Retrograde Zone...	11/30/96 at 16 Virgo	01/13/99 at 24 Libra	
STATIONARY RETROGRADE...	02/06/97 at 05 **LIBRA**	03/18/99 at 12 **SCORPIO**	
Solar Opposition........	03/17/97 at 26 Virgo	04/24/99 at 04 Scorpio	
STATIONARY DIRECT.......	04/27/97 at 16 Virgo	06/04/99 at 24 Libra	
Leave Retrograde Zone...	06/30/97 at 05 Libra	08/03/99 at 12 Scorpio	

JUPITER

Enter Retrograde Zone...	09/09/19 at 08 Leo	10/08/20 at 08 Virgo	11/07/21 at 08 Libra
STATIONARY RETROGRADE...	12/05/19 at 18 **LEO**	01/03/21 at 18 **VIRGO**	02/02/22 at 18 **LIBRA**
Solar Opposition........	02/03/20 at 13 Leo	03/05/21 at 14 Virgo	04/04/22 at 14 Libra
STATIONARY DIRECT.......	04/04/20 at 08 Leo	05/05/21 at 08 Virgo	06/06/22 at 08 Libra
Leave Retrograde Zone...	07/01/20 at 18 Leo	08/03/21 at 18 Virgo	09/03/22 at 18 Libra
Enter Retrograde Zone...	12/08/22 at 09 Scorpio	01/10/24 at 10 Sagittarius	02/13/25 at 12 Capricorn
STATIONARY RETROGRADE...	03/05/23 at 18 **SCORPIO**	04/06/24 at 19 **SAGITTARIUS**	05/10/25 at 22 **CAPRICORN**
Solar Opposition........	05/05/23 at 14 Scorpio	06/06/24 at 15 Sagittarius	07/10/25 at 17 Capricorn
STATIONARY DIRECT.......	07/07/23 at 09 Scorpio	08/07/24 at 10 Sagittarius	09/09/25 at 12 Capricorn
Leave Retrograde Zone...	10/03/23 at 18 Scorpio	11/01/24 at 19 Sagittarius	12/02/25 at 22 Capricorn
Enter Retrograde Zone...	03/22/26 at 17 Aquarius	04/30/27 at 23 Pisces	06/26/28 at 00 Taurus
STATIONARY RETROGRADE...	06/16/26 at 27 **AQUARIUS**	07/24/27 at 03 **ARIES**	08/30/28 at 10 **TAURUS**
Solar Opposition........	08/15/26 at 22 Aquarius	09/22/27 at 28 Pisces	10/28/28 at 05 Taurus
STATIONARY DIRECT.......	10/14/26 at 17 Aquarius	11/19/27 at 23 Pisces	12/25/28 at 00 Taurus
Leave Retrograde Zone...	01/05/27 at 27 Aquarius	02/10/28 at 03 Aries	03/18/29 at 10 Taurus
Enter Retrograde Zone...	07/11/29 at 06 Gemini	08/13/30 at 10 Cancer	09/13/31 at 12 Leo
STATIONARY RETROGRADE...	10/05/29 at 16 **GEMINI**	11/08/30 at 20 **CANCER**	12/09/31 at 22 **LEO**
Solar Opposition........	12/03/29 at 11 Gemini	01/06/31 at 15 Cancer	02/07/32 at 17 Leo
STATIONARY DIRECT.......	01/31/30 at 06 Gemini	03/07/31 at 10 Cancer	04/08/32 at 12 Leo
Leave Retrograde Zone...	04/26/30 at 16 Gemini	06/02/31 at 20 Cancer	07/06/32 at 22 Leo
Enter Retrograde Zone...	10/12/32 at 13 Virgo	11/11/33 at 13 Libra	12/13/34 at 13 Scorpio
STATIONARY RETROGRADE...	01/08/33 at 23 **VIRGO**	02/07/34 at 23 **LIBRA**	03/10/35 at 23 **SCORPIO**
Solar Opposition........	03/09/33 at 18 Virgo	04/08/34 at 18 Libra	05/10/35 at 18 Scorpio
STATIONARY DIRECT.......	05/10/33 at 13 Virgo	06/10/34 at 13 Libra	07/11/35 at 13 Scorpio
Leave Retrograde Zone...	08/07/33 at 23 Virgo	09/07/34 at 23 Libra	10/07/35 at 23 Scorpio
Enter Retrograde Zone...	01/15/36 at 14 Sagittarius	02/18/37 at 17 Capricorn	03/28/38 at 22 Aquarius
STATIONARY RETROGRADE...	04/10/36 at 24 **SAGITTARIUS**	05/15/37 at 27 **CAPRICORN**	06/21/38 at 02 **PISCES**
Solar Opposition........	06/10/36 at 19 Sagittarius	07/15/37 at 22 Capricorn	08/21/38 at 27 Aquarius
STATIONARY DIRECT.......	08/11/36 at 14 Sagittarius	09/13/37 at 17 Capricorn	10/19/38 at 22 Aquarius
Leave Retrograde Zone...	11/06/36 at 24 Sagittarius	12/07/37 at 27 Capricorn	01/09/39 at 02 Pisces
Enter Retrograde Zone...	05/05/39 at 28 Pisces	06/11/40 at 05 Taurus	07/16/41 at 11 Gemini
STATIONARY RETROGRADE...	07/29/39 at 08 **ARIES**	09/04/40 at 15 **TAURUS**	10/10/41 at 21 **GEMINI**
Solar Opposition........	09/27/39 at 03 Aries	11/03/40 at 10 Taurus	12/08/41 at 16 Gemini
STATIONARY DIRECT.......	11/24/39 at 28 Pisces	12/31/40 at 05 Taurus	02/05/42 at 21 Gemini
Leave Retrograde Zone...	02/15/40 at 08 Aries	03/24/41 at 15 Taurus	05/01/42 at 21 Gemini
Enter Retrograde Zone...	08/17/42 at 15 Cancer	09/18/43 at 17 Leo	10/17/44 at 17 Virgo
STATIONARY RETROGRADE...	11/12/42 at 25 **CANCER**	12/13/43 at 27 **LEO**	01/12/45 at 27 **VIRGO**
Solar Opposition........	01/11/43 at 20 Cancer	02/11/44 at 22 Leo	03/13/45 at 22 Virgo
STATIONARY DIRECT.......	03/12/43 at 15 Cancer	04/13/44 at 17 Leo	05/14/45 at 17 Virgo
Leave Retrograde Zone...	06/07/43 at 25 Cancer	07/10/44 at 27 Leo	08/12/45 at 27 Virgo

JUPITER

Enter Retrograde Zone...	11/16/45 at 17 Libra	12/17/46 at 17 Scorpio	01/20/48 at 19 Sagittarius
STATIONARY RETROGRADE...	02/11/46 at 27 **LIBRA**	03/14/47 at 27 **SCORPIO**	04/15/48 at 28 **SAGITTARIUS**
Solar Opposition........	04/12/46 at 22 Libra	05/14/47 at 22 Scorpio	06/15/48 at 24 Sagittarius
STATIONARY DIRECT.......	06/14/46 at 17 Libra	07/15/47 at 17 Scorpio	08/16/48 at 28 Sagittarius
Leave Retrograde Zone...	09/11/46 at 27 Libra	10/11/47 at 27 Scorpio	11/10/48 at 28 Sagittarius
Enter Retrograde Zone...	02/23/49 at 22 Capricorn	04/02/50 at 27 Aquarius	05/11/51 at 04 Aries
STATIONARY RETROGRADE...	05/20/49 at 02 **AQUARIUS**	06/27/50 at 07 **PISCES**	08/04/51 at 14 **ARIES**
Solar Opposition........	07/20/49 at 27 Capricorn	08/26/50 at 02 Pisces	10/03/51 at 09 Aries
STATIONARY DIRECT.......	09/18/49 at 22 Capricorn	10/24/50 at 27 Aquarius	11/14/51 at 04 Aries
Leave Retrograde Zone...	12/11/49 at 02 Aquarius	01/14/51 at 07 Pisces	02/20/52 at 14 Aries
Enter Retrograde Zone...	06/16/52 at 10 Taurus	07/21/53 at 16 Gemini	08/22/54 at 19 Cancer
STATIONARY RETROGRADE...	09/08/52 at 20 **TAURUS**	10/15/53 at 26 **GEMINI**	11/17/54 at 29 **CANCER**
Solar Opposition........	11/08/52 at 15 Taurus	12/13/53 at 21 Gemini	01/15/55 at 24 Cancer
STATIONARY DIRECT.......	01/05/53 at 10 Taurus	01/10/54 at 16 Gemini	03/16/55 at 19 Cancer
Leave Retrograde Zone...	03/29/53 at 20 Taurus	05/06/54 at 26 Gemini	06/12/55 at 29 Cancer
Enter Retrograde Zone...	09/22/55 at 21 Leo	10/20/56 at 21 Virgo	11/20/57 at 21 Libra
STATIONARY RETROGRADE...	12/18/55 at 01 **VIRGO**	01/16/57 at 01 **LIBRA**	02/15/58 at 01 **SCORPIO**
Solar Opposition........	02/16/55 at 26 Leo	03/17/57 at 26 Virgo	04/17/58 at 26 Libra
STATIONARY DIRECT.......	04/17/56 at 21 Leo	05/19/57 at 21 Virgo	06/19/58 at 21 Libra
Leave Retrograde Zone...	07/15/56 at 01 Virgo	08/11/57 at 01 Libra	09/16/58 at 01 Scorpio
Enter Retrograde Zone...	12/22/58 at 22 Scorpio	01/24/60 at 23 Sagittarius	03/01/61 at 27 Capricorn
STATIONARY RETROGRADE...	03/18/59 at 01 **SAGITTARIUS**	04/20/60 at 03 **CAPRICORN**	05/25/61 at 07 **AQUARIUS**
Solar Opposition........	05/18/59 at 27 Scorpio	06/20/60 at 28 Sagittarius	07/25/61 at 02 Aquarius
STATIONARY DIRECT.......	07/20/59 at 22 Scorpio	08/20/60 at 23 Sagittarius	09/23/61 at 27 Capricorn
Leave Retrograde Zone...	10/15/59 at 01 Sagittarius	11/14/60 at 03 Capricorn	12/16/61 at 07 Aquarius
Enter Retrograde Zone...	04/08/62 at 02 Pisces	05/16/63 at 09 Aries	06/21/64 at 16 Taurus
STATIONARY RETROGRADE...	07/02/62 at 12 **PISCES**	08/09/63 at 19 **ARIES**	09/14/64 at 26 **TAURUS**
Solar Opposition........	08/31/62 at 07 Pisces	10/08/63 at 14 Aries	11/13/64 at 21 Taurus
STATIONARY DIRECT.......	10/29/62 at 02 Pisces	12/05/63 at 09 Aries	01/10/65 at 16 Taurus
Leave Retrograde Zone...	01/19/63 at 12 Pisces	02/25/64 at 19 Aries	04/04/65 at 26 Taurus
Enter Retrograde Zone...	07/26/65 at 21 Gemini	08/26/66 at 24 Cancer	09/26/67 at 25 Leo
STATIONARY RETROGRADE...	10/19/65 at 01 **CANCER**	11/21/66 at 04 **LEO**	12/22/67 at 05 **VIRGO**
Solar Opposition........	12/18/65 at 26 Gemini	01/20/67 at 29 Cancer	02/20/68 at 00 Virgo
STATIONARY DIRECT.......	02/15/66 at 21 Gemini	03/21/67 at 24 Cancer	04/21/68 at 25 Leo
Leave Retrograde Zone...	05/11/66 at 01 Cancer	06/17/67 at 04 Leo	07/20/68 at 05 Virgo
Enter Retrograde Zone...	10/25/68 at 26 Virgo	11/25/69 at 26 Libra	12/26/70 at 26 Scorpio
STATIONARY RETROGRADE...	01/20/69 at 06 **LIBRA**	02/19/70 at 05 **SCORPIO**	03/23/71 at 06 **SAGITTARIUS**
Solar Opposition........	03/21/69 at 01 Libra	04/21/70 at 01 Scorpio	05/23/71 at 01 Sagittarius
STATIONARY DIRECT.......	05/23/69 at 26 Virgo	06/23/70 at 26 Libra	07/24/71 at 26 Scorpio
Leave Retrograde Zone...	08/20/69 at 06 Libra	09/20/70 at 05 Scorpio	10/20/71 at 06 Sagittarius

JUPITER

Enter Retrograde Zone...	01/29/72 at 28 Sagittarius	03/06/73 at 02 Aquarius	04/13/74 at 07 Pisces
STATIONARY RETROGRADE...	04/25/72 at 08 **CAPRICORN**	05/30/73 at 12 **AQUARIUS**	07/07/74 at 17 **PISCES**
Solar Opposition........	06/24/72 at 03 Capricorn	07/30/73 at 07 Aquarius	09/05/74 at 12 Pisces
STATIONARY DIRECT.......	08/25/72 at 28 Sagittarius	09/28/73 at 02 Aquarius	11/03/74 at 07 Pisces
Leave Retrograde Zone...	11/18/72 at 08 Capricorn	12/20/73 at 12 Aquarius	01/25/75 at 17 Pisces
Enter Retrograde Zone...	05/21/75 at 14 Aries	06/26/76 at 21 Taurus	07/30/77 at 26 Gemini
STATIONARY RETROGRADE...	08/14/75 at 24 **ARIES**	09/19/76 at 01 **GEMINI**	10/24/77 at 06 **CANCER**
Solar Opposition........	10/13/75 at 19 Aries	11/18/76 at 26 Taurus	12/23/77 at 01 Cancer
STATIONARY DIRECT.......	12/10/75 at 14 Aries	01/15/77 at 21 Taurus	02/20/78 at 26 Gemini
Leave Retrograde Zone...	03/02/76 at 24 Aries	04/04/77 at 01 Gemini	05/17/78 at 06 Cancer
Enter Retrograde Zone...	08/31/78 at 29 Cancer	09/30/79 at 00 Virgo	09/24/80 at 00 Libra
STATIONARY RETROGRADE...	11/25/78 at 09 **LEO**	12/26/79 at 10 **VIRGO**	01/24/81 at 10 **LIBRA**
Solar Opposition........	01/24/79 at 04 Leo	02/24/80 at 05 Virgo	03/26/81 at 05 Libra
STATIONARY DIRECT.......	03/26/79 at 29 Cancer	04/26/80 at 00 Virgo	05/27/81 at 00 Libra
Leave Retrograde Zone...	06/21/79 at 09 Leo	07/24/80 at 10 Virgo	08/25/81 at 10 Libra
Enter Retrograde Zone...	11/29/81 at 00 Scorpio	12/31/82 at 01 Sagittarius	02/03/84 at 03 Capricorn
STATIONARY RETROGRADE...	02/24/82 at 10 **SCORPIO**	03/27/83 at 10 **SAGITTARIUS**	04/29/84 at 12 **CAPRICORN**
Solar Opposition........	04/26/82 at 05 Scorpio	05/27/83 at 06 Sagittarius	06/29/84 at 08 Capricorn
STATIONARY DIRECT.......	06/27/82 at 00 Scorpio	07/29/83 at 01 Sagittarius	08/29/84 at 03 Capricorn
Leave Retrograde Zone...	09/24/82 at 10 Scorpio	10/24/83 at 10 Sagittarius	11/22/84 at 12 Capricorn
Enter Retrograde Zone...	03/11/85 at 07 Aquarius	04/18/86 at 12 Pisces	05/26/87 at 19 Aries
STATIONARY RETROGRADE...	06/24/85 at 16 **AQUARIUS**	07/12/86 at 22 **PISCES**	08/19/87 at 29 **ARIES**
Solar Opposition........	08/04/85 at 12 Aquarius	09/10/86 at 17 Pisces	10/18/87 at 24 Aries
STATIONARY DIRECT.......	10/03/85 at 07 Aquarius	11/08/86 at 12 Pisces	12/15/87 at 19 Aries
Leave Retrograde Zone...	12/25/85 at 16 Aquarius	01/29/87 at 22 Pisces	02/26/88 at 29 Aries
Enter Retrograde Zone...	06/30/88 at 26 Taurus	08/03/89 at 00 Cancer	09/04/90 at 03 Leo
STATIONARY RETROGRADE...	09/24/88 at 06 **GEMINI**	10/29/89 at 10 **CANCER**	11/30/90 at 13 **LEO**
Solar Opposition........	11/23/88 at 00 Gemini	12/27/89 at 05 Cancer	01/29/91 at 08 Leo
STATIONARY DIRECT.......	01/20/89 at 26 Taurus	02/24/90 at 00 Cancer	03/30/91 at 03 Leo
Leave Retrograde Zone...	04/14/89 at 06 Gemini	05/22/90 at 10 Cancer	06/26/91 at 13 Leo
Enter Retrograde Zone...	10/04/91 at 04 Virgo	11/02/82 at 04 Libra	12/03/93 at 04 Scorpio
STATIONARY RETROGRADE...	12/30/91 at 14 **VIRGO**	01/28/93 at 14 **LIBRA**	02/28/94 at 14 **SCORPIO**
Solar Opposition........	02/29/92 at 09 Virgo	03/30/93 at 09 Libra	04/30/94 at 09 Scorpio
STATIONARY DIRECT.......	04/30/92 at 04 Virgo	06/02/93 at 04 Libra	07/02/94 at 04 Scorpio
Leave Retrograde Zone...	07/29/92 at 14 Virgo	08/29/93 at 14 Libra	09/28/94 at 14 Scorpio
Enter Retrograde Zone...	01/04/95 at 05 Sagittarius	02/08/96 at 07 Capricorn	03/16/97 at 12 Aquarius
STATIONARY RETROGRADE...	04/02/95 at 15 **SAGITTARIUS**	05/04/96 at 17 **CAPRICORN**	06/10/97 at 21 **AQUARIUS**
Solar Opposition........	06/01/95 at 10 Sagittarius	07/04/96 at 12 Capricorn	08/09/97 at 17 Aquarius
STATIONARY DIRECT.......	08/02/95 at 05 Sagittarius	09/03/96 at 07 Capricorn	10/08/97 at 12 Aquarius
Leave Retrograde Zone...	10/28/95 at 15 Sagittarius	11/27/96 at 17 Capricorn	12/30/97 at 21 Aquarius

JUPITER

Enter Retrograde Zone...	04/23/98 at 18 Pisces	05/31/99 at 25 Aries
STATIONARY RETROGRADE...	07/18/98 at 28 **PISCES**	08/25/99 at 04 **TAURUS**
Solar Opposition........	09/16/98 at 23 Pisces	10/23/99 at 29 Aries
STATIONARY DIRECT.......	11/13/98 at 18 Pisces	12/20/99 at 25 Aries
Leave Retrograde Zone...	02/03/99 at 28 Pisces	03/12/2000 at 04 Taurus

SATURN

Enter Retrograde Zone...	09/19/19 at 04 Virgo	10/01/20 at 18 Virgo	10/14/21 at 00 Libra
STATIONARY RETROGRADE...	12/23/19 at 11 **VIRGO**	01/04/21 at 24 **VIRGO**	01/17/22 at 07 **LIBRA**
Solar Opposition........	02/28/20 at 08 Virgo	03/12/21 at 21 Virgo	03/25/22 at 04 Libra
STATIONARY DIRECT.......	05/07/20 at 04 Virgo	05/20/21 at 18 Virgo	06/03/22 at 00 Libra
Leave Retrograde Zone...	08/11/20 at 11 Virgo	08/26/21 at 24 Virgo	09/09/22 at 07 Libra
Enter Retrograde Zone...	10/26/22 at 13 Libra	11/08/23 at 25 Libra	11/18/24 at 07 Scorpio
STATIONARY RETROGRADE...	01/29/23 at 20 **LIBRA**	02/11/24 at 02 **SCORPIO**	02/22/25 at 14 **SCORPIO**
Solar Opposition........	04/07/23 at 16 Libra	04/19/24 at 29 Libra	05/01/25 at 11 Scorpio
STATIONARY DIRECT.......	06/16/23 at 13 Libra	06/29/24 at 25 Libra	07/11/25 at 07 Scorpio
Leave Retrograde Zone...	09/22/23 at 20 Libra	10/04/24 at 02 Scorpio	10/17/25 at 14 Scorpio
Enter Retrograde Zone...	11/29/25 at 19 Scorpio	12/10/26 at 01 Sagittarius	12/23/27 at 12 Sagittarius
STATIONARY RETROGRADE...	03/06/26 at 26 **SCORPIO**	03/18/27 at 07 **SAGITTARIUS**	03/28/28 at 19 **SAGITTARIUS**
Solar Opposition........	05/14/26 at 22 Scorpio	05/26/27 at 04 Sagittarius	06/06/28 at 15 Sagittarius
STATIONARY DIRECT.......	07/24/26 at 19 Scorpio	08/05/27 at 01 Sagittarius	08/17/28 at 12 Sagittarius
Leave Retrograde Zone...	10/30/26 at 26 Scorpio	11/11/27 at 07 Sagittarius	11/22/28 at 19 Sagittarius
Enter Retrograde Zone...	01/02/29 at 23 Sagittarius	01/13/30 at 05 Capricorn	01/25/31 at 16 Capricorn
STATIONARY RETROGRADE...	04/09/29 at 00 **CAPRICORN**	04/21/30 at 11 **CAPRICORN**	05/03/31 at 23 **CAPRICORN**
Solar Opposition........	06/18/29 at 27 Sagittarius	07/01/30 at 08 Capricorn	07/13/31 at 19 Capricorn
STATIONARY DIRECT.......	08/29/29 at 23 Sagittarius	09/09/30 at 05 Capricorn	09/21/31 at 16 Capricorn
Leave Retrograde Zone...	12/04/29 at 00 Capricorn	12/16/30 at 11 Capricorn	12/27/31 at 23 Capricorn
Enter Retrograde Zone...	02/06/32 at 28 Capricorn	02/18/33 at 09 Aquarius	03/02/34 at 21 Aquarius
STATIONARY RETROGRADE...	05/14/32 at 04 **AQUARIUS**	05/27/33 at 16 **AQUARIUS**	06/08/34 at 28 **AQUARIUS**
Solar Opposition........	07/24/32 at 01 Aquarius	08/08/33 at 13 Aquarius	08/18/34 at 24 Aquarius
STATIONARY DIRECT.......	10/02/32 at 28 Capricorn	10/14/33 at 09 Aquarius	10/26/34 at 21 Aquarius
Leave Retrograde Zone...	01/07/33 at 04 Aquarius	01/18/34 at 16 Aquarius	01/30/35 at 28 Aquarius
Enter Retrograde Zone...	03/15/35 at 03 Pisces	03/28/36 at 15 Pisces	04/10/37 at 28 Pisces
STATIONARY RETROGRADE...	06/21/35 at 10 **PISCES**	07/03/36 at 22 **PISCES**	07/17/37 at 05 **ARIES**
Solar Opposition........	08/30/35 at 06 Pisces	09/12/36 at 19 Pisces	09/25/37 at 01 Aries
STATIONARY DIRECT.......	11/07/35 at 03 Pisces	11/19/36 at 15 Pisces	12/02/37 at 28 Pisces
Leave Retrograde Zone...	02/10/36 at 10 Pisces	02/27/37 at 22 Pisces	03/06/38 at 05 Aries
Enter Retrograde Zone...	04/24/38 at 11 Aries	05/08/39 at 24 Aries	05/22/40 at 07 Taurus
STATIONARY RETROGRADE...	07/30/38 at 18 **ARIES**	08/14/39 at 01 **TAURUS**	08/27/40 at 14 **TAURUS**
Solar Opposition........	10/08/38 at 14 Aries	10/22/39 at 27 Aries	11/03/40 at 11 Taurus
STATIONARY DIRECT.......	12/14/38 at 11 Aries	12/28/39 at 24 Aries	01/09/41 at 14 Taurus
Leave Retrograde Zone...	03/18/39 at 18 Aries	03/30/40 at 01 Taurus	04/13/41 at 14 Taurus
Enter Retrograde Zone...	06/06/41 at 21 Taurus	06/21/42 at 05 Gemini	07/06/43 at 19 Gemini
STATIONARY RETROGRADE...	09/10/41 at 28 **TAURUS**	09/25/42 at 12 **GEMINI**	10/08/43 at 26 **GEMINI**
Solar Opposition........	11/17/41 at 25 Taurus	12/01/42 at 09 Gemini	12/15/43 at 23 Gemini
STATIONARY DIRECT.......	01/23/42 at 21 Taurus	02/06/43 at 05 Gemini	02/20/44 at 19 Gemini
Leave Retrograde Zone...	04/27/42 at 28 Taurus	05/11/43 at 12 Gemini	05/24/44 at 26 Gemini

SATURN

Enter Retrograde Zone...	07/20/44 at 03 Cancer	08/03/45 at 17 Cancer	08/18/46 at 01 Leo
STATIONARY RETROGRADE...	10/23/44 at 10 **CANCER**	11/06/45 at 24 **CANCER**	11/20/46 at 08 **LEO**
Solar Opposition........	12/29/44 at 07 Cancer	01/12/46 at 21 Cancer	01/26/47 at 05 Leo
STATIONARY DIRECT.......	03/05/45 at 03 Cancer	03/20/46 at 17 Cancer	04/03/47 at 01 Leo
Leave Retrograde Zone...	07/08/45 at 10 Cancer	06/23/46 at 24 Cancer	07/08/47 at 08 Leo
Enter Retrograde Zone...	08/31/47 at 15 Leo	09/05/48 at 28 Leo	09/26/49 at 12 Virgo
STATIONARY RETROGRADE...	12/04/47 at 22 **LEO**	12/17/48 at 06 **VIRGO**	12/30/49 at 19 **VIRGO**
Solar Opposition........	02/07/48 at 19 Leo	02/21/49 at 02 Virgo	03/07/50 at 16 Virgo
STATIONARY DIRECT.......	04/17/48 at 15 Leo	05/02/49 at 28 Leo	05/15/50 at 12 Virgo
Leave Retrograde Zone...	07/22/48 at 22 Leo	08/06/49 at 06 Virgo	08/20/50 at 19 Virgo
Enter Retrograde Zone...	10/09/50 at 25 Virgo	10/21/51 at 08 Libra	11/01/52 at 20 Libra
STATIONARY RETROGRADE...	01/12/51 at 02 **LIBRA**	01/24/52 at 14 **LIBRA**	02/05/53 at 27 **LIBRA**
Solar Opposition........	03/22/51 at 29 Virgo	04/01/52 at 11 Libra	04/14/53 at 24 Libra
STATIONARY DIRECT.......	05/29/51 at 25 Virgo	06/10/52 at 08 Libra	06/23/53 at 20 Libra
Leave Retrograde Zone...	09/03/51 at 02 Libra	09/15/52 at 14 Libra	09/29/53 at 27 Libra
Enter Retrograde Zone...	11/13/53 at 02 Scorpio	11/24/54 at 14 Scorpio	12/06/55 at 26 Scorpio
STATIONARY RETROGRADE...	02/17/54 at 09 **SCORPIO**	03/02/55 at 21 **SCORPIO**	03/12/56 at 02 **SAGITTARIUS**
Solar Opposition........	04/26/54 at 06 Scorpio	05/09/55 at 17 Scorpio	05/20/56 at 29 Scorpio
STATIONARY DIRECT.......	07/06/54 at 02 Scorpio	07/19/55 at 14 Scorpio	07/30/56 at 26 Scorpio
Leave Retrograde Zone...	10/12/54 at 09 Scorpio	10/25/55 at 21 Scorpio	11/05/56 at 02 Sagittarius
Enter Retrograde Zone...	12/17/56 at 07 Sagittarius	12/28/57 at 19 Sagittarius	01/08/59 at 00 Capricorn
STATIONARY RETROGRADE...	03/24/57 at 14 **SAGITTARIUS**	04/04/58 at 25 **SAGITTARIUS**	04/16/59 at 07 **CAPRICORN**
Solar Opposition........	06/01/57 at 11 Sagittarius	06/13/58 at 22 Sagittarius	06/26/59 at 03 Capricorn
STATIONARY DIRECT.......	08/11/57 at 07 Sagittarius	08/24/58 at 19 Sagittarius	09/05/59 at 00 Capricorn
Leave Retrograde Zone...	11/17/57 at 14 Sagittarius	11/29/58 at 25 Sagittarius	12/11/59 at 07 Capricorn
Enter Retrograde Zone...	01/20/60 at 11 Capricorn	01/31/61 at 23 Capricorn	02/13/62 at 04 Aquarius
STATIONARY RETROGRADE...	04/27/60 at 18 **CAPRICORN**	05/09/61 at 29 **CAPRICORN**	05/21/62 at 11 **AQUARIUS**
Solar Opposition........	07/07/60 at 15 Capricorn	07/19/61 at 26 Capricorn	07/31/62 at 08 Aquarius
STATIONARY DIRECT.......	09/15/60 at 11 Capricorn	09/28/61 at 23 Capricorn	10/09/62 at 04 Aquarius
Leave Retrograde Zone...	12/21/60 at 18 Capricorn	01/02/62 at 29 Capricorn	01/13/63 at 11 Aquarius
Enter Retrograde Zone...	02/25/63 at 16 Aquarius	03/09/64 at 28 Aquarius	03/22/65 at 10 Pisces
STATIONARY RETROGRADE...	06/03/63 at 23 **AQUARIUS**	06/15/64 at 05 **PISCES**	06/28/65 at 17 **PISCES**
Solar Opposition........	08/13/63 at 19 Aquarius	08/24/64 at 01 Pisces	09/06/65 at 13 Pisces
STATIONARY DIRECT.......	10/21/63 at 16 Aquarius	11/02/64 at 28 Aquarius	11/14/65 at 10 Pisces
Leave Retrograde Zone...	01/25/64 at 23 Aquarius	02/04/65 at 05 Pisces	02/17/66 at 17 Pisces
Enter Retrograde Zone...	04/04/66 at 22 Pisces	04/18/67 at 05 Aries	05/01/68 at 18 Aries
STATIONARY RETROGRADE...	07/11/66 at 29 **PISCES**	07/25/67 at 12 **ARIES**	08/07/68 at 25 **ARIES**
Solar Opposition........	09/19/66 at 26 Pisces	10/02/67 at 09 Aries	10/15/68 at 22 Aries
STATIONARY DIRECT.......	11/26/66 at 22 Pisces	12/09/67 at 05 Aries	12/21/68 at 18 Aries
Leave Retrograde Zone...	03/01/67 at 29 Pisces	03/12/68 at 12 Aries	03/25/69 at 25 Aries

SATURN

Enter Retrograde Zone...	05/16/69 at 02 Taurus	05/31/70 at 15 Taurus	06/15/71 at 29 Taurus
STATIONARY RETROGRADE...	08/21/60 at 08 **TAURUS**	09/04/70 at 22 **TAURUS**	09/19/71 at 06 **GEMINI**
Solar Opposition........	10/29/69 at 05 Taurus	11/11/70 at 19 Taurus	11/25/71 at 03 Gemini
STATIONARY DIRECT.......	01/03/70 at 02 Taurus	01/17/71 at 15 Taurus	01/31/72 at 29 Taurus
Leave Retrograde Zone...	04/07/70 at 08 Taurus	04/21/71 at 22 Taurus	05/04/72 at 06 Gemini
Enter Retrograde Zone...	06/29/72 at 13 Gemini	07/13/73 at 27 Gemini	07/28/74 at 11 Cancer
STATIONARY RETROGRADE...	10/02/72 at 20 **GEMINI**	10/17/73 at 04 **CANCER**	10/31/74 at 18 **CANCER**
Solar Opposition........	12/09/72 at 17 Gemini	12/23/73 at 01 Cancer	01/06/75 at 15 Cancer
STATIONARY DIRECT.......	02/13/73 at 13 Gemini	02/27/74 at 27 Gemini	03/14/75 at 11 Cancer
Leave Retrograde Zone...	05/18/73 at 20 Gemini	06/02/74 at 04 Cancer	06/17/75 at 18 Cancer
Enter Retrograde Zone...	08/13/75 at 26 Cancer	08/25/76 at 09 Leo	09/07/77 at 23 Leo
STATIONARY RETROGRADE...	11/14/75 at 02 **LEO**	11/27/76 at 16 **LEO**	12/11/77 at 00 **VIRGO**
Solar Opposition........	01/20/76 at 29 Cancer	02/02/77 at 13 Leo	07/16/77 at 27 Leo
STATIONARY DIRECT.......	03/27/76 at 26 Cancer	04/11/77 at 09 Leo	04/25/78 at 23 Leo
Leave Retrograde Zone...	07/01/76 at 02 Leo	07/16/77 at 16 Leo	07/31/78 at 00 Virgo
Enter Retrograde Zone...	09/21/78 at 07 Virgo	10/04/79 at 20 Virgo	10/15/80 at 02 Libra
STATIONARY RETROGRADE...	12/24/78 at 13 **VIRGO**	01/06/80 at 27 **VIRGO**	01/18/81 at 09 **LIBRA**
Solar Opposition........	03/01/79 at 10 Virgo	03/15/80 at 24 Virgo	03/27/81 at 06 Libra
STATIONARY DIRECT.......	05/09/79 at 07 Virgo	05/22/80 at 20 Virgo	06/05/81 at 02 Libra
Leave Retrograde Zone...	08/14/79 at 13 Virgo	08/27/80 at 27 Virgo	09/11/81 at 09 Libra
Enter Retrograde Zone...	10/27/81 at 15 Libra	11/08/82 at 27 Libra	11/20/83 at 09 Scorpio
STATIONARY RETROGRADE...	02/02/82 at 22 **LIBRA**	02/12/83 at 04 **SCORPIO**	02/24/84 at 16 **SCORPIO**
Solar Opposition........	04/09/82 at 18 Libra	04/21/83 at 01 Scorpio	05/03/84 at 13 Scorpio
STATIONARY DIRECT.......	06/18/82 at 15 Libra	07/02/83 at 27 Libra	07/13/84 at 09 Scorpio
Leave Retrograde Zone...	09/24/82 at 22 Libra	10/07/83 at 04 Scorpio	10/19/84 at 16 Scorpio
Enter Retrograde Zone...	12/01/84 at 21 Scorpio	12/12/85 at 03 Sagittarius	12/24/86 at 14 Sagittarius
STATIONARY RETROGRADE...	03/07/85 at 28 **SCORPIO**	03/19/86 at 09 **SAGITTARIUS**	03/31/87 at 21 **SAGITTARIUS**
Solar Opposition........	05/15/85 at 24 Scorpio	05/28/86 at 06 Sagittarius	06/09/87 at 17 Sagittarius
STATIONARY DIRECT.......	07/25/85 at 21 Scorpio	08/07/86 at 03 Sagittarius	08/19/87 at 14 Sagittarius
Leave Retrograde Zone...	10/31/85 at 28 Scorpio	11/13/86 at 09 Sagittarius	11/24/87 at 21 Sagittarius
Enter Retrograde Zone...	01/04/88 at 25 Sagittarius	01/15/89 at 07 Capricorn	01/27/90 at 18 Capricorn
STATIONARY RETROGRADE...	04/11/88 at 02 **CAPRICORN**	04/22/89 at 13 **CAPRICORN**	05/04/90 at 25 **CAPRICORN**
Solar Opposition........	06/20/88 at 29 Sagittarius	07/02/89 at 10 Capricorn	07/14/90 at 22 Capricorn
STATIONARY DIRECT.......	08/30/88 at 25 Sagittarius	09/11/89 at 07 Capricorn	09/23/90 at 18 Capricorn
Leave Retrograde Zone...	12/04/88 at 02 Capricorn	12/17/89 at 13 Capricorn	12/29/90 at 25 Capricorn
Enter Retrograde Zone...	02/08/91 at 00 Aquarius	02/20/92 at 11 Aquarius	03/04/93 at 23 Aquarius
STATIONARY RETROGRADE...	05/17/91 at 06 **AQUARIUS**	05/28/92 at 18 **AQUARIUS**	06/10/93 at 00 **PISCES**
Solar Opposition........	07/26/91 at 03 Aquarius	08/07/92 at 15 Aquarius	08/19/93 at 26 Aquarius
STATIONARY DIRECT.......	10/05/91 at 00 Aquarius	10/16/92 at 11 Aquarius	10/28/93 at 23 Aquarius
Leave Retrograde Zone...	01/09/92 at 06 Aquarius	01/20/93 at 18 Aquarius	01/31/94 at 00 Pisces

SATURN

Enter Retrograde Zone...	03/17/94 at 05 Pisces	03/30/95 at 17 Pisces	04/12/96 at 00 Aries
STATIONARY RETROGRADE...	06/23/94 at 12 **PISCES**	07/06/95 at 24 **PISCES**	07/18/96 at 07 **ARIES**
Solar Opposition........	09/01/94 at 09 Pisces	09/14/95 at 21 Pisces	09/26/96 at 03 Aries
STATIONARY DIRECT.......	11/09/94 at 09 Pisces	11/21/95 at 17 Pisces	12/03/96 at 00 Aries
Leave Retrograde Zone...	02/12/95 at 12 Pisces	02/24/96 at 24 Pisces	03/07/97 at 07 Aries
Enter Retrograde Zone...	04/26/97 at 13 Aries	05/10/98 at 26 Aries	05/25/99 at 10 Taurus
STATIONARY RETROGRADE...	08/02/97 at 20 **ARIES**	08/15/98 at 03 **TAURUS**	08/30/99 at 17 **TAURUS**
Solar Opposition........	10/10/97 at 16 Aries	10/23/98 at 00 Taurus	11/06/99 at 13 Taurus
STATIONARY DIRECT.......	12/16/97 at 13 Aries	12/29/98 at 26 Aries	01/12/2000 at 10 Taurus
Leave Retrograde Zone...	03/20/98 at 20 Aries	04/02/99 at 03 Taurus	04/14/2000 at 17 Taurus

ASTROLOGY THE COSMIC PATTERN
Correspondence Courses on Cassette Tape
by Joanne Wickenburg

A complete Correspondence Course in Astrology, presented on cassette tapes. The "Cosmic Pattern" takes you through the fundamentals of Astrology, chart calculation, the interpretation of a horoscope, and finally to examine the chart in motion through transits and progressions. Individual workbooks accompany each course, providing (1) outlines of the taped material, (2) illustrations, (3) self testing material, (4) self analysis quizzes, and (5) homework.

"The Cosmic Pattern" has been designed for those interested in pursuing Astrology in-depth, either for professional or personal reasons. After completing the entire course, you will (a) be prepared to begin practicing Astrology on your own, and (b) have a complete format for teaching others.

COURSE DESCRIPTION

Astrology I: An introduction to astrology, including in-depth information on signs, houses, planets and their interrelationships. 6-1 hour tapes + Workbook.
Astrology II: The construction of a horoscope based on the date, time and place of birth. This is the only course requiring reference books. Write for titles. 6-1 hour tapes + Workbook.
Astrology III: Basic interpretation techniques, including chart patterns, tone, qualities and elements, Moon phases and nodes, retrogradation and interceptions. 6-1 hour tapes + Workbook.
Astrology IV: Psychological interpretation of the birth chart using rulerships, major and minor aspects, nodes and parts. Includes 5-1 hour tapes + Workbook.
Astrology V: Detailed chart analysis, including vocational, health, relationships and chart comparison. Includes 5-1 hour tapes + Workbook.
Astrology VI: Calculating and interpreting primary and secondary progressions, and investigating transits to find the conditions surrounding life at any given time. Includes 6-1 hour tapes + Workbook.
Supplement: Preparing for professional certification. Write for details.

For more information contact: